IN THE
SHADOW
OF THE
MOUNTAIN

IN THE
SHADOW
OF THE
MOUNTAIN

A Memoir of Courage

SILVIA
VASQUEZ-LAVADO

HENRY HOLT AND COMPANY

NEW YORK

Henry Holt and Company
Publishers since 1866
120 Broadway
New York, New York 10271
www.henryholt.com

Henry Holt® and ⏹® are registered trademarks of Macmillan Publishing Group, LLC.

Library of Congress Cataloging-in-Publication Data

Names: Vasquez-Lavado, Silvia, author.
Title: In the shadow of the mountain : a memoir of courage / Silvia Vasquez-Lavado.
Description: First edition. | New York : Henry Holt and Company, 2022.
Identifiers: LCCN 2021036935 (print) | LCCN 2021036936 (ebook) | ISBN
    9781250776747 (hardcover) | ISBN 9781250776754 (ebook)
Subjects: LCSH: Vasquez-Lavado, Silvia. | Mountaineers—United States—Biography. |
    Hispanic Americans—Biography. | Everest, Mount (China and Nepal) | Women in
    technology—United States.
Classification: LCC GV199.92.V37 A3 2022 (print) | LCC GV199.92.V37 (ebook) |
    DDC 796.522092 [B]—dc23/eng/20211020
LC record available at https://lccn.loc.gov/2021036935
LC ebook record available at https://lccn.loc.gov/2021036936

Our books may be purchased in bulk for promotional, educational,
or business use. Please contact your local bookseller or the Macmillan Corporate
and Premium Sales Department at (800) 221-7945, extension 5442, or by e-mail at
MacmillanSpecialMarkets@macmillan.com.

First Edition 2022

Designed by Meryl Levavi

Printed in the United States of America

1   3   5   7   9   10   8   6   4   2

For all those who have yet to climb
. . . you are not alone.

CONTENTS

1: Chomolungma 1

2: Borron y Cuenta Nueva 10

3: Summit Mittens 27

4: Sunday's Prey 48

5: The High Himalayas 72

6: Lancaster 90210 86

7: Ridum 104

8: Top Shelf 119

9: Nothing We Do Is Small 135

10: Peruvian Cowgirl with No Past 157

11: Walking Together 169

12: When Things Fall Apart 182

13: Testosterone 200

14: The Great Wall 206

15: Kind If You Let Her 221

16: Los Divorciados 242

17: The Valley of Silence 259

18: The Death Zone 279

19: At the Top of the World 297

Acknowledgments 307

Chapter 1

CHOMOLUNGMA

If I can count to one thousand, I can get through this.

1, 2, 3 . . .

I'm going for a walk. That's it. Just a walk. A very long, very steep, potentially deadly walk up Lhotse Face, a four-thousand-foot vertical wall of blue ice rising from the Western Cwm.

The Valley of Silence.

My mind is anything but silent, and from where I stand, Lhotse is a slick, shimmering beast.

An alpine skyscraper.

Just before the wall is a bergschrund, a gaping crevasse where the glacier has cracked and pulled away from the mountain. The morning's gluten-free oats sit heavy in my gut as I stare down into its immensity. Its wide mouth gapes, hungry.

Then a sound.

A glove falls and slips into the void. I watch it disappear and stare long after it's gone, hoping it will magically re-emerge.

None of the other climbers says a word, and one by one we climb over a field of shaggy rocks and cross a ladder over the bergschrund.

I focus on the ropes. Two skinny lines snaking up the icy face of Lhotse. One for us, the climbers going up, the other for those descending. The ropes are no thicker than my thumb but will guide us up a vertical mile like a handrail on a flight of stairs. In my mind, they morph into velvet ropes leading us toward a mysterious, exclusive nightclub where both the dancers and the drinks are flowing. A blackout drunk experience is way less terrifying than this.

A few steps off the route, unclipped, and I would become the glove. A quick and quiet slip into a vast and endless death.

In other words, it's all up from here.

17, 18, 19 . . .

Mike, the head guide, is leading us up Lhtose, followed by Danny and Brian, the fastest and strongest of the climbers, with Ang Dorjee close behind. Mark and I keep pace in the middle, our sweet spot, and bringing up the rear is Lydia Bradey, an Everest legend—the first woman to summit without oxygen. Rob, another member of our team, who had been struggling, wasn't healthy enough to climb past Camp 2.

33, 34 . . .

At breakfast, Mike said it would take just under five hours to scale the Face. I extend the safety carabiner from my harness, then open the jumar and feed it with the first fixed rope on my left. Attached to the climbing harness that cradles my hips and upper thighs, the jumar is a hand brake, or a ratcheting handle, which slides up the rope one way and pulls taut when weight is applied. Slowly I begin to walk, sliding my jumar up the rope, pushing my fingers deep into the glove so I can feel what I'm gripping through the bulky material. My gloves are baggy as always. Elite mountaineering gear is still designed for men, and even the extra-small gloves gape around my hands.

I've learned to make do.

When I first started climbing, the jumar was a symbol. The thing that made me a "real climber." A tool to master for entrance into the cool-kid climbers' club. After a decade of climbing and reaching five of the Seven Summits—the tallest mountain on each continent—I'm still a nerdy kid trying to fit in, but the jumar is no longer a flashy piece of equipment. It's an extension of me. My lifeline, my anchor, it doesn't unclip unless I do.

I respect the jumar. I bow to the jumar.

And every time I feel its steel teeth bite down on rope, I let out a hushed *yes*.

55, 56, 57 . . .

Leveraging my ice axe like a cane, I chop it into the wall and kneel into the incline to stabilize myself. Walking in crampons—strap-on metal cleats—is a tedious art. They dig into the hardened snow and ice to provide traction. Luckily, I share the same short gait as most of the Sherpas, who have already climbed ahead to set up camp for the night. I space out my steps to hit the tiny ledges their boots have cut into the ice. Not having to chop into virgin ice saves a sliver of energy, and I'm hoarding whatever juice I can. Every step must be precise and mechanical.

Deep breath and exhale. Emotions are dangerous at this elevation. Focus. Count. *61. 62.* No feelings. Count. *70.* No emotions. Count. *84. 85.*

We're thirty-six hours from summit, I think. Two camps to go. I'd try to calculate the miles, but they mean nothing anymore. This high on the mountain, distance is abstract. Granular, even. Our days are measured in landmarks and elevation gain. *Camp 3. 24,500 feet. Camp 4. Yellow Band. Geneva Spur. South Col. 26,300 feet.* Altitude owns us. It's hard to grasp what is near and what is far. Time expands and contracts. Perspective shifts quickly. Zoomed out, we're ants in formation, tiny black dots pushing up the side of a colossal mountain range. But my field of vision is microscopic—all I see is the shimmer and the crumble of the wall I'm climbing at this very moment.

At this altitude, we're higher than most birds will ever fly.

I wonder if birds do this. Get obsessed with height. Try to fly higher than each other.

93, 94, 92 . . .

Shit. Start again.

1, 2, 3 . . .

Somewhere behind this wall is the summit. Or is it above?

Why didn't I memorize this route better?

Lhotse is the final obstacle before Camp 3 and where our oxygen tanks are waiting. Above 24,000 feet, the climb is a race against diminishing oxygen. This high, we rest, but we don't recover. We are deteriorating. Strapped to our backs like newborns in a manta, the oxygen tanks will become our most precious cargo. Without them, we'd be done. Everyone except Lydia, maybe. The last chance for rescue is behind us, anyway. Helicopters don't fly higher than Camp 2. Any kind of rescue now, even to bring back a dead body, has to be done step-by-step, on foot, down the ropes.

24, 25, 23 . . .

Shit. Again. Keep beginning again.

1, 2, 3 . . .

The wind is picking up.

The day's usual banter and shit-talking have gone silent, replaced by baritone huffs and grunts. Everyone is focused on their next step.

"Rock!" Brian shouts suddenly from above. He swerves to the right as a basketball-sized rock tumbles down Lhotse.

Rock! Rock! Rock! The word echoes through us. We all swerve right. *22, 23, 24 . . .* Another team slips quietly past on the descending rope, coming down from Camp 3. It's unsettling to watch them descend while everyone else on the mountain is thinking *up up up*. It's May 17. This is *the* summit window. Going down means something has gone wrong. As they pass, I realize I haven't seen any other teams this morning. We're the only ones on the Face.

Fifteen minutes later, the wind begins to whistle and groan.

"Ice!" hollers Ang Dorjee.

Ice.

Ice.

Ice.

Something isn't right.

Halfway up, we hit a bulge, a dangerous rocky outgrowth covered in the ethereal sky-blue ice that forms when snow falls onto a glacier. The bulge is a beautiful icy scab we have to wriggle our bodies over while executing a complicated change of ropes.

Each fixed rope up Lhotse is about 150 feet long. At the end of a segment, we have to unclip our jumar from the climbing harness and attach it to the next rope. The moment between ropes is the most dangerous. It is a two-step process: you must always remain attached to the fixed line by at least one device to avoid slipping down the wall.

Being unclipped here is suicide.

I dig my crampons into the ice as hard as I can to keep my balance while clipping out. Just then, the wind starts to shriek, launching rocks the size of a gallon jug of water straight toward us. Shards break away from the wall and thud against my helmet. My goggles rattle. I kneel down and press my head against the Face. Up ahead, Camp 3, which I'd easily seen from this spot on our second rotation, is a blur. I squint to make it out, but the clouds are thick billows of cotton candy. A sight that would be sweet, beautiful even, anywhere else, but is not a good sign here.

We can survive the wisps of spun-sugar clouds that break away from the clump. Those are mild mini storms and pass fast. But if the whole cap descends on us, there's nowhere to go. Up this high, scenery takes on a different meaning. Mystical cloud formations harbor avalanches, piles of whipped-cream snow are pocked underneath with icy fractures that might eat a leg or, worst case, an entire body.

Beauty and death are two sides of the same coin.

This morning, Mike predicted the sun was going to open up later. Instead, thick cloud caps descend on Lhotse, and before I can steady my feet on the wall, the wind's shriek becomes a hollow scream. It blows divots into the marshmallow sleeves of my jacket. Thwaps against the rope. Whips the snow into icy tornadoes. Large hunks of ice and debris speed violently down the wall around us and disintegrate as they plummet hundreds of feet.

In every Everest disaster movie, this is the scene where people die.

Visibility approaches zero.

All I can see is the rope in front of me.

Praying the ground is solid, I step onto a rocky, exposed ridge where Camp 3 is supposed to be. I spot the first settlement of tents, where Ang Dorjee said our oxygen tanks would be waiting. Through frosted goggles, I see them—little silver and yellow cartridges lying in the snow like a pack of AAA batteries. Lifelines. My breath is ragged and thin. I stumble toward the tanks and fall into the group huddle. We wait for directions from the guides, but the wind swirls against us in wild icy dervishes, obliterating all sound. I strain to hear Mike, even though he looks to be shouting now. I don't dare take off my neck gaiter and thick hood to hear him. Hypothermia hits instantly at this altitude.

"Grab your bottle and go!" Mike barks, and I hear his voice crack with panic. "Go, go, go! It's getting worse, keep moving. We're in a dangerous spot. Go, now!"

Over the last five weeks, we've been training for this moment, for our summit push. Mike has been stern, strict even, but never *ever* has he lost his cool. Hearing the panic in his voice launches me into a frenzy, shuttling me back to girlhood, to Lima, to home, where my father motivated us by screaming. Following orders was a nonissue in my house. There was no discussion, only repercussion. I always did as I was told.

I rush to scoop up my oxygen tank and move robotically through the steps as fast as I can.

Step One. Open backpack.

Step Two. Wedge oxygen tank into center.

Step Three. Connect regulator and mask to the tank.

Step Four. Tighten regulator so no oxygen is wasted.

My heart is pounding. I can hear my breath against the buff covering my neck and chin. Something in my mask still isn't clicking. I fiddle around with the regulator, but my teammates are moving already, so I strap my mask on, unsure if oxygen is flowing, and follow them into the blizzard. Camp 3 is a shallow bowl perched on the edge of the mountain with a bird's-eye view—usually. Our tents are pitched at the far end of the camp, another 500 feet up the embankment. Up ahead, I see a shadow breaking trail through the blizzard. I can't see if it's Danny or Brian. Flutters of snow become sheets and then, finally, a solid colorless wall.

The sky is bleached.

Fear flares through my body, hot and uncontrollable. Panic is deadly at altitude. I know this. It steals your oxygen, poisons your limbs. I've trained for moments just like this. But this knowledge can't override the adrenaline shuttling through my veins.

As we pass the first settlement of tents, there's a final traverse to cross. A thin ledge of rock we have to perch ourselves onto and then clip into a rope overhead. My mask is foggy, its airway thick and dull. When I draw a breath, I feel like I'm suffocating instead of pulling in oxygen. Maybe I didn't start the regulator? *Damn.* I stop and pull my backpack off to check.

"Silvia, what the hell do you think you're doing?" Lydia snaps. "You're in a dangerous spot. Keep moving!"

From the men, brusqueness is expected, but from Lydia, it's jarring. I'm gasping for air, so I rip off my mask and gulp down a thin breath. Hunks of debris slam down the wall fast and frantic, some exploding into deadly splinters, others thudding and blooming like tiny bomb clouds in front of my face. I grab the rope and walk toe-point, slowly—one foot in front of the other. I can't see anything but my hands grasping the ropes immediately above me, and then, suddenly, those end too. Through brief gaps in the swirling snow, I see the next fixed line. I have to clip out.

My toes clench inside my boots like they're trying to cling to the mountainside. Unlocking my jumar, I hold one long terrified breath. For a moment, I'm untethered and alone.

What if I just stop?

Just lean back and let go right now? Plummet into the void with the ice and scree. For the first time it clicks; I understand that not only has death always been on the table, but maybe that's why I'm here.

More ice, endless ice it seems, falls around me at warp speed. I imagine I'm next. No one would hear or see me. I'd just be here and then I'd be gone. Easy. Maybe it would be easier to end it like this. Go out with a bang.

They say years that end in six are bad luck for climbing Everest. Both 1996 and 2006 were devastating for the climbing community when storms killed dozens of climbers and Sherpas. Some of their corpses are still black and frozen on the mountain, too cold to ever properly rot.

But it's 2016 and here I am.

Back in Peru when my mother was battling cancer, I went to see a psychiatrist named Dr. Hugo. He determined that climbing Everest, for me, was a death wish. *Isn't it for everyone?* I laughed, dismissing him as a typical Peruvian machista. Of course he'd balk at my ambition. I'd been underestimated by men like him my entire life. But maybe Dr. Hugo was right. Maybe I'm here to let the mountain do for me what I can't do for myself.

By the time I click my jumar into the last stretch of rope, my skull is a symphony. The tat-tat-tat of my heart ricochets against its bony insides. Inside the gloves, my fingers are completely numb. My skin flashes hot, then cold, and my chest heaves like it might split down the center. Is the ground up or down? Everything is gyrating. My feet are walking on sky. Everything is white. Shiny bright white. Like the color of our national school uniform on the first day of school. White like the pristine gloves that school brigadiers wore during our annual patriotic march. Exclusive markers, those gloves were the ultimate recognition of being an exemplary student, something I ached to be.

White was clean, like the snow I'd only seen in movies.

White was tranquility, belonging, calmness.

White was order. Goodness.

But now inside the white, there is shouting.

The snowy silhouettes of my team flit in and out of sight. They're somewhere ahead in the whiteout. The wind pushes me off-balance; it's almost too strong to stand. I try to glue myself to the wall.

This is crazy. Totally fucking crazy. To climb a mountain—to climb *this* mountain—makes no sense.

1, 2, 3 . . .

I teeter on the lip of the traverse. Snow-blind, I click into the final rope, complete the traverse, then drop to all fours and bear crawl toward where I pray the tents are pitched. Finding my tent is the only goal. I block all other thoughts and sounds. There is no more counting. I'm nothing but a body moving through space. For once, blacking out comes in handy.

"Get inside any empty tent!" someone yells as our team Sherpas run past. "Descending to Camp 2, no safe!"

Finally, I spot a cluster of shapes. I fumble around for the double zippers of the first tent I reach, push them apart with a finger to unzip the frozen flap, and roll into the tent. I quickly pull my crampons off so the spikes don't tear the tent, and fling my backpack to the ground. My oxygen tank pops out. My teeth chatter as blood starts circulating into my limbs. I can't stop shivering. The winds are ferocious, thwapping against the nylon walls. My heart is in overdrive. I want to scream for help, but no one will hear me.

I can't do this.

I need someone, anyone to help me.

Snotty tears roll down my cheeks.

I curl up on my side. This is as far as I'm going to make it. This is the end. Who was I to think that I could summit Mount Everest? The tears build into a heaving deep-belly sob. Not since the first day at Base Camp, alone and overwhelmed in my tent, have I cried like this.

Before I left San Francisco, I drafted a will—a formality my climber friends recommended. Too scattered to do anything official, I threw together a holographic will. Leaving my apartment to my nonprofit, I wrote something general about how it should continue to be used for good. But the will didn't seem real. More like a half-assed precautionary measure a responsible adult would take. Now, the words *last will and testament* loom large.

What will I leave a testament to?

There were nights in San Francisco that I prayed for the San Andreas Fault to open up and swallow me whole. For my heart to quietly stop beating in my sleep. Some mornings I woke up with mysterious bruises all over my body. Other mornings, I woke up in a hospital not knowing how I had gotten there. So many days I wasted retracing the steps of my blackouts like a forensic scientist. All the friends and family who begged me not to climb

Everest, who were afraid it might kill me, didn't understand that I'd been killing myself for years.

I wrap my arms around my body as tightly as possible.

It's not enough. It's never been enough.

I pick up the canary-yellow oxygen tank and clasp it against my chest. Pretend it's holding me, and cling to it like life support. What I need to keep breathing right now is not oxygen, but touch. *I need to be held.* I need a hug that wants nothing in return. A hug that is pure and protective.

The hug of a mother.

Everest has many names, but they all mean mother. Sagarmatha—Mother of the Sky; Chomolungma—Mother of the World. For some reason, I haven't feared her. I have reverence for her power, her sheer hulking breadth. Instead of terror, I've felt protected by her size. There's something nurturing and steady about eons of rock, about Everest's immovable brutality and beauty. I'd come to envision her as the strong spiritual guide I had never had. And in return, I thought she would see me with the clear-eyed compassion of a mother.

What an outrageous fantasy.

What arrogance and delusion to think that a mountain could save me from myself. To believe that this sprawling formation of rocks and ice would open its so-called arms and provide me with safety. That it would give a shit if I lived or died. She's killed so many. People come to Everest for many reasons—they want peace, adventure, honor, glory, transcendence. But like a good mother, she gives us what we need, not what we want.

Maybe Everest really is my glorified death wish. Maybe what I've been chasing is a way to go out on top. Literally.

Why did I expect Chomolungma to save me?

After all, she was not the first mother to let me down.

Chapter 2

BORRON Y CUENTA NUEVA

After a swift knock, the front door creaked open. J's hi-ho whistle danced through the house and into the kitchen where I sat with Mamita as she brewed café pasado and scooped out maracuya for morning jugo.

"Hola, pasa a la cocina, J," she called. "Estoy haciendo un cafecito."

"Buenos días," said J, ambling into the kitchen and dropping a kiss on my mother's cheek.

"Hola, J!" I chirped, pecking his cheek as he leaned toward me. His aftershave was a thick, spicy cloud. Lean, with a handlebar mustache, bushy black hair, and mahogany skin, J was younger than my gray-haired grouch of a father. His jovial bounce and whistle lightened the dark corners of the house. Mamita's shoulders dropped when he was around.

"Jala el banquito!" she said. *Pull up a stool.* At that, I giggled. Our kitchen table, a low, rustic wooden table, was built for short people. When I sat on the backless kid-sized stools, my legs slid under with ease. My little brother Miguel was a toddler. Before we hired a housekeeper, Mamita hardly sat at all, flitting around to make sure the dishes were warmed and properly seasoned to my father's standards. And my father, Segundo, was hardly five feet five. We all just fit. But the sight of J, at five feet eight, sitting at the table with his knees folded up to his chin, sipping from a delicate china cup, was silly.

My father didn't allow visitors often, and my mother seemed to bask in J's company. Mamita laid out two pan francés on the table—French-style rolls spread with butter, ham, and cheese—for J before he started work. She poured a tiny stream of coffee essence, café pasado, into my cup and an adult serving into J's, topping off both with boiling water from a thermos. Then, she leaned in, ready to gossip, and they launched into the droning chatter of adults, leaving me to my café and pan. I snatched the can of evaporated milk from the table and splashed some into my cup. Mama promised I could have a full cup of café when I turned six the next year.

"Azúcar?" I said, holding a bowl of sugar cubes up for J but eyeing the glittering hunks for myself.

"No, no. Gracias," J said, ruffling my hair. "No quiero engordar."

J was convinced sugar would make him fat.

Mamita always giggled at this.

My mornings were spent here, content while J and Mama sipped and chatted—him eating, her hassling him to eat more. Meanwhile, I basked in the sun streaming through the window of the inner courtyard next to the kitchen, soaking in a feeling I didn't have during the rest of the week. I noticed new things. Little things. Like the way my mom's chestnut eyes gleamed or the extra tint of rose on her full high cheeks; the warmth of sun on my hand, the sweet-sour tang of the maracuya and the grainy crunch of its seeds between my baby teeth. I could feel these things wriggling into my mind—imprinting as color, light, joy.

J had been cleaning our house since I was a toddler. He was introduced to my father by a distant but trusted cousin as someone reliable. In the 1970s, Lima had a hierarchy that ranked mestizos, light-skinned Peruvians with mostly Spanish blood, above indígenas, darker-skinned Andean people, and drew lines between working, middle, and upper class, with stark definition. Skin color was synonymous with class. Even though my father was from the mountains, his light skin and education let him slip easily into Lima society, but Mama remained on the fringes, more comfortable with the working class than the elite. Most families in Lima who could afford staff did not take a cafecito with them. But Mama treated all people, rich or poor, equally and demanded I do the same.

Financial security is only as thick as a hair, she'd say.

Memories of poverty hunted her like a ghost dog—so close I think that she could still smell it. To her, J was a peer, both of them doing whatever it took to rise above the struggle. Young, hardworking, and much closer to her age than my father, J was the sort of strong, gentle country man she wished my father could be.

That at first maybe she thought he was.

* * *

To the people of his hometown, Santa Cruz de Chuca, a small village in the Andes, or La Sierra as we call it, my father had done more than well for himself. First, making it out of the mountains and into the capital city, he got an education, opened his own accounting firm, and built our home in Santiago de Surco, a colorful middle-class district with upper-class aspirations. But while my father became an important man driven by achievement and status, his heart went soft at the chance to help young men from La Sierra, where money was slim and opportunities were few. He brought many men to Lima and used his connections to get them jobs. He knew what it was like to be treated as second-class. It was his namesake. Segundo. *Second.* At first, my father was wary of letting another man into the house. For him to cede any part of his turf was major. But like Mamita, he must have seen something of himself in J, because in time, he embraced him as part of the family.

Somewhere, there's a picture of me as a toddler holding my father's hand as I chase after a red plastic ball. In the background J is watching us, smiling.

J came to clean every week, and it took him all day. Our house, a two-story modernist design, created by a known Lima architect, was my father's opus, and he demanded it be kept pristine. Floor-to-ceiling windows wrapped the house, letting in floods of searing white light, but the dark cherrywood floors quickly swallowed it up in shadowy pockets.

J started with the windows. I stood in the driveway and watched in awe as he leaned a long metal ladder against the front of the house, then climbed rung by rung to clean and shine the outside of the windows with vinegar and stacks of old newspaper. Wet ink stained his hands for the rest of the day. Then, the floors. He polished the parquet floors and stairs and the heavy swooping banisters to a glossy shine with la cera roja, a thick, pungent, carnauba wax that smelled like spilled gasoline. It was oxblood red, and when J squeezed it onto the floor, it reminded me of the thick and goopy glue I used for my art projects. But as he slowly worked the waxer over the floors, it went slick and spread out, disappearing into the wood. For days after, my socks slipped around wildly, and my shoes made a rubbery clean squeak. But it was the smell I remember most. Astringent, heavy, alcoholic, it clung to my nostrils, my clothes.

"To work!" J bent down and in one beat swooped me up off my stool and lifted me onto his shoulders. From there, I could see on top of the fridge, could almost rake my fingers across the ceiling. I laughed, gleeful. Just as fast, he plopped me back onto the ground and bent to scoop up his cup and plate.

"Dejalo no más," Mama said, waving him away. "*Leave it.* Silvita, give J a hug and then stay out of his hair, okay? He's got lots to do!"

But J was already whistling his way to the front hall closet, where he shed his khaki pants and long-sleeve button-down shirt and swapped them out for ragged work pants and a T-shirt. Every week, after he finished, he showered on the third floor in the azotea where all the laundry was done, rolled his things into a makeshift bundle, and dressed again in his khaki pants and button-down shirt. When he left, it was close to sunset, and his thick, inky hair was coiffed to perfection.

The next year, just as the Shining Path murders began in the mountains surrounding Cusco, I started first grade at María Reina, the Marianistas' Catholic school across town. It was a long drive, but my father was the accountant for the school, and he got a discount. Education was the most important thing to him. And a prestigious one at a good price was something he was willing to drive for—even for a daughter. To prepare for classes, I needed a uniforme único. A legacy of Peru's militaristic government, a nationwide school uniform was enacted in 1970 as an attempt to reform our deeply embedded social-class system. By dressing all the students the same way, they figured, Peruvian school kids would be twinned, blurring social, racial, and economic differences. There would be no reason to discriminate against anyone. The uniform was to be worn throughout elementary school—first grade to sixth grade—and all through high school.

At a department store, two premade uniforms might cost 300 soles. But at Mercado Central, where Mama took me with cash from my father tucked into her purse, material for knockoffs could be purchased and sewn for a quarter of the price.

"Agarrate fuerte de mi!" *Hold on tight,* my mother warned, clutching my left hand and locking onto her purse with the other.

Ever vigilant of the pickpockets and purse snatchers who swarmed the mercado, Mama was expert at weaving through the streets. Around the market, tricycles, ambulantes, and buses converged in smoky clusters while people sprinted through traffic. "Caserita!" "Caserita!" Vendors hollered, employing their pet names for customers to lure us in. Wooing and sweet-talking was simply a part of shopping.

"Caserita preciosa. Ay mi reina, que te puedo servir?"

My gorgeous customer, my queen, how can I help you?

I stood a bit taller. I knew my mother was gorgeous, and hearing them holler after her, trying to catch her attention, even if it was only for business, tickled me with pride. She used it to our advantage. That was also part of shopping.

Mama set the material for two skirts and two shirts on the counter. As the vendor added up the bill, she threw on two more bolts of fabric. Both larger pieces.

"How much?" Mama asked the vendor.

"Two hundred soles."

"Que cosa? Carisimo! No way. Vámonos. *Let's go*, Silvita."

She grabbed my hand and started to pull me from the store. I turned my nose up and marched beside her.

"Wait, wait!" He cried. "One hundred fifty."

"You think I'm a millionaire?" Mama huffed. We kept walking.

"Ay! One twenty-five."

She spun on her heel, glancing over her shoulder, still ready to bolt.

"One hundred. Y nada mas. He looks like he'd love my business," Mama added, pointing to an indentical stall across the alleyway.

"Okay, okay, calm down. Come back."

Leaving was staged. The walkout was integral to the song and dance of the bargain. Only a sucker paid the first ask. Even I knew that. We had to perform the act of leaving to get what we wanted.

"Put the larger cuts in a different bag, por favor," Mama said as she separated and folded them neatly on the counter, her hands running tenderly over the heavy material.

She paid and thanked the vendor, and we ducked back into the choked streets, two packages tucked under Mama's arm, my small hand folded into hers.

"Mama, but why? Why two packages? Who for?"

"Shush shush, hijita." She clucked her tongue. "Be alert right now. You have to learn to pay attention in the city. Your life is too soft." She'd been raised in La Victoria, an industrial hood skirting Old Lima's city limits. It was nothing like the manicured streets of my neighborhood. In Lima, industries clustered together in districts: cobblers, fabric merchants, stone and tile. La Victoria was the automotive part of town. We called it the Recycling Center. If you wanted to track down something stolen, you went to La Victoria. You had to watch your back there. Family were the only ones to be trusted. Even then, loyalties fluctuated.

We crossed the main avenue, weaving through cars, horns bleating as we rushed toward the intersection of Calle Capón. A smile crept over my face. I knew this corner. We were heading toward my favorite Chinese bakery. Surrounding the Mercado, Lima's massive Chinatown was full of chifas, Cantonese-Peruvian hybrid restaurants.

"No need to tell your father we came downtown," she said, handing me my favorite pork bun.

I wondered if we should bring my father a snack. His office was just down the street. But he didn't like us to stop by unplanned. Or, really, at all. And I'd learned to stop asking.

"Mmmm hmmm," I hummed, my mouth full, savoring every bite of the pillowy bun.

* * *

Father dropped me off at school early every morning on his way into the office, taking Avenida Angamos all the way. Rush hour was minimal then—a few colectivos, the communal vans that acted as mini city buses, clogged the road, and at the stoplights men weaved around the cars to sell the morning paper through the window. In the afternoons, he picked me up and came home for almuerzo—a long, late afternoon lunch—before going back to the office to work late. Sometimes, he didn't come home for dinner at all. These were the nights that Mama paced the kitchen; other times, she would busy herself with my brother, Miguel.

A flash of a woman, my mother was hard to catch. She was always flitting in and out of the house, running endless errands. Rushing between here and there. Sometimes she left us at home with J instead of loading us into the car to tag along.

So much of that time was a blur of motion, light, and noise.

One afternoon, she set up a little art station for me on a desk in the guest room with a sketch pad and crayons.

"*Mamita, puedo ir contigo hoy?*"

I desperately wanted to go with her.

"No." She hushed me, turning my head to the paper and pastels. "Not today, hijita. You stay here with J. Another day you can come."

"Mamita . . . ," I pleaded.

"Ya vengo." She pecked me on the cheek and ran out before I could protest further. "Un ratito!" she called, already halfway down the stairs. Un ratito. Mama was always going out *for a little while*. Just a *minute. A tiny, little minute.* Everything was diminutive. Just a little bit of cake. Just a teensy sip of pisco.

How could such a tiny bit of anything hurt anyone?

I don't remember how long she was gone before I heard J's whistle coming down the hall.

"Silvita?" He called my name, his voice a deep baritone.

"Ah, here you are." He came in and shut the door behind him. He lifted his index finger to his mouth. *Shhhh*, he whispered, his eyes twinkling like it was a game. *Shhhh*. I giggled, nodding along. What were we playing with no sounds? The silent game. I knew that one. Maybe hide-and-seek.

"Come here." His whisper was raspy, muffled.

"What?" I said.

"Sientate." He patted the bed. I dropped the crayon and plopped down next to him.

He put his hand on my leg over my school skirt. His palm swallowed my thigh, and the end of his fingers grazed my knee. His hand was cold and rough from the cleaning and climbing. Against my warm skin, it made me shiver.

His eyes held mine as he leaned down and brushed his lips across my cheek. I could feel the wiry hairs of his mustache and swallowed a giggle, trying my best to stay silent. To follow the rules of the game. Then, something new. His lips moved to mine. Pinched and dry, they scraped the soft tissue inside my lip. I froze. He watched my face, like he was looking for something. I'd seen my parents kiss. I had kissed my aunt. But his kiss felt different. I played along. Slowly, he pushed the long gray pleat of my school skirt up one leg. Motioned for me to lay my head on the pillow. There was no more laughing, no more sound. He stopped whispering but continued to press the *shhhh* finger against his lips to let me know we were still playing. After a while—three minutes, five minutes, an hour, an eternity, I don't know—he pulled my skirt back down and without breaking eye contact, tucked a stray curl into my ponytail.

There was a sticky white glob on my leg, and as I reached down to touch it, J quickly wiped it away with the inside of his T-shirt. "No digas nada," he whispered, leaning so close the hot steam from his mouth wet my ear. "Tus papas saben lo que estoy haciendo y están de acuerdo."

No need to say anything. Your parents know what I'm doing and it's okay. They've asked me to.

With J, I'd always been ready to play. He'd kissed me before, on the cheek, pet me, played with me, flung me into the air, and we all laughed. Me and Mama. Our laughter meant play. And now, he was following orders. Listening to my parents, to my father, the way I always had. I didn't understand why they would ask for this but didn't dare question it.

En conversación de adultos se callan los menores, my father always said.

In adult conversations, kids are quiet.

After that, J never had to hiss *shhhh* again. All he had to do was bring a finger to his lips and the sound rattled through my mind, a great shushing snake that drowned out any thoughts, any urge to speak, to question. Even my quieting was quiet.

And that is how it began.

A long, silent, strange game, one I never knew the rules to. The only thing I knew for sure was that the sound of the garage door opening meant *the end*. The house began to turn inside out on me. Its corners darkened. When my parents fought, it drove numbing needles into my fingers. I hated the screaming, the violent rages, vases shattering, bones cracking. But I learned there was something worse.

The sound of a whistle.

Silent games.

The muffled choke of a girl quieted by a hand.

Every night before bed, I'd kneel in front of the nightstand, between the twin beds where Miguel and I slept, and pray to the Ángelito de la Guarda.

> Ángelito de la Guarda,
> dulce compañía,
> no me desampares
> ni de noche ni de día.
> No me dejes solo que me perdería.

I asked her to protect Padre, Mamita, Miguel, and J. I asked her to protect me. *Please don't leave me lonely during the night and during the day, because if you leave me alone, I'll lose myself.*

* * *

By 1983, I was in third grade, and Sendero Luminoso—*the Shining Path*—had made their way down from the mountains of Ayacucho and started to infiltrate Lima. It was all over the news. Electric towers exploding. Rolling blackouts. Kidnappings. Car bombs. A domestic terrorist movement based on the principles of Chairman Mao, the Shining Path was ignited by a philosophy professor in the central Andes surrounding Cusco. He believed that by taking land and governmental power out of the hands of the bourgeois and returning it to the proletariat, Peru could become a more equitable nation. The Shining Path's methods were bloody and unyielding.

It was a time of tyrannical precision and violent outbursts. The current of danger was luminous, both inside and outside my home.

One afternoon, I was waiting to go with Mamita to visit her sister, my Tía Irene. The clock in the kitchen read three-thirty, no, no . . . six-fifteen. I often mixed up little and big hands. My stomach grumbled, but I didn't dare call upstairs for my mom. Time was irrelevant to Mamita anyway. A fluid suggestion rather than a fixed moment. I'd learned to wait patiently.

"Segundo, nooo, noo, noo!" A scream from upstairs ripped through my hungry haze. "Qué haces? Noooo."

Mama!

Our staircase swept from the front door to a second-floor landing. Cautious, I ran halfway up on my tiptoes and peeked through slats in the railing. On the landing above, my mother was on her knees, while my father rained blows down on her back, the top of her head, her arms, anything he could reach.

"You fucker," he barked.

I ran up two more stairs. As he pummeled her, she became still, pulling her body in tighter and tucking her fingers into her palms. Like a turtle retreating into a shell.

"Noo!" I screamed, charging up the stairs, my socked feet slipping out wildly beneath me, landing me onto my hands and knees. I crawled up the final stairs. "No a mi mami!"

Not to my mom, you won't.

His bushy eyebrows were scrunched together, and fury appeared in his eyes. Desperate, I threw my body between them. *Maybe he'll listen now. Maybe he'll stop . . .* His fist hit my nose, and I heard the crunch before I felt a hot black wave wash over me. I fell to the floor and curled into a ball next to my mom. Blood streamed from my nose; its fiery red color was shocking against the glossy cognac wood.

"You imbecile!" Mama was on her feet again, making the most of his momentary shock. "Look what you've done. Le has roto la nariz a tu hija."

You broke your own daughter's nose.

"Mi hijita, ay, mi hijita. Lift your head." Mama rushed to the green bathroom and grabbed a handful of cotton balls. She tore one in half and made a tiny ball that she pressed just inside my left nostril, then pulled me to the couch and cradled me, propping my head into the crook of her elbow.

But the bleeding didn't stop. I began to wail.

"Vamos al doctor." Mama stood up abruptly and, without a word to my father, carried me down the stairs, out the front door, and tucked me into the front seat of my father's car.

"Ten la cabeza arriba."

"Mom, am I going to die?"

"No hijita, you'll be fine."

I leaned my head back against the seat and pinched my nostrils, careful not to bleed on the beige seats.

At the ER, we stepped up to the admissions desk.

"My daughter fell from the stool and hit her face," Mama explained calmly. "I plugged it with cotton, but the bleeding hasn't stopped. She might have broken something."

Upset that the nurses would think this was my fault and confused about why Mama didn't remember what had just happened, I tugged at her jacket. "But Mama, I didn't fall down . . ." She looked down at me, her eyes watery, and stroked my hair. My mouth was metallic with blood. Thin clots slid down the back of my throat.

"Shhh, cállate, hijita," she said. "Shhh. No digas nada. Quédate callada." *Shhh. Say nothing. Stay quiet.*

I swallowed my words.

"Quieres unas salchipapas?" Mama asked as we walked out of the hospital.

"Sí!" I exclaimed, the pain already being replaced with the thought of the salty crunch of French fries and sausages drowned in mayonnaise and ketchup.

"But Mama, una preguntita. What about the blood on the floor?"

"Don't worry, hijita, J will clean it up tomorrow."

There were so many things I had to stay quiet about now.

And as I grew quieter, the bombs from the mountains grew louder.

The Shining Path was encroaching on Lima, infiltrating the city and setting fire to buses and bombing residential streets.

The growing chaos outside my home matched the growing chaos inside.

* * *

Tía Emerita always prayed over the chicken before she slit its throat. As the birthday girl, it was my job to hold its wings and hold them tight. She set up a plastic bucket underneath the stairwell in the produce hall outside the kitchen.

"Silvita, come!" Her voice was loud and high-pitched.

"Mama, por qué tengo que hacerlo?" I whined. *Why do I have to do it?*

"Cállate y no te quejes!" Mama snapped. "Don't disrespect your aunt. She's traveled a long way."

If there's one thing she wouldn't tolerate, it was snobbery. Especially not to my aunt, who brought a chicken she raised herself and carried in her lap all the way from Puente Piedra. Tía Emerita's neighborhood sat at the edge of Lima where many families lived in hillside shacks without water, gas, and electricity. To get here, my aunt had taken the covida bus, an old school bus that traveled in one general direction but with no real schedule, stopping at random street corners so often that the twenty-five-mile trip to our house took two hours. She had to double-wrap the chicken's body in plastic bags and tie them together like a satchel—a little chicken purse—and put it in a big gunnysack. During the ride she'd give it some air by setting the satchel on the seat next to her, or if the bus was crammed, on her lap. After, she would put it back and show up at our door with the gunnysack slung over her shoulder and a wide grin on her face.

Emerita was Miguel's godmother and my father's first cousin. She had left Santa Cruz de Chuca after elementary school to come live with my father in Lima, where she stayed until she fell in love and had my cousin Felipe. They moved to a modest brick house, where Tía sold chickens, pigs, rabbits, and turkeys from her adjoining corner store. In La Sierra, where Tía was from, it was customary to bring something you'd grown as a birthday gift. Papas. Pollo. Humitas. Choclo. Bringing a fruit of your labor, a chicken for slaughter, meant more than any doll or candy or toy.

That didn't mean I wanted anything to do with the chicken. I was a city kid, a limeña, used to eating meat that was already dead and plucked.

"Hija," Mama kneeled down to my eye level, her voice softer. "This is your tía's gift. It's full of love."

In the hall, I could hear the bird squawking. A large metal stockpot of water began to boil on the stove.

I knew better than to fight back. I was nine now and practically a woman. I suppose it made sense. So many other things were happening that I didn't understand. Why shouldn't I be able to kill a chicken?

I walked slowly to meet my fate.

Miguel and our cousin Felipe, who was six years older than me, were crawling over each other for a chance to see the bird. From deep within the smelly sack, Emerita yanked a stunning bundle of white and flame-orange feathers. It smelled like feed pellets and dirt, and its body was diapered in a series of plastic bags. She peeled the bags off slowly, motioning for me to clasp my hands around its body. My hands didn't fit all the way around, and the bird bucked and ca-cawed under my timid grip.

"Hold it tight, girl!" Emerita bellowed. "Que no se te escape."

Quills dug into the delicate flesh of my fingers. I squeezed tighter and felt the bird's heart thump against my sweaty palms. For a minute, our heartbeats merged.

"Are chickens scared to die?" I asked Tía.

"Love is killing it quickly," she replied.

From what I'd seen, love was explosive, seismic; a complex equation of secrets and cover-ups, of ever-shifting moods. Mesmerized by the warmth of the chicken's body pulsing between my hands, I understood love could be something more tender.

Just then the chicken became serene in my hands.

Before I could question Tía again, she yanked its head back with one hand and slit its neck in a clean, swift motion. Brilliant scarlet blood streamed from its convulsing body into the bucket, then slowed to short spurts. Tía pressed her free hand over mine to make sure I didn't loosen my grip.

Little by little its violent jerking slowed, then abruptly stopped. I blinked. I'd been holding my breath. Little dots of scarlet painted my face. War paint. When I finally took a breath, the air was tinny and thick. Tía grabbed the chicken from me and with a butcher knife unceremoniously hacked its head off. She brought the boiling pot from inside and poured it into another metal pot next to the stairs, then dunked the chicken into the steaming water to loosen feathers from skin. We had to work fast, Tía said, as we sat on the steps knee-to-knee and plucked every feather from its body, making certain not to miss a single feather. A feather was evidence of slaughter. No feathers meant no proof of agony.

With the chicken dead and plucked, preparations for the birthday almuerzo began. Mamita and Emerita were making my favorite: arroz con pollo. On the way into the kitchen, Tía pushed the bloody bucket aside with her foot. Later she'd use it to make sangrecita, chicken-blood stew.

Love is killing it quickly, she'd said.

Love must be bloody, I thought.

It was ten a.m.

For the next two hours, Tía and Mama disappeared into a flurry of cooking and local gossip. They chopped garlic, steamed the white rice, butchered the chicken into parts, and assembled a causa de atún, a cold pressed-potato dish stuffed with tuna and mayonnaise. Soon, the house was filled with the earthy green smell of stewing cilantro. As the chicken browned on the stove, its blood simmered in a small pot, slowly clotting and congealing into a jiggly ground-beef-looking stew.

Miguel and Felipe played fulbito in the front drive. My father was, as usual, still in his home office.

Almuerzo would soon be served at the ornate ten-person table in our rarely used "fancy" dining room. Tía laid out my parents' special occasion plates and gold-rimmed coupe glasses. The delicate crystal bowl, the thin ring of gold, was like something a princess might sip from.

"Bring a bottle of pisco, Silvita," called my mother. "The big one." I skipped to the storeroom under the stairs where my parents kept their liquor. It was a dark, gaping space barely taller than me. The low plywood door creaked as I swung it open. Past a maze of canned beans, ten-pound bags of rice and sugar, and stacks of bottles of nuclear-yellow Inca Kola, was a shiny display of magical-looking bottles. A variety of piscos, Cartavio rum, J&B Scotch whiskey, and Campari, with its electric-orange liquid and regal label. The door swung shut behind me, and I didn't move to prop it open. Sounds from the kitchen were muffled. Just a sliver of light spilled under the door. I thrilled in the soft darkness of the room.

Upstairs, I had a room, but it was no longer mine. J could find me there anytime. Under the stairs, the shadows of home didn't feel so daunting. Warm and dark and sweet smelling, it was a portal to another land, but not another place that would swallow me whole. One where we didn't have to worry about my Tía traveling alone while bombs shattered the city. Where I wasn't stuck waiting for someone, anyone, to tell me why J did what he did. For the adults, it must have been a special room too. Because all those bottles—the astringent and syrupy concoctions, their wines, their whiskeys, their pisco, which smelled the worst of all—always seemed to brighten the mood.

"Silvia!"

I grabbed the first bottle my fingers touched and bolted out of the room, latching the door behind me. In the kitchen, the blender was whirring. I set the pisco on the counter, and Mama measured aloud her recipe for the perfect strawberry pisco sour, a celebratory birthday drink: "Two cups strawberries, half a cup of sugar, one cup pisco, one cup of water, three cups of ice, and the squeeze of two limones." I licked my lips at the sight of the strawberries and all that sugar.

"Segundooooo! Segundo! La comida ya está lista."

My father sauntered out from his office, stiff and unsmiling. He surveyed the landscape. As everyone sat to eat, there was a restlessness in my mother's face as she watched him take his first bite. He nodded and took another, and the table broke out into chatter.

"Salud comadre, salud compadre!" they cried.

Everyone held up their fancy glasses, filled to the brim with slushy strawberry pisco, mine just a third of the way. *Un poquito.* A kid's portion. As I sipped, the cold hit me first, then the sweet bloom of sugar and the searing heat as it melted down my throat. I choked a bit, and my father chuckled, proud almost. The liquor was an electric shock down my spine. A tickle in the brain. A tiny humming over my skin. A swell of comfort.

Of pleasure.

Across the table, my parents toasted each other and kissed lightly on the lips. Seeing them touch lit me up. Borron y cuenta nueva, Mom liked to say. *Kiss and make new.* They did that on special days. Forgot the fighting. The screaming. The past didn't matter. It was a clean slate. For this day, at least.

I gulped down another sip. I wanted to forget. I wanted to make new.

"Salud to you, my dear Silvita!" cooed Mamita. "You're nine now. What a beautiful age. You're becoming a young woman."

"Keep studying," grumbled my father. "A young woman, yes. Now you can keep your room clean."

In all the morning cartoons and fairy tales, the princess left home on the arm of a handsome prince. I kept trying to wedge our portrait into the frame, but no fairy tale fit my story. My father looked more like Mamita's father than her prince. His hair silver where hers was still dark brown. At school soccer games he didn't roughhouse or join in like the other dads. An older man, a younger woman. Maybe they met like me and J? If J was who my father had chosen for me, did that make him my prince?

Everyone finished their piscos, and Sandra, our housekeeper, plunked two-liter bottles of Inca Kola down on the table. But before we got to dessert, Emerita stood suddenly. She wanted to be home before dark. The Shining Path had continued to set off car bombs at random around the city. Nighttime bus routes were dangerous and unpredictable. Especially for a woman and child alone.

"Senderistas, aye," Emerita cried. "Están destruyendo todo!"

She, like most people she and my father had grown up with, was a proletariat, one of the Peruvians Sendero Luminoso said they were fighting for, but she cursed their bloody approach. "How are we free if that means killing many of our own?"

As the room broke into debate, Miguel and Felipe ran to the living room, and I snuck to the kitchen and poured the last of the pisco sour from the blender straight into my mouth. Its sweet and sour warmth felt like a hug from the inside. I ran the seeds over my tongue, savoring their gritty crunch and remembering mornings with J, before. When he and Mama and I sat in the middle of our sunny kitchen, the maracuya bursting in my mouth.

My parents didn't notice I was gone, so I backed slowly out the side door and into the interior hall where we'd killed the chicken. I ran up the three flights of stairs to the azotea. Just past the washbasin, there was a short ladder that led to the roof. Careful not to snag my birthday outfit on the splintery wood, I crawled up it and onto the shimmery tin roof. Still fuzzy from the pisco, I stepped slowly to the edge of the roof and leaned into the fading sun. I could see past the tops of the fiery red poinciana trees to the cerros—*hills*—in the distance. Massive and smog-cloaked, the cerros on the outskirts of Lima were home to a village of thousands who'd claimed the land by squatting. They first built shantytowns, with no running water or electricity, until eventually the place became theirs.

I looked at the cerros and imagined a place free of secrets. Somewhere far from here. Somewhere I could breathe my own air. Down on the sidewalk the heladero man pushed his yellow cart past, blowing his silver horn like a magical flute. *Whoo whoooot!* Neighbor kids ran from their houses, soles in hand for a box of bombones or Peziduri.

Whoo whoooot!

That whistle meant ice cream, meant summertime was here, or spring was on its way. Meant the end of the dry season. Meant, if we were lucky, trips to El Bosque, an enchanting forested pool club far outside the city, where I was free to run and play, to notice the sounds of birds, the colors and smells of the plants, acts of noticing that were lost to me in the punitive precision of home.

A whistle from the heladero was a call to play. To revel in childhood.

But as I listened that night from my spot on the roof, the sound started to warp. To morph into something more complex and sinister. I leaned out a little farther and squeezed my eyes shut. I wanted to hold on to the sweet ice cream whistle just a little bit longer. But it was too late. The hi-ho of J's whistle danced alongside, twisting and bending it, until the two whistles became indistinguishable. Until they became one.

The whole world swirled below me—whistles and blood spatter and pisco.

Love is killing it quickly.

There would be no kiss and make new for me.

Chapter 3

⁂

SUMMIT MITTENS

I was wide awake at seven a.m., my ears still ringing from the cacophony of last night's schlep into Kathmandu. The meep-meep of moped horns. The long smoker's sigh of exhausted buses huffing and puffing their way down crowded streets. Kathmandu is dense. Kathmandu is dirty. Kathmandu is chaotic.

I feel right at home.

It's Lima in the 1980s. Not the manicured side, the Miraflores, or the Barranco. But Puente Piedra. Downtown Lima. Combi-style vans blaring their horns and buzzing past three to a lane, motorcycles driving the wrong way to cut through traffic, whole families riding helmetless. Pedestrians playing Frogger just to cross the street. The Lima where vendors swarmed the streets and traffic was unregulated. Shit, everything was unregulated. If you could drive in central Lima, you could drive anywhere with a steering wheel on the left-hand side.

Groggy, but too buzzed to sleep, I roll over in bed and try to relish the 400-thread-count sheets. It's my last night in a real bed for two months. For the two-week trek to Base Camp, I will sleep on hard cots in tea houses, and then for the six weeks training to summit Everest, I will be in a tent. I try to hang onto this minute. To soak in the comfort of hotel sheets and fluffy down, to capture a moment of stillness and breathe the cool hum of fully oxygenated air. But chilling has never been my strong suit. There's too much to do.

Ang Dorjee Sherpa is coming to check my gear soon, and everything's a mess. I crawl out of bed and part the heavy curtains, letting light filter in through the sheers. My window overlooks the swimming pool, and beyond that, acres of lush, manicured lawn. Far from the chaos of downtown, the Hotel Annapurna is one of Kathmandu's few luxury hotels. Worth it for a couple nights of comfort before the trek, I figured. I brush my teeth, slip on a Courageous Girls T-shirt and down vest, and dump the contents of my suitcases onto the two double beds. It's like an REI garage sale: mounds of down—thin jackets, thick jackets, vests, pants—piled high against the wooden headboards. Boots and headlamps and tiny hills of freeze-dried snacks. On Everest, defective gear can be the difference between not only summit and failure, but life and death.

It's no time to go cheap. Especially on my very first attempt.

For the two-month expedition to summit, we have to pack four different sets of gear: a Base Camp hike bag, an everyday life at Base Camp bag, a rotation-training bag, and a summit bid bag. It's a logistical nightmare, and organization is not my strong suit.

I set to work sorting everything into piles.

Something's missing. I can't put my finger on it yet, but it's a dull hum at the back of my brain. A familiar lurking. I've forgotten something important. Forgetting equipment is my trademark. Sometimes I wonder if it's really forgetfulness or the result of feeling unfinished. Like there's a part of me out there that I haven't found yet.

There's a sharp tap at the window.

Damn.

It's exactly nine. Not 9:20. Not even 9:05. Ang Dorjee Sherpa sure as hell isn't on Peruvian time.

"You have the list?" he asks as I crack my door slowly. His voice swoops up, almost a British lilt to his Nepali accent. I nod. "Please, come in," I say, bowing instinctually.

Ang Dorjee is Everest royalty, born into climbing. His father was Nima Tenzing Sherpa, the guide who helped British mountaineer Chris Bonington summit in the 1970s and '80s, back when climbing Everest was even more rare and prestigious. A Master Sherpa, Ang Dorjee has summited Everest twenty times and was one of the heroes during the disastrous 1996 season that Jon Krakauer memorialized in *Into Thin Air*. He lives in the States now with his American wife and two kids but comes to the Himalayas every season to guide climbers up Everest and visit his family.

Our crew is an elite team of eight led by Adventure Consultants, one of the original Everest guiding companies. I know I've put in the work to earn my place, but I still feel lucky they let me join at the last minute. The rest of the summit team set out two days ago with the lead guide, Mike, on the forty-mile hike to Base Camp. I should have been with them, but I couldn't leave the States any earlier. Ang Dorjee was gracious enough to delay his departure to greet me in Kathmandu, review my gear, and pass it on to the Sherpas to transport to Base Camp.

He stakes a wide cowboy stance at the end of the bed and pulls a piece of paper from a file folder with my name on it. A shadow of mustache darkens his broad mahogany face. Smile lines whisker away from his thin, dry lips.

Determined to show him I'm prepared, I dig around my backpack for the spreadsheet I'd printed back home in San Francisco. "Ta-da!" I say awkwardly, producing a crinkled wad of paper from the bottom of my carry-on. With the slightest hint of a smirk, he takes the list and smooths it out between muscular, weathered hands. We move through the hundred-item list at an efficient clip as I dash between the double beds, digging frantically through my piles and holding up the items for him to check off.

"Negative-four-degree sleeping bag," he says.

"Check, sir, yes sir!" I call, hitting my best at-attention stance.

Not even a chuckle.

"Negative-forty-degree bag," he says.

For nights above Camp 3.

"Check!"

"Pee bottle."

"I should have bought these in bulk." I laugh.

Ang Dorjee plows ahead. He doesn't laugh.

"Too big," he nods to the thermos I'd handpicked knowing it was bulky but overruled by visions of endless tea on frigid mornings.

"On to boots," he says.

Boots are not a line item on this expedition but an entire category.

"Down bivvy boots?"

"Check."

"Snow gaiters."

"Check.

"Climbing boots."

"Check, check, check," I cry, scooping boots up from the floor, under the bed, atop my pillow. "And these boots are officially made for walking!"

My act is bombing. No friendly crinkling of his weathered face. Not even a pity laugh. He makes a final scrutinizing sweep of my gear as I gnaw at my cuticles. Americans often mischaracterize Sherpas as overly warm and docile, almost cartoonish in their nurturing, and I did too, at first, but there's no mistaking that Ang Dorjee is one macho man. His skin is tanned to leather from years of climbing, but something about his stern, authoritative nature reminds me of my father. His sturdiness strikes a chord. Suddenly, I'm back in a classroom. Fourth grade at María Reina in Lima. My uniform pressed and starched. Raising my hand, proudly reciting all the right answers, gunning for that extra credit. For validation. Does Ang Dorjee think what I'm attempting is absurd? Does he think it's possible? I want to ask, but I gulp down the expanding balloon of my anxiety. *You're a grown-ass woman, Silvia, keep it together.*

"Jackets," he continues.

Another category all their own.

"Base camp down? Gore-Tex? Midweight?"

"Check, check, check!"

"Summit pants."

"Huh?"

"Pants?"

"What?"

"PANTS."

"Pants, yes, uh, errrr . . . of course."

Summit pants. Shit. That's it.

Shit, shit, shit, SHIIIIT!

Summit pants are not optional. At the Everest summit, the air is less than 7 percent oxygen. At that elevation, everything is a battle between weight and warmth. Wearing clothing that is too heavy results in a struggle to breathe; too light and you'll freeze instantly. Summit, or 8,000-meter pants, provide insulation without bulk. Stalling for time, I rifle through my duffel and trace my steps from Kathmandu to Hong Kong to San Francisco to my cozy Twin

Peaks two-bedroom on a steep road overlooking Glen Canyon Park. In the kitchen, on the table, I see my laptop. There's a tab open at Backcountry .com, where a pair of absolute-zero parka pants, "specifically designed for elevations above 26,000 feet," sit in my shopping cart.

I'd never completed the order.

"Damn!" I throw my hands up.

Ang Dorjee smiles politely as I try to laugh off my embarrassment at forgetting one of the most vital pieces of gear for our life-or-death climb. For the first time, his thin lips part to reveal a mouthful of pristine white chiclet teeth.

"No trip is complete without me forgetting something," I say, laughing. "After ten years of climbing, at least I'm down to just one."

"Mittens?" he asks, the slightest hint of weariness seeping through.

"Yes!" I shout, waving my mittens overhead like a good student, but my confidence is flattened. A souped-up version of the puffy gloves American kids wore on TV for snowball fights, summit mittens are markers of arrival. They're reserved for the final days on Everest when temperatures plummet so fast that any exposed skin is in danger of instant frostbite. People think falling from the top of the world is the biggest risk, but it's the cold that kills most climbers. At 29,000 feet, even water lines must be kept tucked inside a down suit at all times. If the lines escape insulation, they'll freeze instantly.

Same for hands.

Frostbite is the kiss of death.

I tuck the mittens into my summit-bid bag, then slip my hand inside the front pouch to triple-check that my pictures are still there. Flicking their slippery edges between thumb and forefinger, I count *one, two, three.* I focus on why I'm here. To honor, to grieve, to grow. Ang Dorjee motions for me to zip up my bag and secure it with the tiny padlock. My eyes linger on the summit mittens. They nag me, whispering refrains of doubt. *There's no way I'll make it. I won't make it far enough to use them.* I've already purchased a cancellation insurance policy worth $50,000.

Without another word, Ang Dorjee jots down "PANTS and THER-MOS" and hands me the scrap of paper.

"Shopping in Thamel will be our first order of business. The girls need to get a few things as well." I'm guiding five novice hikers—three women from

Nepal and two from San Francisco—on the forty-mile hike to Base Camp before joining Ang Dorjee and my expedition team to begin my first attempt at summiting Mount Everest.

"They are so excited for the hike, Ang Dorjee . . ." I start to ramble.

Ang Dorjee bows suddenly. "I'll be back for your bag at seven p.m.," he says.

I nod in gratitude, but he's out the door before I can squeak out a "namaste."

In thirty years on the mountain, Ang Dorjee has seen it all. He must think I'm an idiot. That I'm reckless to guide the girls up the mountain right before my first summit attempt.

*　*　*

Most people attempting to summit Everest plan and save for years. They think of nothing but the mountain. They breathe, eat, and dream Everest. Become fluent in its legends and lore. Visualize standing at the summit through guided meditations and brutal monthlong training climbs. Hoping that if they can osmose its topography into their DNA, their chances of making it to the summit are better.

I've been dreaming this climb into being for years too, but in a different way.

In 2005, I followed a vision I didn't understand to Kathmandu. It was a leap of faith. And for that leap, for finally trusting myself, I thought I'd be rewarded by some flash of divinity. Towering peaks in all directions. A white light and singing crystal bowls maybe. Instead, I was shuttled back to the chaos of my youth. The buses. The smog. The noise. Stepping into the streets of Kathmandu in 2005 was like falling asleep and waking up in Lima. In my room at the Annapurna now, on my third trip to the Himalayas, I can only laugh at how arrogant I was that first time around. I didn't know then how much pain there is in healing. How much shit and grime.

In order to heal, I would have to wade through chaos. Not just show up at the foot of the mountain ready for my benediction.

But I'm still waiting. Even now. For what? A celestial thumbs-up? For someone—my peers, the mountain, God, Ang Dorjee—to validate me. To feel like I've done enough. Am enough. I've been running on adrenaline, running from myself, since the late '90s. My comfort zone is somewhere between cataclysmic and just wild enough that it all might work out.

And most of the time it does.

But for this trip, it's not just my ass on the line. I have the girls to worry about.

This is so typical.

To take on too much at once.

To push for something already over-the-top and then sprinkle on un poquito más. Just a little bit, right? Like my mother always said. Un ratito. She'd be back in a minute. Un poquito de pisco. Just a little sip.

It's like I only feel alive when I'm juggling so much that something is bound to fall.

In the 1980s, Canadian psychologist Frank Farley identified what he calls Type T personalities. *T* as in thrill seeking. Type Ts are genetically compelled to chase risks and push boundaries. Through his research, Dr. Farley learned that if this thrill-seeking "gene" is recognized early on and Type Ts are given outlets for productive risk-taking, they can be molded into stars and thought leaders. Trailblazers. World-class mountaineers. But if left to their own devices, their first taste of destructive behavior can easily morph into a lifestyle of gambling, crime, or addiction. Many of the world's innovators and criminals are Type T. Social circumstances dictate whether they become a creator or a destroyer, but the payoffs—the adrenaline, the dopamine, the high—are the same in either case.

"Gamblers are often happiest when they're losing," wrote Farley. "Because that's when they're closest to failure."

I'm getting them to Base Camp even if it kills me.

Once we make it, *if* we make it, the girls will turn back, and I'll attempt the summit. My climbing friends don't understand why I'm using my first Everest bid to guide a group of novices on the brutal Everest Base Camp (EBC) hike instead of getting my head in the game.

You'll be exhausted before you even begin.

Why the hell would you do that all at once?

This is EVEREST, Silvia, not a day hike. Not a backpacking trip. Everest.

I'd heard it all. But it didn't matter.

I couldn't explain to them—mountaineers who'd been working their entire lives for the chance to summit Everest—why I was overcomplicating it. They don't understand that what matters most is not the ascent, but the promise. The promise I made to the girls, and to myself a decade earlier.

I'm climbing to make promises mean something again.

There's a gentle rapping at the door.

"Ms. Silvia, they're here," calls a low, warm voice. *Lucy.* "They're here. The Nepali girls are waiting for us in the lobby."

I feel tears streaming down my cheeks. *Jesus, it's only the first day.* I'm the fearless leader. The one who's been drill-sergeanting them on our runs up steep city inclines for months. Pushing them to tears in bootcamp classes twice a week. What kind of leader sobs constantly? I check my reflection in the mirror. Gray roots are spreading into my dark curls. Little do the girls know that I'm less Wonder Woman and more Machito Lloron—the weeping mighty man. Badass on the outside, howling melty mess inside.

"Silvia, HELLO," comes a different voice. Clipped and clear. *Jimena.* "Let's go!"

I brush my tears back with a wrinkled sleeve, determined to be the leader I've signed up to be. The one they believe I am.

"Listo!" I holler, swinging open the door. Jimena and Lucy are leaning on either side of the frame.

In a sleeveless tangerine dress cinched with an embroidered serape belt and dangling turquoise earrings, Lucy beams. Pinned into her freshly curled black hair is a single fresh white flower. Her makeup is perfect, like it has been every day since we first met five months ago. Blushed cheeks and long lashes and perfect winged liner. Jimena is Lucy's tomboyish counterpart. With closely cropped hair, two-tone glasses, and a striped black-and-white sleeveless tee, Jimena presents a sturdy clean-cut image except for the deep purple lipstick—a nod to the punk-rock rebel heart I've gotten to know and love.

I make a mental note to use they/them as Jimena's pronouns. They explained it to me a few times back in San Francisco, but I kept messing up. It's hard to break old habits. In my native Spanish, words themselves are gendered. They end with *a*'s and *o*'s to indicate female or male. With gender so built into my mother tongue, I'm afraid that I'm going to mess up and disrespect Jimena. Or even worse, that someone else will.

My number one job here, above summiting, above anything else, is to protect this group, but I'm nervous that the Nepali girls, or others in the local community, won't understand—or worse, might lash out against Jimena's pronouns or identity. San Francisco is a queer haven. And most liberal U.S. cities are accepting of the LGBTQ+ community, but in many places in the world, it's still dangerous to even be out as a gay person. Like in Peru, Nepali culture is highly traditional compared to the United States.

At least that's what I thought.

I was surprised to learn that the Nepali government was one of the first to have other gender as a choice on their census form. I was five years behind Nepal when it came to pronouns.

"Your room is okay?" I say. "How'd you sleep?"

"Yes, good. Thank you," Lucy says politely, her thick accent sweet and rolling. Jimena is quiet but nods sharply.

We've been here less than twenty-four hours, and I can tell they're a bit shell-shocked at being plunked down in Kathmandu. At twenty-three, Jimena is making their first trip out of the United States, and Lucy, who grew up in Mexico, has never been further than there.

I clap my hands and lead them toward the hotel lobby.

"Wow!" Shailee exclaims as we approach. The rest of the group is clustered around an ornate couch in the marble lobby. She pulls Lucy into a bear hug. "Look at you. All the colors. Is this typical? Where was your color last night?"

"It's called thirty-six hours of travel," says Lucy, flashing a Cheshire cat smile.

"And you too!" Shailee gestures to Jimena's lips. "With the colors. Did the rainbow land last night?"

"The rainbow is always here," Jimena says with a righteous nod.

Shailee lets loose a deep belly laugh, and the sound of it soothes my nerves. It's hard not to feel good around Shailee. Her energy is effervescent. She and another friend, Asha, are my co-guides and translators for the trip. They're both members of the Seven Summit Women's Team, which in 2008 became the only all-Nepali women's team to successfully summit Everest. Their ultimate goal is to climb the rest of the Seven Summits together. Last night, they picked us up from the airport, and today they came back bringing Jimena and Lucy's Nepali counterparts—Shreya, Ehani, and Rubina—whom I met on my second trip to Nepal two years ago. I had just launched my nonprofit, Courageous Girls. My friend Lisa, a photographer, was working on an anti-trafficking film and brought me to visit a shelter in Kathmandu called Shakti Samuha.

Shreya, Ehani, and Rubina were living at Shakti then. At first, there was a shy formality to our conversations. I was an outsider, and they were wary for good reason. What they had survived made my childhood look tame. But once I told them my idea—to hike to Mount Everest Base Camp with other survivors of sexual violence, they came alive. All the soft mannerisms went out the window, and I saw a hunger in each of them. A hunger to defy a system that had told them what they could be their whole lives. A hunger that I also recognized in myself.

In Kathmandu, trekking Everest is seen primarily as a leisure sport for wealthy Westerners. The flight from Kathmandu to Lukla—where the Base Camp hike begins—costs 150 US dollars, and for Nepali citizens, half of that, or 6,000 rupees. That's two months' salary in Nepal.

Technically, Nepal's caste system has been outlawed, but culturally it's still very much alive. It's a highly complex system, and in it, Ehani, Shreya, and Rubina come from the lowest possible caste: the Dalit. The "untouchables."

When they first explained it, I imagined untouchables as the mafia or something elite and high-class. But in Nepal, to be untouchable is a mark of poverty. To be unfit for contact. Historically, Dalit women weren't allowed to enroll in school or even walk on the same side of the street as women of a higher caste. By the time I met Ehani, Shreya, and Rubina in 2014, things were changing. Their generation was breaking through entrenched class barriers. Still, by virtue of their gender and names (which indicate caste), they were expected to accomplish little. Ironically, it was their families' deep desire to build a better life for the girls that made them prey to exploitation.

For all of us, this is so much more than just a hike.

I clear my throat, ready to make introductions, but the group scatters into little pods, everyone hugging clumsily and making their own introductions. "Namaste," they say. *I bow toward your existence. Namaste. Namaste. Namaste*, they repeat. Ehani, twenty-three, who speaks the least English of the trio, reaches out and softly takes Jimena and Lucy by the hand. There's a tender maturity about her. Something clear and steady about her beauty that's communicated in few words.

At nineteen, Shreya is the baby of the crew, but her delicate face veils a shrewdness that saved her life.

Rubina, also twenty-three, looks like Lucy's American Eagle counterpart in a fleece-lined denim trucker jacket and an orange flower pinned into her hair. Her forehead is high, and her face is compact, all its features gathered at the center, almost masklike. Her bold brown eyes are hard to read. The well-worn creases around them remind me of my own guardedness and distrust at her age.

As I watch, the group becomes an organism, chattering and fusing with ease, and I realize I've been holding my breath. I expected our introduction to be rusty, or at the least that I'd have to bridge cultural divides. But as Rubina steps forward to shake hands with Jimena and Jimena pulls her in for a hug, I'm instead struck by a surety I haven't felt since I first had the idea for this journey.

We might just make it. But it may not be because of me.

Before my eyes, they morph into girls on the first day of school becoming instant best friends. I can't help but chuckle to myself at the sweetness of it all. It's almost saccharine. Hard to imagine. A bond I never had as a girl. Our motley sisterhood is complete.

We are daughters, sisters, friends.

We are Mexican, Peruvian, Indigenous, Colombian, Nepali, Indian, Hindi, Buddhist, Catholic, Atheist.

Young, old, queer, straight, nonbinary.

And Everest, the mother, is knitting us together.

But there's something else too.

I imagine there's a hum of anxiety just under the surface of our gathering—a sense of foreboding within all this instant vulnerability. But maybe that's just me. I push back a rush of thoughts and plaster on my best smile. *Fake it 'til you make it.*

"Let's go," I say a little too loud. A little too bright. The girls eye me suspiciously.

It's a fast reminder that my work is to be nothing less than honest with them.

We have all learned our hypervigilance the hard way.

And these girls can spot bullshit a mile away.

* * *

After we finish shopping for our last-minute gear in Thamel and I find a decent pair of summit pants, we head to the Shakti house. The staff there want to wish the girls luck on their journey. Tucked off a busy street of crumbling brick buildings and colorful awnings, Shakti Samuha is a two-story stone house. It is the world's first organization established and run by survivors of human trafficking. Shailee and Ehani lead us down an interior alley into a simple stone room.

The safe house.

There are always twenty to thirty girls living at the shelter—some as young as ten years old. As we walk down the dingy stone hall, they poke their heads out from doorless openings, giggling and casting their eyes down sharply as if it's an insult to meet ours.

At Shakti, Shreya, Ehani, and Rubina are local legends.

In trafficking cases, prosecution is rare. It's complicated to untangle the web and hard to track the women as they're moved frequently, and trafficking ringleaders often hold powerful positions in politics and the community. When I first met Shreya, Ehani, and Rubina, they were living in the shelter's transitional housing for older women after escaping from brothels in India, where they'd been trafficked. And with the help of the Shakti staff, they prosecuted their captor and won.

For them to take on such a rich and dangerous man was a potential death sentence. They risked it anyway. Their fire was the genesis of our group. Its namesake. The original Courageous Girls. The ones I wish I could have been.

A revered Hindu goddess, Shakti is a divine feminine energy that does not conform to traditional ideas that a mother is only soft and tender. She shape-shifts into mother, warrior, or destroyer, whichever is most needed to get the job done.

The Shakti Samuha mission is to turn tears into power.

It was all of our mission on this trek.

As we enter, the executive secretary, Binsa, greets us with hands clasped. "Namaste," she says. "Welcome." She and six other women drape light-yellow silk khatas, or scarves, around our shoulders and smear sindoor, the vibrant scarlet powder used for bindis, down our foreheads in a line. Khatas are a traditional Tibetan offering of welcome—or in our case, wishes for a safe journey. We settle into a circle, a dozen women cross-legged on yoga pillows. After joyful *namaste*s all around, Binsa welcomes us in Nepali with Shailee translating to English. "Shreya, Ehani, and Rubina, our three Shakti Samuha sisters going on this special hike, are younger than me, but their courage inspires me," Binsa says.

They all grin and nod their thanks.

"We're so excited to see Silvia here," says Binsa. "And a warm welcome to our two new friends, Jimena and Lucy. Best of wishes with the trek and whatever objective you have for it. I hope it comes true." Directing her attention to the group of women before us, she asks if they will introduce themselves.

One by one, the women share their names and offer a token of support for our trip. Some I recognize from other visits. Most are former trafficking victims who now help run the organization. They are women who turned what happened to them inside out. Who understood that no one was coming to save them and leaned on each other instead. I wondered how much pain I could have avoided if I'd had a group like them instead of surrounding myself with power-hungry party friends and dot-com escapists. Maybe I would have had the courage to confront my past sooner.

Introductions are loose and organic, and something about the informality and the simplicity of the room shaves the edge off for Jimena and Lucy.

They look almost at home.

"Thank you for welcoming us," says Lucy. "I worked super hard to get here, and I didn't know what to expect, really. But being here now, and seeing Kathmandu, has already opened my eyes to a lot outside the States."

She picks each word out carefully. There's a decorum to her speech. An intentionality I haven't seen in her before.

Jimena nods in agreement, their face twisting in thought as they prepare to speak. The women in the circle turn to Jimena, their faces warm and open. "I just want to say that I'm truly honored to be here with all of you. Because I *see* you. I *see* you—you know what I mean?" Their hand draws a circle in the air to emphasize the deeper meaning of the word. *See.*

Jimena speaks in plain language, but often it feels like metaphor. Their voice opens words up and unpacks them, riffs, and flows, and follows them somewhere deeper than where they began. I wonder how their sentiments will translate into Nepali. I wonder if they will need to be translated at all. Jimena has a way of making you feel their words.

"I'm slightly overwhelmed," Jimena says. "Not overwhelmed because it's a new place, but because I can see the sincerity in your eyes. Thank you for welcoming us and reminding me that sisterhood is not just a phrase. It's a lived everyday experience. Sometimes in the United States we forget that, but here it appears to be effortless."

Back in San Francisco, Jimena and Lucy are involved in activist work. Lucy hopes to build a career in social justice, maybe politics, advocating for immigrant and houseless communities, while Jimena is engaged in Latinx queer community building. Over the last several months of training with them, I've listened to how their language does something mine does not. In my childhood, the language of construction was present. But *building* for my father meant amassing wealth to construct his castle and become king. I was bred to consider my own station in life, to blaze forward, to do the best, be the best, but the way Jimena and Lucy use the word *build* is communal. Building is talking and sharing experiences. It's gaining trust. Using the ideas and knowledge of others as building blocks to construct something that can be shared and serve all.

Their words unfold as an invitation, rather than a declaration.

It's clear that the women at Shakti understand what Jimena is saying without translation. That they register its intent. As they nod along, their eyes are soft and gazing. I wonder then about language. About how much of what we're doing here is not about *what* happened to us, but *how*. How it metastasized inside of us. How it cancered our lives. How we got away. How we are still fighting every day of our lives.

"Activism is not a tagline," says Jimena, their voice rising like they are behind a podium. "It's in everyday action. In every word, every thought. For me to be sitting here with you, I never thought it would happen." Their eyes swell with tears. Shailee pats their arm and in one single breath translates everything into Nepali.

Before we go, I want to offer something. I know most of the women in the room will never step foot on Everest.

With Shailee's help, I explain.

"This is what I'll take to the summit of Chomolungma," I say, holding up the yellow khata they gifted us. "It'd be an honor to bring a piece of you all with me to the top of the world. Speak your wishes into the khata, and I'll carry them to Mother Everest. Assuming I make it myself!" I stand and walk around the circle, stopping to hug each woman as she closes her eyes and speaks her wish into the yellow khata. I wrap each one in its own corner of rough silk.

"Silvia, you have the energy of all of us behind you to reach the summit," says Binsa.

The first time I told the story of my sexual abuse, I thought that would be it. That it would be done. I could bury it away.

The End.

But in the presence of the women at Shakti, I remember that the telling was just the beginning. Healing is circuitous. There are so many roadblocks, stops and starts. A decade earlier, I'd followed a vision to the mountains and promised that I would return. But in the time since, I have encountered new peaks and valleys, have fallen off course in both commitment and spirit. Fighting for myself hasn't always been enough to keep me going. But fighting for women around the world might be. Fighting for these women before me might be.

Before bed, I get word that the weather for tomorrow's flight to Lukla—the starting point for the hike—looks bleak. Tons of flights have been canceled. A dull ticking begins in the back of my brain. It's a timer. For me to meet my expedition team at Base Camp for the puja ceremony, a mandatory group blessing for all teams attempting to summit, the girls and I have two weeks to make the hike. Not a day more. Tonight, I pray for surrender, and as I lie down to sleep, I try again to imprint the feeling of the soft, warm bed into my bones. It will be a long time before I lie on one again. Instead, I toss and turn, a familiar dread creeping over me. Things are in order, as much as they can be, so I try to relax, sleep, pray more.

Nothing works. I try to tell myself it's just anxiety over tomorrow's flight. But the truth is, for me, beds have always been complicated places.

And every time I close my eyes, I can only see the faces of the ten-year-old girls who must live in safe houses.

* * *

Flying into the town of Lukla in Nepal leaves no room for error. The length of a football field, its tiny air strip slams into a mountain on one end and plunges thousands of feet into a rocky ravine at the other. All trips to Everest begin with this flight. It's part of the thrill. An aerial initiation. Flying in a ten-seater into the thick soup of Himalayan weather, the plane rattling like screws might pop loose at any moment, is preparation for the physical and emotional turbulence ahead. During our one-hour flight, Lucy scrunches up next to a window clutching the good-luck teddy bear she'd brought from home, while Jimena sits silent and unmoving, their eyes half-closed, but watching.

Jimena is always watching.

Shreya, Ehani, Rubina, and Asha have been held back in Kathmandu due to a logjam at the airport. By law, Nepali locals are charged half the airfare of tourists, and because the Himalayan economy is so dependent on climbers, when the airport is packed, locals are the first to get bumped. Everest is the Mother of the World, and she's also an economy. I was ready to throw a fit at the ticket counter when the agent bumped them, but Shailee diffused the situation and encouraged us to keep moving. "They'll get an afternoon flight and be there after lunch. Just in time to kick off the hike!"

After catching our breath from the landing, we sling our packs on and walk on wobbly legs to the nearest teahouse to have breakfast and wait for the others. As we climb the creaky steps, through the window I see a face I'd recognize anywhere. *What are the chances?* An aroma of spicy lentils and garlic soup fills the low wooden room as we walk in. Warmth from the yak dung burning in the woodstove at the room's center envelops us in a pungent hug. Shaking off the chill of the plane ride, I push past a camera crew milling over pots of ginger tea.

"I'll be right back," I say to Shailee, Jimena, and Lucy as they settle around a low round table.

"Richard!" I cry. Richard Hidalgo is one of Peru's most famous mountain climbers. He leaps up to embrace me, un besito to one of my cheeks.

"Are you climbing?" he asks, pulling over a stool from the next table. "Here, sit."

"Yes, yes," I say, scooting onto the seat. "It's time. My first attempt."

"And you have a crew with you?"

"Not like yours!" I tease, pointing to the cameras. Richard is attempting to climb the world's fourteen highest peaks, all in the Himalayas, without supplemental oxygen, to celebrate the 2021 bicentennial of Peru's independence. Climbing without oxygen is rare and very dangerous. Our country takes immense pride in Richard's accomplishments. He's beloved. Hailed as the toughest of the tough. A national hero.

"Who are the young women?" he asks.

"A sisterhood." I smile. "Women who've been through a lot. We're hiking to Base Camp before my summit push."

"Now?" he asks. "On your first bid? Is that not a lot to do?" His eyes crinkle as he gracefully pours me a cup of ginger tea.

I don't know what to say.

Richard's trip is sponsored. Most Everest expeditions are. In the last ten years, I've summited five of the world's seven highest peaks with no professional backing. Although the Peruvian mountaineering community has cheered me on the whole way, they've never given me any money. In 1975, the year after I was born, Japanese climber Junko Tabei became the first woman to summit Everest. I remember reading about how hard she had to fight to get her expeditions funded. How, at first, male climbers in Japan assumed she'd joined their mountaineering club to find a husband. Women climb, of course, and from all over the world, but the majority of climbers attempting 8,000-meter peaks like Everest are still straight, wealthy white men. Having access to the money for gear and guides, time off to train and climb, and the support of a family back home to keep daily life chugging along is something few women are lucky enough to possess.

The mountains may be my lineage, but expedition climbing is different from having Andean blood. People who spend hundreds of thousands for a chance to stand on top of the world are often set on conquering, not merging, with the mountain. I don't expect Richard to understand that, for me, climbing Everest is bigger than national glory or personal bragging rights. Peru, my home, both formed and destroyed me. After leaving my country in desperation, I spent years in fracture, searching for an identity in a place that only ever saw me as an immigrant, an outsider. Wherever I go, I represent my country, but I have more than just a flag in my bag. I have special photos. And now my yellow khata from Shakti Samuha.

That's what I'll leave at the top.

Some people are drawn up the mountain for glory; others are pushed up by pain.

By the time we finish breakfast, it's noon. Asha messages that their flight has been delayed again. We will have to start walking if we want to have any chance of keeping our schedule. We still have enough time, I tell myself. Shailee and I padded the itinerary with plenty of cushion. Even at a comfortable stroll, if we leave now, we can make it the five and a half miles to our first stop, Phakding, in about four hours.

After wishing Richard "Buena suerte!" we begin to walk.

Descending into a lush valley surrounded by pine and hemlock forest, we set our pace on a zigzagging dirt trail. Yielding to the jingle of the cow bell, we step aside for yaks, loaded down with sacks full of supplies. Livestock own the trail. "Namaste," I call out to porters as they rush past with giant loads strapped to their heads, their bodies bent into the incline.

We can learn something from them, I think. Leaning into difficulty to balance ourselves. At the bottom of the valley, we come to the first of a series of wobbly suspension bridges and cross over the vibrant Dudh Koshi Nadi, the River of Milk, named for its milky turquoise waters.

I let Jimena and Shailee walk ahead, their steps shaky as they cross over the wooden slats of the bridge. They grip the wire railing with both hands. Prayer flags whip in the wind, cheering them on in rainbow form. Less than an hour in, Lucy is lagging behind, panting. I walk back to check on her.

"I'm spent," she says, her eyes fluttering. "Already, I can't do this."

I bite my tongue. The last week of training, Lucy showed up to our last trekking practice hungover. She tried to deny it, but if anyone knows a hangover, it's me. Back in San Francisco, we'd been working on strength training for months. Lucy had been busting her ass. For the final month leading up to the trip, I outlined a strict dietary schedule that included a minimum of three liters of water a day and no booze. All this, I told them, was to help the body prepare for hiking at altitude. Something that's almost impossible to prepare for.

I'd warned her that partying would slow her down. Now I resist my hair-trigger impulse to chastise her. To ask why she couldn't stay out of the clubs for two more weeks. It's a question I've asked myself many times.

"Here," I say, taking her pack and slinging it on over my stomach. "Don't think about how much farther. Just take one step, then another."

For the next hour every step is a struggle. Jimena hangs back and we step aside constantly to let other hikers and locals pass. Kids in tattered shorts lap us. Today is one of the easiest days of the hike. I want to ease them into what will be a brutal ten days, but if Lucy can't make this, how is she going to survive the High Himalayas, where the oxygen saturation plummets?

"You need to stop?" asks Jimena.

"No," says Lucy.

I know she will never say die.

When I first invited them on this trip, they eyed me suspiciously. It was 2015, and my vision to hike to Everest Base Camp with the Courageous Girls was in motion. Shreya, Rubina, and Ehani were on board, but I hoped to bring some girls from the United States as well. During a lunch break, I left eBay's

San Francisco office to visit a small nonprofit women's center on the corner of Fourth and Folsom. I talked to a group of six girls about trauma and mountaineering. About how climbing mountains had changed my life. They were young, mostly teenagers, some just barely in their twenties. I remembered all the pain I held at their age, with nowhere to put it. Most of them were building their lives back up; some had fled abusive homes, and some were transitioning from living on the streets. I told them that if they committed to the process and trained with me for three months, I'd take them to hike to Mount Everest Base Camp and make sure their trip was paid for.

They looked at me with the blank stares of women who'd never gotten anything for free.

"Like Mount Everest in Nepal?"

"Yes," I said.

"Where even is Nepal?" said another.

"It's in Asia," said a quiet girl.

"We'll be flying there?" shouted another.

"Yes."

"Fly to Nepal? For reals? In a plane?"

"Yes."

"So if we train every weekend," asked another girl, "then you are going to give us a ticket to fly to Nepal to walk to the base of the mountain?"

The girls stared, waiting for the catch. Life always had a catch. In their experience, people didn't give. They only took. I understood their distrust.

"Yes," I said. "That's my promise to you."

"Promise? Ha, ha, ha!" The girl who had been quiet laughed angrily. "This lady is so full of shit."

She walked out of the room.

I didn't blame her. I knew plenty of white people in the Bay Area tech world who had visions of "saving" marginalized young women. Especially women of color. Those visions rarely panned out, and the attempts often did more harm than good. A promise means more when you have nothing to lose. But I was no one's white savior. I had one message for them, a message that, as corny as it sounds, I was compelled to deliver—the message of the mountain. I wanted for them what I had found in the mountains. To see something bigger than themselves. To understand themselves as I had begun to understand myself—as so much more than what had happened to me.

"Training starts next week," I pushed on enthusiastically. Three more girls walked out. Jimena and Lucy were the only ones who stuck around. There was something in them that believed. As teens, they'd experienced a similar path, both running away from homes and ending up on the streets of San Francisco.

Jimena was putting themself through San Francisco State, had aspirations to write, and was a fierce advocate for the homeless. They were a queer Brown Colombian American whose eyes sparkled as they told me how they loved the outdoors but suffered from depression and lived in transitional housing. Jimena had never been out of the United States. Going to Asia would be a dream, they said.

From day one, Jimena was game to train. They never faltered.

Lucy was equally enthusiastic, and her warm energy was contagious. Like me, she was an immigrant. She'd migrated from Guadalajara, Mexico. The oldest of her siblings, she wanted to be a role model for the rest of her family. She was enrolled in classes at a local community college, was learning code, and had dreams of becoming an entrepreneur. There was a fire in her eyes, and I saw myself reflected there immediately. She was headstrong, a warrior for better or worse.

Immigrants are also often Type T. You take a huge risk that alters the course of your life and the generations that come after. Whether you're running away from or toward something, it takes cojones to leave your home and start from scratch. And whether you leave out of hope or fear—for opportunity or asylum—you always, always carry your country with you.

I left the meeting eager to get started.

But now I can see that maybe we hadn't trained hard enough.

Shreya, Ehani, and Rubina look strong. Over the last year, they've been following the detailed training regimen I had sent them to build immunity and lean muscle. When we first met, their legs were string beans, but now they are solid and sinewy.

Jimena and Lucy, not so much.

I try to remind myself that not every challenge is one we're totally prepared for. That that too is an important lesson, and even if we don't make it, the girls will be galvanized by their own strength. That will be enough, I tell myself. But secretly I want more. I want us to make it. I want it all. We can do this—that's the message I want to inject. We can do anything. Especially women like us—built on the bones of survival. That is what I really want them to know.

They're both loopy and exhausted now. Dragging behind.

We don't make it to Phakding. After four hours, we stop in Ghat for the night, less than halfway to our first rest point, where we'll wait for the rest of the team. I hadn't even considered that we wouldn't make it to the first checkpoint. For months I've been so consumed with the preparations for the girls that my anxiety about attempting to summit myself had gone subterranean. But suddenly it barrels through my chest and floods my limbs. Why didn't I press Purchase on those pants? I'd managed to arrange flights, gear, guides, and months of training for five novice hikers, two of whom had never traveled outside North America. But I'd conveniently forgotten the one piece of equipment necessary to reach the summit of Everest, something I'd been working toward for a decade? How can I make sure the girls are safe when I can't even remember my own fucking pants?

The truth is that for all my souped-up visions of the trip, I simply can't picture myself on the summit.

It's not forgetting my summit pants that ignites panic.

It's the idea that maybe I forgot them because I didn't believe I was ever going to use them.

⊘⊘⊘⊘

Chapter 4

SUNDAY'S PREY

On Sundays, my father woke at seven to water his roses. In the gated drive-way in front of our house, there was a stone planter with half a dozen bushes whose creamy ivory, yellow, and pale pink blooms were his prized possession. But his fingernails didn't carry dirt from tending them. He fussed over the flowers from afar, dictating to Sandra how to prune them just so. They were objects for his pleasure, not living things that demanded sweat equity and tenderness.

Still they seemed just as, if not more, important to him than we were.

One morning Miguel and I were playing fulbito with the new leather ball he'd gotten for his eighth birthday. My legs were hungry for motion. I loved the feel of them on the move. Our concrete driveway became an open-air stadium, the cracks in the ground our boundary lines. Weaving and ducking around Miguel's advances, I pushed toward the goalpost and, with my sights set, cranked my leg back and kicked as hard as I could. The ball soared into the rose bushes, cracking a yellow flower at its stem.

"Carajo, mierda!" My father screamed from upstairs. He'd been napping in the TV room and had looked out to check on us at that exact moment. My ears were ringing as I rushed to fix the rose.

"Imbéciles," he shouted. "Pedazos de mierda!"

Imbeciles. Pieces of shit.

His footsteps rang like death chimes.

Miguel scooped up the soccer ball, and I frantically tried to prop the flower up, but it hung by a thread of woody stem. *Maybe it could heal. Maybe it's not that bad*, I thought, as my father burst into the courtyard clutching his best belt. One I knew well. It was an elegant black belt, handmade by Pedro P. Diaz, Lima's premier leather maker, and my father used it for all our whippings. Even my father's discipline was aspirational. His typically seamless face was crinkled and red with rage, his bushy brows knitted together. He didn't care that I was trying to right the wrong. He didn't ask what happened or wait for me to speak before he unleashed the thick leather on my naked legs. Once, twice, three times, its sharp tongue licked from my calves to my shins.

The pain was numbing.

"Noooo, Papa, please. Ayyyyyy! NO."

It wasn't the first time I'd screamed no and he hadn't stopped.

No meant nothing to him.

When he stopped to catch his breath, I bolted inside and up the stairs, but he trapped me halfway. Another whipping. Rapid-fire explosions until panting ensued, then he finally threw the belt down and stomped to his room, screaming behind him: "Ve a tu cuarto, pedazo de mierda." *Go to your room, piece of shit. Piece of shit.* Pedazo de mierda. That was one of his favorite insults. It rolled so easily off his tongue, and every time he said it I imagined a cake made of shit and me as a piece of it. Now he wouldn't love me for a while. He never did after a beating. I shuffled to my room, ashamed for disappointing him yet again, and looked at my legs. My playful fast legs, my skinny little legs, were laced with thick scarlet welts, dots of blood rising under the surface of the skin.

Home was the safest place to be, Mamita always said. Our castle, our protection. People outside were a threat. "Pay attention. Don't talk to strangers!" she'd chastise me. Strangers did bad things. Sendero Luminoso was expanding in Lima. Car bombs exploding in the streets. Kidnappings for ransom or the threat of them were a daily terror. In the Andes, the guerrillas had overtaken private land and claimed it as communal. My father's village, Santa Cruz de Chuca, was occupied in a coup, and the small piece of land that he and his brother owned was seized. He got cryptic phone calls warning him to stay away. They said they'd kill him if he came back to claim his land. Once I picked up.

"We're watching you," a male voice rasped. "Be careful with the little baby." It was 1984 and my baby brother, Eduardo, had just been born.

I froze, gripping the phone in fear as the dial tone blared.

Regardless of what Mama assured me—that home was a protective fortress—I felt little safety inside or outside of my house. The rice undersalted? Our games too loud? My father's roses disrupted? It was too easy to earn the belt. My father, Segundo, was always trying to outrun his name. If he couldn't be first anywhere else, at least in his tiny kingdom of home he would reign. The secret to my happiness, I'd learned, was doing exactly as he said. My survival hinged on compliance. So, when J closed the door and shushed me and said he was just following Segundo's orders, I knew exactly what he meant.

* * *

I was out in the garden searching for insects. My parents had given me a microscope, and I wanted to examine a roly-poly under its magnifying glass. I loved the way the bugs curled into a tiny ball when touched. I wanted to see up close how they protected themselves.

From above came the dulcet chirp of J's whistle. I looked up, shielding my eyes from the smoggy white sun. He waved from the second-floor balcony.

"Que estás haciendo?"

"Digging for a chanchito!" I yelled.

"Aw, you're a good girl."

"Yes," I said, nodding proudly to myself. "Yes, I am." I giggled at his acknowledgment. Maybe my father told him to say that. Maybe he'd sent J as a proxy to tell me what he couldn't. That he was proud of me. That I was good. Maybe that was his way of loving me.

"Come up here," J called.

I set down my makeshift cardboard bug catcher and ran upstairs to the second floor, where J was cleaning my parents' room, a room I was forbidden to enter unless Mama invited me in, which she did only when my father wasn't around. I was dying to explore the inside.

"Sientate acá," said J, patting the bed next to him.

I obliged.

He locked the door behind us and moved toward me. Cupping his hands under my armpits, he laid me down diagonally and began to kiss me softly on the mouth. Only lovers kissed like this. Husbands and wives on TV, couples at church, my parents in their rare moments of peace. I watched, still and quiet, as he pulled down my pants and pink-flowered underwear, bringing the *shhhh* finger to his lips before dropping to his knees. He kissed down my body in a line until he reached my private area. His mustache was brillo-y and sharp against my tender, hairless skin. And then there was something softer, something wet, almost watery, swimming against me. He placed my hands on the top of his head. His dark hair was coarse and poufy. My eyes opened wider as a flashing pulse lit my lower body.

J glanced up at me, his mouth open wide, tongue peeking out. He dipped down again between my legs. And the feeling was not pain. This thing my parents had ordered him to do sent a current through my torso. Sparking explosions. Tickling electricity danced through my belly, up the sides of my legs, and along my inner thighs. My breath became quick, and the top of my head did a disorienting dance. I didn't know if this was love, but J looked so pleased. "Don't worry," he said. "Your parents know. They told me to do this. Don't worry," he repeated like a mantra as he stood, unzipped himself, and pulled his penis from his white briefs.

* * *

I was in fourth grade. My religion teacher said it was the most important year of our young lives. We'd reached "the age of reason," the age when the Catholic Church said we were old enough to understand that the Eucharist was not a melt-in-your-mouth cracker, but the actual body of Jesus Christ. It was our moral coming-of-age. When we could decide between right and wrong for ourselves, which also meant that we could officially sin. We had an hour of religion class every day at school in preparation to receive our first Holy Communion. We were learning the Ten Commandments, and I repeated them to myself all day, determined to memorize them first. I'd been waiting years for a rulebook aside from my father's erratic commands. At least what God expected of me was crystal clear.

The First Commandment: You shall have no other gods before me.

The Second Commandment: You shall not take the name of the Lord your God in vain.

Communion was one of the seven holy sacraments, or required steps, in the life of a good Catholic: Baptism, Communion, Penance, Confirmation, Anointing of the Sick, Holy Orders, and Matrimony. Of course, the Holy

Orders only applied to men. To be pure enough to receive communion, first we had to admit to our sins and be forgiven. The priest, Father Selestino, said asking for forgiveness was simple, but the more I learned about God, the less likely it seemed that he easily forgave. Every year, during Easter Holy Week, Charlton Heston's *The Ten Commandments* played on TV, a in a two-night, four-hour saga. Charlton Heston was huge in Peru. We worshipped his gravitas. His muscular piety. Thursday and Friday night, we'd gather on the couch in the family TV area. Squeezed onto the sofa between my parents, with Miguel sprawled on the floor and baby Eduardo rocking in my mother's lap, I watched Heston transform into Moses. Sipping a whiskey, my father grunted his way through the movie, snarling at the parts I loved most. *Don't worry*, I whispered into Eduardo's soft spot as I stroked his head. His fine wispy hairs were velveteen against my hand. *I'll never let him hurt you.* As Moses kneels before the burning bush, God's echoing baritone commands him to lead the Israelites out of Egypt.

"But how will I know what to say?" asks Moses. "What words will I speak to them?"

"I'll teach you," booms the God-voice. "I'll show you the way."

Moses does everything God says, but after leading the people for forty years, he makes one terrible, arrogant mistake by tapping his staff on a rock and pretending that it is his own power that draws water from the stone. For this, God banishes Moses from entering the Holy Land. Forever.

"But why? Mama? Why did God betray him?" I tugged at my mother's shirt, but she shushed me and went on rocking Eduardo to sleep.

God did not seem forgiving to me.

My school was small: 40 kids per class, 160 per grade. First graders all the way through high school shared the same campus. While my classmates and I prepared for communion, our parents had to attend weekly catechism meetings. "I hope you'll use this as an opportunity to review some of the principles," the priest said as he broke the parents into groups. "This weekend when you go to church with your family, you can talk about what we're learning." My parents knew everyone but were close with no one. We lived all the way across town, and at school soccer games and barbeques, my father left early or sat on the sidelines while the other fathers, still agile and dark-haired, taught their kids how to kick and dribble. Mama seemed hungry for the company of other mothers. Always buying Sublimes (Peruvians' favorite chocolates) to send to school on my birthday. Trying to organize playdates with little success. When it was her turn to host catechism meetings, she laid out an ornate spread and made sure the house was spotless.

"Best behavior!" she said to me.

"Yes, Mama."

My parents greeted the families formally at the door, and while the kids played out front, I trailed the adults on a tour of our house.

"The architects used the finest cherrywood here," said my father. "Lasts generations. Sound investment. And this angle here was calculated for maximum light intake." He twisted his hands into stiff shapes to frame the house's geometry for a group of nodding parents.

I'd never seen my father like this. The formal door greeting. The strange tour.

Next to me, Gisela's parents whispered to each other. Her father stroked her mother's hair and kissed her tenderly on the cheek. In that flash of a moment, I was flooded with hope. Maybe this would bring my family together. Maybe all my parents needed was a reminder of how to live a good and godly life. Of how to love. Maybe we could be one of those families.

The adults returned to the living room to eat and drink, and I joined the kids outside in a game of fulbito. "Careful of the roses!" I called, shooing them away from the flower beds. Later, as the couples filed out hand in hand, I imagined my parents growing more active in the church. I saw my father speaking at fundraisers, joking around with the priest. I would sing in the choir and learn to play guitar.

We started attending Sunday Mass together. As we sat on the stiff wooden benches listening to the sermon, I thought of God and Moses. When Moses descended the mountain, he was a changed man. Watching him slouched over, commandments in hand, gave me hope that even my father could change.

But after attending catechism classes for three weeks, my father dropped out. When my mother pressed him, he snapped. "Por que voy a ir a esa mierda? Anda tú sola, diles que tenía que trabajar!" *Why am I going to attend that shit fest? Just go alone, tell them I had to work.* And just like that, we stopped attending Mass as a family. While my father tended his roses from afar, I ran over the commandments, tried to tally my sins and prepare for confession.

My fear of slipping up at home, at school, at church, was relentless. A gnaw-ing anxiety that wound its way into my school days and dreams.

* * *

My father's business was growing, and he built a third-floor apartment above our house next to the azotea. Miguel or Eduardo or I would live in the apartment with our own families one day, he said. Until then it sat empty and unfurnished except for the bedroom closest to the front door. A double bed and simple wooden nightstand sat wedged against the window. Thick woolen drapes hung from metal rails with tiny fingernail hooks. The drapes opened with string pulleys, and I remember the slow screech of hooks scrap-ing against metal as J closed them to block out the sun, leaving just a crack open so he could watch the driveway.

I don't remember the first time J brought me to the third floor, but it doesn't matter because every time was the same. And each time was every time, all over again. As soon as Mamita left to run errands, he called for me to follow him up the stairs and into the empty bedroom. While I lay there on the bed, in my uniforme único, stockings itching at the knees, he stood in the far corner with his back to me. First, I heard the metal teeth of his zipper unclenching, then watched the rhythmic pumping of his shoulder blade. When he glanced back to look at me, I could see he was holding his penis, stroking it. He didn't look me in the eyes but scanned my limp body instead as if he were searching for something.

Waiting for me to react.

He came toward me, walking slowly. His long body cast a shadow over my face as he knelt at the edge of the bed. Oily, metallic fumes of la cera roja, the thick red wax, wafted from his shirt. "Lift up your butt," he said. I was light-headed as I thrust my pelvis up. He slid his hands under my skirt and in one long yank, pulled my underwear down around my ankles. J never took our clothes off all the way. He'd push my skirt up and leave his pants mid-drop so we could dress quickly if my parents pulled in. My father parked his VW Beetle on the street, and sometimes he'd run into the house quickly to get something he'd left from his office. He moved with little noise, a regal stride. I pictured him rifling through his office downstairs, wondering if he knew where I was.

He never called for me.

Mom drove the Impala, a cruise ship of a car that took up too much space on the street. She parked in our open-air gated driveway. The gate was manual, so she had to get out of the car to open it, pull the car in, and get out to shut and lock it. The gate was ornate, like the entrance to a castle, all metal-edged wood with rivets. It was low and scraped against the concrete, sounding another long warning to stop. Maybe J liked it that way. Almost being caught. Maybe that was part of the thrill for him. Seeing how far he could push it. Gambling for more. More time. More of my body.

At school, all the little girls huddled together during breaks, whispering visions of the futures we'd been fed. How one day we'd marry and live happily ever after. Find our prince, or, rather, he would find us. Like Sleeping Beauty, we would be awakened by one kiss. J was doing what I'd only seen adults do, so the place in my brain that tried to make sense of things decided that I must be an adult. A married adult.

No one had ever told me how my parents met, but as I watched J's penis grow stiff and raise itself parallel to the bed, I wondered if their story was like this. My father so much older than Mamita. Had they met this way too?

Grabbing my ankles, J pulled me down the bed and carefully laid on top of me. With his free hand, he shushed me again. If my parents had ordered them, then J's kisses must mean that he was going to be my prince. I'd be married in a full sparkling gown, J in a blue suit.

All the most handsome princes wore blue suits.

My blue prince.

He started moving faster, rocking his body against mine. Again, the electrical tickling sensation. My breath grew heavier. My body took on a life of its own as I watched from above. He pressed harder against me, his body heavy, and I felt a dull pressure around my private area. Then something sharp, and I swallowed a gasp, trying to remain calm. He froze and gave a little shiver, groaning. Clumps of what looked like snot dripped onto my leg and the inside of my skirt. J wiped them up with a cleaning cloth he pulled from his back pocket.

Two levels down, the front door swung open. I could tell it was my father by the precise click of his loafers against the glossy wood.

J yanked my underwear up, and I felt cold soggy patches cling to my skin. "*Shhhh, shhhh,*" he sang. "Anda sigue jugando." *Go back to play.*

My father went straight to his office and slammed the door as usual. The windows of the house trembled. I wanted to run down and make him happy, tell him that I was following his orders with J. That we both were. I wanted to tell him about the electric tickling. About the strange sticky clumps. I wanted him to be proud of me for doing as I was told. But he was locked in his office. And we were never to bother Segundo in his office.

* * *

When my parents stopped attending Mass, I often walked to church alone. Church was a place where obeying orders was soothing. Stand up, sit down, kneel, up, down, kneel, up, down, kneel. I wanted to be an obedient girl and took to the rhythm of Mass as if it might shape me into a daughter my father would embrace. Then, maybe, we'd have a chance at happiness.

Soaking in the dappled shade, I kicked aside the red tassels of shedding poinciana trees that lined my street, Domingo de la Presa—*Sunday's prey.* My focus was scattered as I cut through the alley and looked both ways before crossing into Parque Mariano Santos, one of the lush neighborhood parks dotting our corner of Lima. Palm trees hulaed in the wind behind sculpted hedges, but I hardly noticed. I no longer felt the breeze. Sensation seemed to blur. Birdsong was monotone. Balmy walks were temperatureless, stagnant.

The outside world was like a cloak settling over me.

Something murky. A dampening I was trying to claw my way out of.

J was not a stranger, but a "persona de confianza," as my mother called him. A trusted person. Between moments of silence and explosion at home, he provided attention and tenderness I'd never felt from my father. The small girl in me craved it. I yearned to please him. Longed to be seen. To be held. I don't remember when I stopped giggling, though. When it became more than just the silent game.

I'd been waiting patiently for my mother to call me to the couch. To explain what was going to happen in my life. To translate J's secrets and my father's rage into a sense of order. Mama was my translator. My father never apologized or explained. His actions were complete. His intentions, even how he felt about me, were opaque. She was the only conduit for what little understanding existed between us. Between me and the outside world as a whole. I kept waiting for her to speak. I dreamt of it so often that I began to mix the real and the imagined.

It would be a sunny day when she sat me down. One of those days when light poured into our house in hazy streams like the pictures of Christ ascending. Those days when things seemed brighter, more free. She'd call me to the couch in the TV room. Our usual spot.

"Silvita, come." She'd pat the cushion next to her and squeeze me close as I breathed in her sweet scent.

"Yes, Mamita," I'd say.

"I've been waiting until you were older for this. But you're becoming a woman now," she'd say. "You're growing up. We know what J has been doing to you."

"Okay, Mama."

"We love J. He's a good man. And we know he has told you to be quiet. It's because your father and I have chosen J to be your prince. Just like in the fairy tales, hijita. Just like your father and I got married, you will marry J."

"Okay," I'd say, nodding quietly, but swelling inside with relief. "Now I understand, Mama. All this time, J was doing what you and my father asked."

"We told him to keep it quiet because we wanted to tell you ourselves what's been happening. You will have your own children with J."

"So he was teaching me?"

"Yes, hijita. You're a good girl for listening," she'd say. "You've done good. We are so proud of you. Your father too. Even if he doesn't say it."

I'd breathe a sigh of relief. J had already told me they knew. But now I could stop worrying. I'd just needed to be patient. And so I was.

As I gave myself to the ritual motions of Mass every Sunday, other questions bubbled up. Questions I didn't dare ask. Even in my own daydreams, I didn't ask them. I didn't ask my mother what the sticky stuff was. Or how old I'd be when we got married. Whether the other girls in my class had a J. Whether my father had been hers.

Like my father always said, "In adult conversations, kids are quiet."

* * *

I wanted so badly to behave. To be good. But I began to throw wild fits before Mamita left to run errands. I couldn't stop myself from sprinting to the front seat and locking the door. She'd bang and bang on the window, but I wouldn't unlock it until she promised to take me along. I couldn't. Something was overtaking my body. A surge of energy.

"So dramatic," she said one day when I finally let her in. "You've been watching too many telenovelas. There's nothing to be scared of, you know? Come along, then."

She backed the Impala out of the driveway. "Buckle yourself," she said. We drove with the windows down.

Dusk was falling. I started to nod off but woke up as we passed mechanics alley. We were near her old district, La Victoria. But instead of turning down her street, we swung a right on Avenida Esmeraldas and into Balconcillo. She pulled down a half-dirt road, and I bounced in my seat as she swerved around deep potholes and small piles of stone before parking along a string of one-story stone buildings. Sheets of paint peeled from the stucco walls. In the center of the road there was a long concrete median packed with dirt and pockets of unfinished construction, nothing like the lush parques surrounding my house. In the distance, I heard the tinny whistle of the heladero.

Mamita turned the car off, and we climbed out.

"See that door there?" She pointed to a red-and-white building with a basement-level entrance. "Hijita, I need you to run over and ring the bell. And then come right back. Don't wait for an answer." I looked up at her, wondering if it was a joke. Small clusters of people gathered on the corners. Salsa music blared from the windows. Three kids about eight or so, Miguel's age, ran past laughing and screaming, their shirts stretched at the neck, shorts sagging and stained. Mama leaned back against the hood and scanned the street slowly in all directions. She was dressed as usual in a cotton blouse and jeans, sneakers so she'd be always ready to move. No jewelry or makeup. Neither of us liked dresses and only wore them when we had to. Housewife butch, that was Mama. A practical woman with endless errands to run.

"Well?" She said, lifting an eyebrow.

Looking both ways, I dashed across the dusty road. I pushed the small black button and heard a bell jingle in the house, then a thud and kids screaming. I ran back across the street, and a couple minutes later Marianela, who was twenty, and Ramiro, sixteen, ran out. My cousins! Was this where they lived? I only got to see them on holidays at my grandma's or aunt Irene's house.

Marianela scooped me up and twirled me around, letting buzzing bees loose in my belly.

"Where's Rolando?!" I giggled.

"Out," Marianela said, rolling her eyes. "With some girl."

"Who's this girl now? I can't keep up," Mama said, hugging Ramiro. "How's soccer? Severo says you've been invited to play on an under-seventeen team?"

Ramiro gave a proud little smirk.

Mama squeezed Marianela's shoulder. "You okay? How's work?"

"Come play with me!" I tugged on Ramiro's shirt.

"You go play!" Mama snipped. "Dig for roly-polies! I'm talking to your cousins."

"Jeez," I muttered and set off kicking a rock down the center of the street. I ran to the dusty median and started scanning the dirt for insects. After kicking around trash with no sight of a chanchito, I heard Mama's laugh and looked back to see her talking to Uncle Severo. I raced back to fling my arms around his waist.

"Tío!"

"Silvita, let us talk," Mom said. She pulled a handful of coins from her pocket. "Here, take your cousins to buy something from the corner store."

"Gansito," I cried. "Race you!"

Ramiro peeled off down the street. He was halfway to the store by the time Marianela and I got going, leaving cartoon clouds of dust in his wake.

As we walked back to the car, sweets in hand, Ramiro hoisted me onto his shoulders, and Marianela chattered on about life in the United States. "United States?" I said. "How far is that?" "Very far!" She laughed. Frowning, I ate the Gansito little by little, my fingers sticky with pink jam filling.

"Un besito," Severo said, pecking my cheek. Ramiro swung me to the ground with the sound of a fighter jet, and Marianela kneeled down to give me a hug. The three of them walked back toward their house. Mama and I climbed into the car, the hot leather of the seat searing the back of my legs.

"Mom, where's my cousins' mother?" I asked.

"Not sure. I think she's out of town," she said, turning up the radio as she pulled away from the curb. AM news anchors were reporting another Shining Path bombing. "Oh, if Papa asks, we went to see Grandma today in La Victoria."

"But we didn't," I said. "We saw my cousin Ramiro. And I miss Rolando. When can I see Rolando?"

She pumped the brake, and the car jolted to a stop.

"Silvita," she said, her voice steely. With her eyes fixed on mine, she repeated, "We did not see Ramiro today. We saw your grandma."

The way she said it, as if I'd materialized my cousins, as if I'd imagined Marianela spinning me in circles or dreamt up Ramiro racing me down the dusty road, was so certain, so unwavering that I began to wonder if I had in fact made it up. My mother had written new stories over my own so many times that it was increasingly hard to know the difference. The extra fabric for school uniforms, telling the doctors that I fell when my father hit me. She was the adult. Her truth trumped mine. Maybe we had visited my grandma. Maybe my cousins were all a dream. My allegiance to Mamita was more than obedience.

It was absolute.

The Fourth Commandment: Honor your mother and father.

* * *

We were in the car again. Rushing again. We were always late for something. But this time, my father had on his nicest suit, and his hair was slicked back. Mama was in a fancy black-checked dress, and she even had lipstick and blush on. My father parked, and we dashed up the steps of a church. It was familiar. Saint Anthony of Padua! Saint Anthony is the patron saint of lost things, and this was Father Hugo's church. He'd been to parties at our house many times. My father was always eager to share his fancy bottle of Ye Monks whiskey with Padre Hugo. "Salud, Padrecito!" he'd toast in a sarcastic tone.

Panting, Mama and my father and I dashed up the stairs. A crowd of people was gathered outside the church holding handfuls of rice. What I saw next shocked the breath out of me. Emerging from the ornate wooden doors, hand in hand, were J and a woman.

"J, we're over here," my mother cried. "Over here!"

J ran over, clutching the woman's hand. She was beautiful and beaming in a full white gown. J was in a light blue suit. Just like the one from my daydreams.

"Que felicidad!" Mama said, kissing them both. "From the bottom of our hearts, we wish the best for you and your new family."

My father shook J's hand. "Felicidades."

My arms hung limp at my sides. I was silent until my mother nudged me in the side.

"Congratulations," I choked.

J caught my eye and winked.

"Ay que linda!" said his bride, leaning down to kiss the top of my head.

"Padre!" Mama called. "Padre Hugo. Over here!" El padre strolled over in his elegant costume, and, after exchanging pleasantries, he ushered the couple away to the small chapel behind the church for pictures.

I watched from the distance as they posed for wedding photos in the same chapel where nine years earlier I'd been baptized as a newborn. After the photos, J and his bride ran down the steps toward their waiting car as the crowd tossed handfuls of rice into the air. As I blinked through the tiny white grains raining down around us, I fixated on J's suit.

You were my blue prince, was all I could think. *You were supposed to be my blue prince.*

* * *

After J got married, I couldn't sleep. Nothing made sense. For four years, I'd listened to him. I'd listened because there was a reason, a future. He was going to be my fairy tale. Why else would it all have happened like it had? But now he was gone, and I was left alone in the small dark room of myself, waiting again for some sort of explanation. And there was something else too. A new moral complication. The Fourth Commandment demanded that I obey my parents, and I had. I'd had my own holy trinity: Father, J, God. Listening to J meant listening to my father, and listening to my father was listening to God. But J had married someone else. If he came to my room now, how could I obey him without breaking another commandment? The Sixth Commandment: *You shall not commit adultery.*

At school, they drilled us with stories of heaven and angels, of redemption and beauty, but what I remembered most was damnation. I was petrified of hell. Of burning. God's vengeance was the only force I'd ever seen that was more powerful than my father's rage.

I had to stop J.

I was thinking of what to say as we sped through the barriadas, the slums, one weekend to do errands. The late-afternoon humidity was swampy, and the windows were halfway down to capture any hint of breeze. When we visited the barriadas of Lima, my job was to come along and protect the car while my parents shopped so a car thief wouldn't run off with it. As usual my parents were arguing up front. My father steered the VW onto Avenida Tomás Marsano, a colorful avenue filled with small hardware stores whose storefronts were packed with bins of strange-looking tools. Swerving around motorbikes, he honked and screamed out the window. Combi drivers hollered back. We bumped down a half-paved dirt street, and a row of shirtless men with beer bellies drinking in front of their houses eyed us as we passed.

"Esos borrachos," scowled my father. *Drunken losers.* "No hacen nada. Haraganes. See this slum life, Silvia? This is where your mother is from."

My window didn't roll down, so I distracted myself by counting blue cars. Ten blue cars, then I picked a new color . . . green . . . and counted ten of those. Like patterns and systems, numbers were clean and ordered. In the chaos of my life, calculation was soothing. Counting a salve.

In the fifth green car, there was a family almost like mine. Mother and father up front. Daughter and son in the back. But they were laughing instead of shouting, singing along to a song on the radio. Their windows were rolled up and foggy from the steam of their voices. I tried to picture myself in the middle of such harmony, singing along happily, but then the light changed and my father slammed on the gas.

"Y tú, que tanto hablas, dejando hijos por todos lados!" he shouted.

Look at you and those children you abandoned.

"Cállate Segundo!" *Stop it*, hissed my mother.

"Where are they now? Rolando, Marianela, and Ramiro. Si eres una puta!"

You are a whore.

Rolando? My cousins. I edged forward in my seat to hear better.

Mama slammed her fists into my father's shoulder and started to sob.

"Andate a la mierda, concha de tu madre!" my father shouted.

At the next stop sign, she jumped out of the car and walked away.

"Mom!" I cried.

My father reached over to pull her door shut, then peeled off.

"Mamita!" I called.

"Cállate, carajo!" he barked, looking back at me in the rearview mirror. His face was stone as I turned to watch my mother grow smaller in the distance.

Later that night, she found me reading alone on the couch in the TV room.

We always met there after a blowout, with her sliding beside me to smooth things over. To decode his fury. I wonder sometimes who those talks were for. If she was trying to metabolize his anger for me, or if it was a way to explain it to herself.

"Silvita," she said. "We need to talk."

Pulling me into the nook of her arm, she started with chitchat, telling me this and that about the rest of her day, a way to wind herself into explanation. *This is it*, I thought suddenly as she rambled on. It was just like I'd imagined. Even the dusty shafts of sun falling across our legs. She was finally going to explain the past few years to me. Tell me how all the pieces fit together. I'd been waiting for this moment for so long. She was going to tell me about J. About all the things that had been hushed away.

But she didn't mention J at all. Not that night.

Or the day after. Or any of the weeks or months that followed.

Instead, she told me a long story about being a girl. When she was only fourteen, her father, my grandfather, was murdered in the mountains outside of Cusco, in a business deal. My grandma was devastated, and, too poor to support herself and her five children, she married my mother off at fifteen to an older boy from the neighborhood. The boy was in the army, and at first Mama was so relieved to escape poverty she didn't think of anything else. She despised being poor. She dropped out of high school, and at sixteen gave birth to her first son, and after that a daughter and then another son. The military stationed her husband in the mountains outside of Cusco, not far from where her father had been killed. Mamita was alone there with three babies.

"I was so young," she said. "Almost a baby myself. I didn't know what to do. So I ran. I'm not proud of it, hija, but for a while, I left. I was always going to come back."

She fled to a nearby town in the mountains and got a job as a secretary. Her husband took the kids back to Lima and won custody of them in court. She could only see them on certain days at certain times. When Mama first met my father, Segundo, she was back in Lima, living with her mother in La Victoria and trying to win her kids back.

When they were first dating, my father used to visit her at home, and when she had the kids, he'd help Marianela with math homework. Mama thought they'd be a family. That she would get her kids back, maybe that being with a man like Segundo would help. He was almost twenty years older than she was and a well-respected, self-made businessman.

There was hushed talk against my mother. Specifically, my Tía Emerita, my father's closest family member, didn't think my mother was good enough for him. The stigma against a divorced woman with three children in Peru was strong.

But she'd already fallen for him. For either his looks or his security. Or maybe even for a heart I'd never seen. Either way, he'd wooed her, sweet-talked her children, and promised her a good life. And then he changed his mind and he made her choose. If she wanted to be with him, she couldn't acknowledge or see her three children, Rolando, Marianela, and Ramiro. He made her an offer she said she couldn't refuse. "You won't have to work anymore," he told her.

"I figured that poco a poco he'd warm up toward my kids. That his love for me would overcome. I figured he'd change his mind eventually, hija. I was sure he'd change his mind."

I was silent.

That day she'd taken me with her to Balconcillo, when I'd demanded to ride along, she'd been visiting her children.

That's where she'd been all the afternoons I was alone with J.

"My cholita berrinchosa," she purred, holding me tight. "No need to tell your brothers, okay? They're too little. For now, it's our secret."

I wanted to ask her where I should put all of our secrets.

* * *

J didn't come around after the wedding much, and for a while, as I grew to accept that my cousins, my sweet beloved cousins, were actually my brothers and sister, I forgot about J. Then one afternoon, a month after my tenth birthday, I heard a faint whistle down the hall. Before I could place the sound, he was standing in the doorway of my bedroom. His smile was wide as he stepped in and locked the door as if nothing had changed. My fists clenched. He unzipped his pants, stood against the wall, and began to pump himself hard. "No," I said quietly as he pushed me down on the bed and started to kiss me. I sealed my lips together, pressing them into a frown. Fire flared up the back of my neck, scorched my ears. For once, my faith was stronger than the word of my father or the weight of J's body. God was above them both. Above us all. "No more," I said.

"What?"

"The commandments."

"What commandment?"

"Number six," I said with as much firmness as I could muster. "It's adultery."

"Who said that?" he asked, looking at me. His eyes narrow slits.

"Padre Pablo. I'm going to tell him. I have to. We're going to hell."

J's eyes widened, and he pulled away, looking at me in a way he never had. Fear, yes, but also underneath that was a sort of sadness. As if he'd just seen me for the first time. And my heart lurched at the thought of angering him. But the fear of sin was greater. Burning in hell would be worse than any pain from my father's leather belts.

J jumped back at the sound of the garage door. *Mamita.* Finally. She'd finally come to save me. I could feel it. God was there too, protecting me. J buttoned his pants and rushed out of the room, leaving me to smooth down my hair and straighten my shirt. He never touched me again after that, and when he came to clean, I did everything I could to avoid him.

I was sure I'd done the right thing, but I began to feel worse.

*   *   *

Confession was held at the large basilica next to my school. For weeks, I'd been all nerves. Nervous that the priest would be shocked and ashamed. Nervous that he'd expel me, or worse, ban me from receiving communion. I was scared he'd see me like Mary Magdalene—as impure. "You are no longer a child of God," I imagined him whispering.

"Why's she taking so long?" whispered my mother, pointing at the girl kneeling next to the priest, pouring out her sins. "I mean really, what could be so bad that she's done?"

My father chuckled.

I wondered how many girls were telling the priest about their J.

Instead of the traditional booth with a dark screen and a closed door, our first confession was done at the front of the church, where the priest sat on a chair and we knelt beside him while everyone watched.

I shuffled down the aisle to the carved wood altar. It was hulking and regal, with gold gilding and an aura of dominion. The cathedral ceiling ballooned above me as I became smaller with each step. My fingers and toes went cold, all their warmth gathering into a churning buzz at the base of my neck. I didn't want the priest to look in my eyes and see a despicable sinner.

This was it. A chance for forgiveness. Or judgment day.

"Ave María Purisima." I bowed my head as I knelt in front of the father and whispered. *Purest Holy Mary.*

"Sin pecado concebida," the priest replied. *Without any original sin.*

"Bless me, Father, for I have sinned," I continued. "This is my first confession, and I have done the following sins: I hit my brother Miguel in the back of his head when we were playing; I forgot to wash my school uniform after my mother told me to; I ate an extra bag of Sublimes and blamed Miguel for it; I hid my bed sheets so that I wouldn't have to make my bed and lied to my mother about it." I hesitated then.

"And?" He waited.

My heart was beating through my eyes, my palms slick against each other as I knelt on the cushioned stool next to the padre, trying to ignore the eyes of my classmates and family sitting in the pews behind me. For so long, my father was not only the man of the house, but a deity. The explosions and curses, the vengeful nature and dramatic reconciliations. The power to destroy. A god ruled by rage and vanity. An undeniably human god. One who beat me but whom I continued to adore. But the more I'd learned, the more I saw that my father didn't pave the way to God. The padre, on the other hand, was a direct channel.

My communion dress pressed lacy imprints into my bare knees, and the barrettes holding on my veil dug into my scalp. I was positive I'd catch fire any moment.

"And . . ." I whispered. "Adultery."

"What?" said the priest.

"Adultery. With a married man. The Sixth Commandment, Father. I have been with a married man."

"I see," he said, unfazed. "Dear child, you must pray four Hail Marys and three Our Fathers. I absolve you from your sins in the name of the Father, and of the Son, and of the Holy Spirit. Go and be a good child of God."

My chest collapsed with relief. My mother shot me a wave and wink from the pew. Next to her my father's eyes were half-closed, his head nodding to the side. As I rushed to the nearest pew and knelt to complete my penance, I wondered why el padre hadn't said more. No advice or explanation. Part of me had been hoping he'd fill in the blanks. He was as close as I was going to get to God. I'd been holding out, praying that if I just waited and did as I was told, that if I *honored my mother and father*, that someone would eventually explain what was going on. But here I was, in a place where most found comfort, alone with my thoughts again.

Threading the beads of a pink glass rosary between my fingers, I began: *Hail Mary, Full of Grace* . . .

Mary, the Virgin. Mary, the kind, the loving, the innocent and tender. She'd watched over me. It was the women who did. They were my only chance to be heard. It wasn't my father I'd been hoping would explain things, but my mother. And though it might have been God I was answering to, it was from Mary that I first asked forgiveness.

That weekend, my parents threw a party at our house to celebrate my communion. All of my family members showed up to congratulate me. Toward the end of the day, J arrived, beaming, with his wife.

She was pregnant.

"Congratulations," she said, leaning down to give me a delicate peck on the cheek. "You're a woman now." A wave of goose bumps ran up my arms.

Later, when the adults had forgotten why they originally had come and sat talking loudly over each other, blaring salsa in the living room, I slipped into the kitchen and poured a tiny bit of pisco into my juice. Just a splash. For a brief, glorious moment, the liquid heat of pisco wiped away the lingering chill of J's wife's lips on my cheek.

* * *

By the next year, J had completely stopped coming to the house. I overheard my mother saying his wife was pregnant again. My parents had helped him land more stable work in his neighborhood, which was far from our house. And my mother had started a business of her own, a small catering operation that served cafeteria meals in a school near mine. There were new people in and out of the house every day, people she'd hired to help her cook and package the meals. Some of the new staff helped out with cleaning too, picking up where J had left off.

As they scrubbed the walls hiding echoes of his whistle and cleaned the rooms storing years of his DNA, a new vitality charged through the house. As if all the windows had been flung open and the dust cleared. Mama was

busy and joyful, constantly testing out new recipes. She saved money to send
to her mother and sisters. She'd always been a busy person, always on the
move, but fuzzy to me. The more work she got, the sharper the outline of
her became. Her portrait coming in full color. She began to speak up more.
To fight back. When my former cousin/sister, Marianela, decided to go to
San Francisco, Mama demanded she be invited over for a going-away party.

None of my secret siblings had ever stepped foot in my house before.

Then came the big offer. Mama's catering business had become a word-
of-mouth success, and Wong, the local gourmet grocery chain, offered to
carry her rolled chicken dish. Peru was a big meat-eating country, and rotisserie chicken was our staple and signature dish, but Mama's chicken was
something new. A Peruvian spin on chicken cordon bleu. Wong offered her
a contract to prepare it for their five largest stores. My mother was radiant.
She floated around like she'd been blessed by the pope himself. She began to
imagine opening her own restaurant. Or maybe something smaller, a little
tea shop, un lonchecito. Just the basics.

But while she was preparing for her first big order and dreaming bigger dreams, my father's criticism, which had always ebbed and flowed, grew
unceasing.

"Teresa, carajo, the house is shit. Everything is so filthy," he'd scream
when he came home to her catering team assembling meals in the dining
room. "Why are you cooking for all those assholes? You have a job already
taking care of your family."

Around the same time Mama's business took off, a counselor came to our
fifth-grade health class to talk about an idea I'd never heard before: self-care.
First, she separated the boys and girls into two groups and sent the boys to
another room. The girls sat cross-legged in tidy rows on the cold tile floor,
our long gray skirts blooming around us.

"One day you'll be married," she said. "You'll have babies. Husbands.
A Prince Charming!" The girls all giggled. "But before that, no one should
touch you down here." She waved her arms over her chest, belly, and crotch.
"Do you understand? That's only for when you're older. For making babies."

Everyone nodded along while I sat on my hand to keep it from shooting
up. Bit my lip to keep the words from tumbling out. *But what if I have been
touched?* I wanted to ask her what to do then. I had so many questions. I

wanted to know if the other girls had been touched too. But every time I opened my mouth to call out, I heard J's voice instead. *You haven't told anyone, right? Remember, don't tell anyone.* And I hadn't. Except for my confession to the priest, which had sparked no response, I had told no one.

In school, in church, at home, how I behaved was a direct reflection of Segundo. He never let me forget that. I was not to cause trouble, and too many questions were always trouble. I was a Catholic schoolgirl. My virtue was obedience, not inquiry. That day, I prayed someone else would speak. Would ask the question that I couldn't.

No one said anything.

As I sank down into the tile floor in the classroom of the only school I'd ever attended, and glanced around at the girls I'd known since first grade, I saw they knew nothing of me. And by the blank looks on their faces, I knew that what had happened to me had not happened to them. Like the self-care lady said, what had happened to me wasn't normal or right.

It was bad.

"Show me your wedding pictures with my father, Mamita?" I begged later that night. "What did your dress look like? Was the wedding big? Were you happy?"

"They were lost in a move, I think," she said. "Later, we'll look more later. I'm busy now. Help me cook."

I wanted to shake answers from her like ripe pears from a tree. I wanted to ask her what love meant to her. What it was supposed to mean for a girl like me.

* * *

My parents were out one night and I was home with Meche, the new housekeeper. Both my brothers were asleep. I snuck into my parents' room to watch the only color TV. As I pushed the door open and tiptoed in, my feet sank into the plush, freshly vacuumed carpet. Their room was mysterious. Off-limits. Carefully, I slid open one side of their closet door. Before me, hanging in a row like soldiers at attention, were my father's pressed bespoke suits. I ran my hands over them, watching them swing and knock together. Below each was a matching pair of mirror-shined dress shoes. From a far corner of the closet I pulled out a small suitcase.

I clicked it open. A heady rush of old leather and shoe polish escaped. Inside, it was filled with fancy fountain pen cartridges and pencils, brands like Cross and Parker. There were little mountains of erasers and tidy packages of pins and paperclips. I imagined my father clacking away at his adding machine in the office downstairs, filing through stacks of all the important papers that kept him away from his family or rushing off to important appointments. Holding the suitcase under my arm like someone important, I climbed up onto their bed and turned on the TV. We had only three channels in Peru, one state-run and two commercial. *The 700 Club* was on. My parents often watched *The 700 Club*, but I'd never paid much attention. It was droning grown-up talk, but I knew the people on the show were good, serious Christian people. Evangelicals. People like them visited our home often, and sometimes my mother invited them in for un tecito, a little cup of tea. They left their pamphlets behind, always with pictures of families bathed in a golden ray of God's light. The kind I'd always imagined streaming into the room while Mama explained about J.

"Today we're talking with four women about how they found salvation with the almighty word of God," said the white-haired host, Pat Robertson.

"Mujeres de la Calle," the caption read. *Street Women.*

I was drawn to the message of salvation. To the idea that a benevolent force could swoop down and save me. Could restore a sort of purity I longed for but had never known. I'd stopped relying on my parents for answers. While I still held out hope that Mama might come to me and explain what J had done, both she and my father were caught up in their own dramas. Meanwhile, my desire to make meaning, to understand, to purge and salvage, underscored every moment of every day. I was ravenous for spiritual order. More than absolution, I yearned for explanation.

The four women were blondes with lots of clownish makeup and all from the United States, where according to TV and movies, life could never be *that bad*. One of the women was speaking, and her voice was dubbed in Spanish. "Yes," she said. "I've been on the streets. And I have been a prostitute. But I didn't choose this. It started when I was a little kid when my uncle took advantage of me. He locked me in a room and hushed me as he pulled down my pants. He abused me."

My heart thumped as she described in detail exactly what J had done to me. "I'm trash," she cried, fat tears pooling in her eyes. "I'm damaged. I became a prostitute and a drug addict."

My fist tightened around the leather handle of the briefcase. The woman in health class said none of us should be touched. But my parents had given J permission to touch and kiss me. Now, the American TV blonde was saying what had happened was abuse. J said they wanted it for me. My parents wanted me to be abused? They wanted me to become a prostitute? To be trash? Trash was unwanted. Trash got thrown out. If I was trash, I was leftovers. The scraps that Tía Emerita fed to her chickens before slaughter.

My parents wanted this for me.

My parents wanted this for me.

I clicked off the TV and slid my father's briefcase back into the closet. I went to my room, knelt in front of my nightstand, and began to pray through trickling tears. *Why hadn't I stopped it sooner?* I ran back to my parents' room and snatched up a book of matches from their nightstand. When I was four or five, I remember sticking the end of a match in my mouth and licking off its strange, salty taste as my mother scolded me. "Stop it!" she'd said. "That's going to kill you! It's poisonous!"

I brought the matches back to my room and, one by one, peeled the flimsy cardboard sticks from the base and swallowed them whole, my mouth tingling with the acidic char of sulfur. Suicide was a mortal sin, punishable by burning in hell, but maybe a slow, accidental death would get me into purgatory.

Before then, I'd still believed that somehow this would all make sense.

That this was a story I just had to grow into. I had followed orders. Done what I thought would make everyone happy. And sometimes that made me happy too. Sometimes it even felt good. But it was wrong. Dirty. I was ashamed. Maybe it was all my fault.

Maybe because I couldn't say no, I'd actually said yes.

I lit one match and then another and another and the wisps of smoke hung in the air, winding themselves into a dark hazy ball. A shadow. That day, my heart became a shadow, and I prayed it would swallow me whole.

Chapter 5

〆〇〆〇

THE HIGH HIMALAYAS

Lucy's lips have a bluish-purple tint this morning, which at almost 9,000 feet isn't rare, but it's making me nervous. "Rocking a bold icy lip today, Ms. Lucy!" I say instead of what I'm really thinking. She flashes me a pity grin, and I feel a hundred and two years old.

I'm a walking nerve. An *ancient* walking nerve.

Most people don't get hit with altitude sickness until Namche, but Lucy's been struggling from day one, and it hasn't gotten better. Her pace is sluggish, her eyes weary. We're entering Sagarmatha National Park, the Nepali park that encompasses Everest and the rest of the Himalayan range. The girls squeeze onto an old wooden bench as I present our paperwork at the squat stone registration building. The ranger takes my money and assigns our hiking permits. My hand quivers as I pass him the additional paperwork for my Everest summit. Just thinking about Everest gives me vertigo. Ehani wanders over to stand beside me, and from the corner of my eye, I see her noticing my trembles. In eight days, my hike with the girls will be over, and I'll begin my summit bid. But right now, all I can see is our feet on the trail. We're two days behind schedule and fewer than ten miles in, but with everyone finally together, we're a unit now. An organism of eight. A conjuring.

Today, we hike toward Namche Bazaar, the gateway to the High Himalayas, where the air really starts to thin.

The ranger hands me my Everest permit, and I shove it into my bag without looking it over. Ehani begins to walk toward the park entrance. We sling our daypacks over our shoulders and follow her. "Alright, Ehani!" I say. "You're our pacesetter." Shailee translates for her; then Ehani raises an arm overhead and flashes me a thumbs-up. Shailee and Asha fall into line behind her, and Shreya and Rubina hang close to Jimena and Lucy in front of me. I bring up the rear.

We're about to pass through the kani gate, a plain-looking, walk-through stone hut that marks the spiritual entrance to the park. We stop and take turns reading the sign aloud.

This traditional kani gate marks your entry into the Beyul Khumbu—a sacred hidden valley of the Sherpa people. While visiting this special area, visitors are encouraged to

1. Refrain from taking life
2. Refrain from anger
3. Refrain from jealousy
4. Refrain from offending others
5. Refrain from taking excessive intoxicants

"Too many rules," Lucy jokes, and I'm thrilled to hear a hint of sweet sarcasm. She's still ticking.

The girls snap a group selfie, their tongues poked out to the side and fingers V'ed into peace signs. It's like an ad for sleepaway camp. The kind where happy, shiny American girls spend their summers. The kind of summers none of us had. For some of us, softness has always been unsafe. For many of us, it still is. But maybe here they can get a tiny taste of it.

The underbelly of the kani gate is painted with mandalas of neon pink and umber; gold and rich greens cover the ceiling. Jimena and Lucy turn in place, and I watch to see where their eyes land. Along the walls are vibrant frescoes of Buddha, Miyolangsangma (Everest's female deity on her red tiger), and the local deity, Khumbila, the god of the Khumbu.

One in particular catches my eye.

He looks ominous compared to the others, evil almost, but his darkness is kind of electrifying. With navy blue skin and three eyes, he wears a crown of skulls and a tiger-skin loin cloth. Wild flames plume around him like a mane. Even his hair is a flame.

"Very punk rock," I say, more to myself than anyone.

"Vajrapani," Shreya says, when she sees me eyeing him. "Holder of the thunderbolt."

Of course I'm drawn to the dangerous one.

Nyingma is the religion of the Sherpas, Shailee explains, and these pictures are their stories. A mystical nature-based sect, Nyingma is the oldest form of Tibetan Buddhism. In this part of the Himalayas, the gods are nature embodied. That makes more sense to me than anything I've heard in a while.

On the right-hand wall of the kani, there's a cutout section where a row of metal cylinders are lined up like beads on an abacus.

"What are they?" asks Jimena.

"Prayer wheels," says Shailee. "You spin them to purify your karma. Good karma in, bad karma out. Each one has a mantra on a teeny tiny little scroll tucked up inside."

"I'm a blessings hoarder, you know," I say, rubbing my hands together hungrily. I've accumulated enough negative karma for a few lifetimes, and my karma could use some wringing out.

"Remember to only go clockwise," Shailee says. "And always pass them on the left."

"What happens the other way?" says Jimena.

"I don't know." Shailee shrugs. "It all gets undone?"

"The karma?" Jimena looks concerned.

"Maybe?"

Single file, we walk, brushing our right hands over the wheels. One, two, four, ten of them. They let loose easily, spinning into an easy whir, making a thwacking sound like two wooden balls hitting each other. A fresh breeze blows through the walkway.

"Some of the wheels are bigger, you'll see," says Shailee. "Some move with water and some with wind. When they move they release their mantras into the air. They send goodwill to all."

When I trekked to Base Camp alone in 2005, I never stopped to spin the wheels. Jet fueled by excitement and pain, I tore through the forty miles of the Everest Base Camp hike in four days, walking so fast that my Nepalese guide was hit with altitude sickness and had to stay behind. I went ahead without him. There was something raging in me then, a writhing, incandescent ghoul that shoved me past any warnings or logic. I was in awe of the mountain, of course, but I couldn't wrap my mind around what any of it meant or why, exactly, I was even there. I'd been so focused on my own stuff that I missed out on all the spiritual aspects.

"They want to always be moving," Shailee is saying. "The prayer wheels. To release the sounds of their mantras and goodwill into the air."

"It's like the prayer flags," I say.

"Yes," says Asha. "Same idea."

I like that you don't need a person to make a prayer. That prayer can ride on wind. That a sound can be an invocation of its own. A blessing for all who wind touches. It's so far from the idea of personal sin and penance. Of kneeling in a church with sore knees praying for salvation.

Ehani marches on, and we fall into line, our feet thumping a soft, hollow rhythm against the warm, packed earth. Since we arrived three days ago, it's been taxis and planes and hotels and logistics. But now we're walking. Tromping single file along the path. This is why we're here. To walk. Nothing more. Okay, something more. Much, much more according to my Excel sheets with tabs on tabs on subtabs. But, if all that fails, if this whole thing is a massive disaster; if nothing else, we will have walked together. And that is enough.

So much is written and filmed about Everest, about the one tiny point where the summit pierces the sky, but really it's the roads winding up to the mountain that cradle the culture of the Himalayas, of the Sherpa people, who live twenty-five hundred strong in small riverside villages and towns cut into mountainsides on steep terraced slopes.

Dark, scrubby rhododendron sprout wildly from the sides of the hill as we begin to drop down into a valley. We pass a huge stone bluff etched with rows of delicate white lettering, the precise swoop of Sanskrit. It's the same message repeated hundreds of times. Some sort of scripture. I think of Moses's stone tablets.

"They're mani stones," Asha explains, she and Shailee in full tour-guide mode. "Pass on the left," she says. "Always pass mani on the left."

"What does it say?" I ask.

"Om mani padme hum," she says. "The famous Tibetan mantra."

"Ah, yes," I pretend to recognize it. "That one, I know."

I do know *om* from the sporadic yoga classes I forced myself into back home—trying to align my body and find the promised inner peace. But holding the postures is exhausting. My body is never right. Too stiff, my breath too controlled. Every time the teacher tells me to *just let it all go*, I do exactly the opposite. Where is it supposed to go? They never tell you that part. I'm more into a fast and hard approach. The blood, sweat, and get-it-done style. Finding the body's limits by pushing it to the edge. The chanting of *om* at the end of yoga is the only move I've mastered, though I still haven't figured out what it means.

The trees turn to houses as we approach the tiny riverside village of Jorsalle, a cluster of blocky Monopoly-like buildings with pointed roofs in utilitarian green and red and blue. We follow the bend and curve of the Dudh Koshi. Its swift flow carries us along, the rush of water tumbling the rocks, playing melody to our silence. Up ahead, a long suspension bridge swings over the river. And beyond that another and another, each one higher than the last. We stop and count five of them draped between the forested hills, a natural roller coaster connecting each hill to the next. To get to the bridges, we have to climb through thick, fragrant forest. Blue pines are brushed up the hillside in thick swaths like someone painted them on.

"Our next stop is close," I pant, my first white lie of the day. "You'll see. Four, maybe five kilometers. Literally three miles." The numbers are true, technically. We may hike only three miles today, but if we make it, we gain almost 2,000 feet in elevation. I leave out that tiny numeric detail. Watching Lucy and now Jimena start to drag, I'm startled to realize that there's no way for me to truly know if I'm pushing them too hard. Lucy's instincts worry me, mostly because I share them. I just hope she knows when to push and when to quit. I never have. How can I measure the distance between challenge and threat? And how can I trust that in this strange new environment, they'll know themselves well enough to tell me?

In *The Nature Fix*, Florence Williams tells the story of Ken Sanders, a rare-book seller who spent years as a river guide in the American West. Sanders noticed that after seventy-two hours on the river, people's perceptions began to shift. His neurologist friends ran a study on the theory and found that after three days, the attention network of the brain—the part responsible for daily lists and chores—took a break and allowed other parts to take over. Namely, those that deal with sensory perception and empathy.

Many survivors experience dissociation at some point, and sensory interactions can provide a gateway to regain connection to and ownership of their bodies. Simply talking about trauma isn't always enough. It lives in the body, and we need to work it out through the body.

Sexual trauma scrambles your instincts. Morphs things that you know are wrong into things you must accept. Over time, boundaries dissolve. Boundaries that are not only physical—your skin, my skin, his skin, their skin—but emotional, energetic. Sometimes it happens before you understand the contours of your own body, so as you grow you carry all the terrible things they inflicted upon you. Like a tree growing around a gash in its trunk, first you split, then fuse back together, and eventually envelop the object, the rock, the wound, swallowing it into your belly as if it were your very own.

Ehani whistles, and I see a trio of dzo—half cow, half yak—lumbering down the trail toward us. We scoot to the far right. Livestock have right-of-way. From Lukla to Base Camp, about forty miles total, everything is packed in by animal or on foot. This hike is not a forested jaunt for tourists like us, but a trade route and a highway.

Led by a short sun-beaten woman, the shaggy swaybacked cattle lumber past us, leaving behind a perfume of piss and warm clay.

"Mmm! Musky," jokes Shailee, sniffing the air.

Ehani leads on, whistling occasionally to signal dzo passing or a herd of yaks. After a while, we become a wave, moving off the trail and back in one fluid motion. It's the most confident I've seen Ehani.

Ehani, the silent.

When I first met Ehani, Shreya, and Rubina, they took me home with them to a rural village in Sindhupalchok, three hours outside of Kathmandu. The roads to Sindhupalchok were chewed up and spit out, at times little more than a steep dirt hill with body-sized rocks we had to swerve around or slowly navigate over. More than once, we jumped down from the back of the 4x4 to push it up the road ourselves, waving at other cars to pass. At first I was shocked at how rough it was, then embarrassed at my own shock. Much of Peru was the same. Poor and rural. The roads were similar to the ones leading to my father's childhood home, winding into the Andean countryside, the potholes growing and the space between adobe houses expanding the deeper we went. The membrane separating me from the poverty of my mother's and father's life, from the life of Aunt Emerita raising chickens in her little corner house, was thin. I could almost see through to the life I could have lived. But as we traveled deep into Sindhupalchok, it was clear how firmly my parents had closed the door on poverty.

One of Nepal's least developed districts, Sindhupalchok has been a hub for human trafficking since the eighties. It was an agricultural district, but because it was so mountainous, the land wasn't very fertile, and the yield was low. It was remote and poor, and for all these reasons, ripe for exploitation.

Their village was at the top of a hill overlooking a valley of moon-shaped terraces. Rice paddies. And beyond that, a panorama of foothills—great crinkly ridges carpeted with lush forest. Fog clung to the creases of the mountains. Ehani grabbed my hand in hers, the warmth of her palm steady, as she led me down a wide dirt road through the village, a collection of huts perched on a steep hill at constant risk of landslide in the heavy annual rains. We passed young girls in red woven outfits and old women in tika, or bindis, and gold nose rings, hauling rocks up the steep hill on their shoulders. They were still rebuilding from the big 2015 earthquake. Two local women stopped us. Their questions seemed to ignite Ehani. She nodded toward me, moving her hands in slow, swooping motions. Her posture was ballet-esque, graceful and steady, her speech vibrant and rolling—so different from the shy person I'd first met. I wondered how much of her timidity had been a language gap and how much was protective distance.

I wasn't the first person who had told her I was there to help.

Every year, thousands of girls were lured away from Ehani's district and trafficked into sex work in India through the promise of jobs or a chance at a better education. Bajir Sing Tamang, a very powerful, very dangerous man with serious political connections, had been responsible for trafficking hundreds of girls, including Rubina, Shreya, and Ehani. Most of the families had no idea what was going on when they sent their daughters away. Some, though, Ehani told me, did. There was a clip of sadness in her voice when she said it.

I nodded. I understood how a place could both be home and the pain you needed to escape.

When Ehani was twelve, her father died. And in Nepali tradition, that made her brother the man of the house. It was his job to step up to support the family, but he didn't take to that role, she said. He had never paid attention in school and didn't want extra responsibility. Her mother struggled to keep food on the table alone, so at fourteen, Ehani ran away to Kathmandu, where she worked for a year in a carpet factory and sent money home.

"When I was young, my father always told me I needed to be a big person," she said. "To be important. But I didn't know what he meant then. There were no big people around."

* * *

We approach the Hillary Bridge. "Hydration," I call. "Last stop." This final climb is where the altitude is going to hit hard. As we stand in a huddle, chugging from our liter bottles, two lanky white men hike past and tape a flyer with a Harvard logo to a makeshift garbage can. I noticed the same flyer back in a teahouse at the beginning of our trek. It had information about an altitude study a group of doctors was doing in Namche Bazaar.

"Are you the doctors?" I ask.

They laugh. "Not yet!"

"Still on our second year," says the taller one. "I'm Peter, by the way."

"Silvia."

"Gabe."

"You know, there is a doctor, though," Peter says. "She's behind us and moving a bit slow, because she's carrying all her gear."

"Refused to use a porter," says Gabe.

"Sounds like my kinda doc," I joke, but inside I'm screaming with relief.

"Where is she staying?" I ask. If there's a female doctor, maybe I can talk her into checking out the girls. Just to make sure I'm not missing any warning signs. All the altitude sickness warnings are neon signs in my mind now, sputtering and buzzing at random.

"Panorama Lodge," says Peter, "Her name is Dr. Jackie."

Peter and Gabe wave good-bye. We cram our waters into our bags and begin to climb a set of stone stairs. Not a right-angled flight, but rounded rocks jutting out from the ground like a row of crooked teeth. Part scramble, part staircase.

"Remember, slow and steady," I say in my calmest voice. "Pressure breathing—deep breath and then a strong exhale."

"Ay, otra escalera más!" grumbles Lucy.

"Ya, llegamos. Arriba no más." *We're almost there.* My second lie. What is a lie, anyhow, except another possible truth?

Jimena groans, and I think this is what it must be like to raise teenagers.

"We're embracing our *friluftsliv*!" I say.

They ignore me and continue to huff up the stairs, even though I was prepared to give a heartfelt lecture on the Norwegian term for the value of spending time in nature.

Two miles left.

The blood is coming back to Lucy's face, but Jimena seems distracted. At each person that passes, their forehead crinkles in concentration, as if they are trying to solve the puzzle of this place. Over the next twenty minutes, I notice a small wheeze developing at the end of each breath Jimena takes.

"Breathe in through your nose, out through the mouth!" Shreya chants. She's got her oversized movie-star glasses on and tips them down her nose at Jimena to flash a look of concern.

"Drink," says Rubina, stopping to pull the Nalgene from Jimena's bag. "Always be drinking water."

"Wait, are we going to climb to that thing way up there?" Lucy lets out a gasp, pointing at a pair of long suspension bridges zigzagging through the trees like garlands.

"Yes," I say. "And just beyond them, not too far, is the entrance to Namche."

At the Hillary Bridge, everyone goes silent. It's a spectacular thing. A narrow corridor of wire mesh strung over a four-hundred-foot deep rocky ravine. Hundreds of silky khatas and prayer flags tied to the railings. It's a tradition to hang Tibetan prayer flags on high places. Prayer flags, like the prayer wheels, have mantras printed on them in tiny script. By hanging them where the wind will blow through them, Himalayan people say the spirit of those blessings gets scattered across the earth. When the flags grow old and eventually fade in the sun and rain and snow, the prayers are absorbed back into the universe. As we file along one at a time, the bridge droops and bounces as the wind rushes up from the ravine below, whipping the prayer flags around our faces like wild manes of hair.

Far below hangs the rickety, threadbare skeleton of the old Hillary Bridge, the one I'd crossed on my 2005 trip. It was while crossing that bridge that I realized that my trauma was not the same as my identity. That's what I hope for these girls. Watching Jimena and Lucy and Rubina and Shreya and Ehani cross the new bridge with wonder and trepidation, I remember being so eager to get to the top. To know what was over the next hill. To know if I was going to be okay.

We fan out across the bridge, each holding part of a long prayer flag. The wind tears through in sudden gusts. The sun has already swallowed us whole. At high altitude, the sun is harsh. More white than golden, it overtakes the whole sky and envelops you instead of beaming down in cute little cartoon rays.

"Everyone, quick, offer something special to the mountain. And if you're called to, maybe ask for a wish as well." I'm shy to speak the last part, but I push myself as I think a leader would. Before we tie the flag to the bridge, we take a collective pause so everyone can focus their intentions. An offering and a wish. What do we bring and what will we take away?

My only wish right now is for the girls to stay alive.

* * *

Across the bridge and halfway up to Namche, there's a woman sitting behind a rickety card table selling overpriced apples and juice. The equivalent of one US dollar for an apple and two dollars and fifty cents for a can of juice. That's ten times what it would cost in Kathmandu. But there's nowhere to fill up our water bottles for another hour and a half. Supply and demand in action. This is trail economics, and I admire her market savvy.

"Apple juice for all!" I say, handing over the equivalent of fifteen US dollars for an armload of juice.

The woman smiles and tucks the bills into a little pouch around her waist. "Namaste."

"Namaste," I say, giving a little bow.

"Hydrate, hydrate," I preach, passing out the juice. Lucy lies down on a low stone wall. "I'm hydrating horizontally," she says.

After a brief rest, I get them walking again, anxious to reach Namche before dark. The packed earth becomes pocked with stones, then turns to a solid stone path. By dusk there are stairs with stone sidewalls, and suddenly we're in front of the entrance to Namche. There are many houses, a small village. The last light of the sun reflects across the village—like the shimmery blue of a swimming pool at night. It bounces off the stone buildings while children run through dry patches of short grass.

Buddha's eyes watch as we enter the bustling horseshoe-shaped village on the edge of a high cliff. Namche is the biggest town on the trail, and its streets are packed with massage parlors and international yoga cafés serving pizza and offering twenty-four-hour Wi-Fi. Streams of yaks strapped with supplies clomp through the narrow stone streets. Children scatter around us, offering flowers in exchange for candy. We pass another wall of prayer wheels and stick out our right arms to spin them as we walk by. A metallic whir chimes our arrival. Pemba, the owner of the Khumbu Lodge, a cozy, cushy spot, hugs me like we're old friends.

"I know! I know. Water and nap. I am on it!" Lucy heads to her room after Pemba passes out the keys.

"Rest!" I call after Jimena as they disappear without a word.

They were quiet toward the end of the trip to Namche. But I've seen Jimena go quiet before. During our weekend practice hikes in the Bay Area, sometimes Jimena would walk ahead on their own. We're birthday twins, almost twenty years apart, and I get Jimena. I think.

"Girls, everyone else, free time," I say.

* * *

That night, we meet back in the dining room and eat under portraits of all the famous climbers who have been through Namche, some of whom never made it back. I cram that thought to the bottom of the growing barrel in my mind. Suddenly, I remember the doctor.

"Can you make a call for me, Pemba?" I give him the name of the lodge, and he dials and speaks in Nepali at length before handing me the phone.

"Hello?" I say.

"Hi, yes this is Jackie. Who's this?"

After I tell her about the girls and explain my concerns, Dr. Jackie offers to come down to our lodge. I'm so relieved I almost scream. I'm seeing it now, all the things that can go wrong. The whole trip is a tightrope, and at each water break, I'm just praying we make it to the next stop. The Nepali girls seem alright. Happy, even. Self-sufficient. Maybe they're putting on a good front, hiding their true feelings under the pressure of hosting us. Or maybe it's pride. This is their mountain, after all. But Lucy and Jimena are far from everything they know. I didn't think enough about how pushing their comfort zones could affect their desire or ability to climb.

It sounds absurd when I say it back to myself, but I think I assumed the mountain would be our therapist. That she would somehow guide our emotional and mental needs. I've taken the Mother much too literally.

I have no plan B.

If we don't make it, the whole thing, my Everest climb, too, is a wash.

Dr. Jackie joins us for dinner and gives the girls an all-clear after quick physicals. She decides to join us for the rest of the trek. It's another person in the mix, yes, but she's a caretaker, a personal expedition doctor who will be here if anything goes wrong. I'm ecstatic. My manifestation powers are back.

Jimena is quiet during dinner, though, and afterward they ask me to come to their room.

"What's up?" I say, perching on the edge of Jimena's twin bed.

"I have to be honest with you," they say. "I told myself I'd be honest. I'm not really feeling it. Not sure I want to stay here."

"I see," I say calmly, but Jimena's words are a gut punch. Just what I've been afraid of. But I'd expected them from Lucy, not Jimena. I see the hesitance in their eyes, the way they dart back and forth, how they drop their head while they speak. Every word matters right now. I must choose mine carefully.

"Did something happen?" I ask. "Are you in pain?"

"The air is bugging me. I can feel my asthma coming. But also, I'm just not really feeling it. I think I want to go home. I'm homesick."

Now that just annoys me, even pisses me off. The air, the struggle, I can understand. But homesick? Jimena had been eager and ready to train since the day I first met them five months ago. How could they give up now? If Jimena leaves, Lucy probably will too, and I can't let them return alone, so there goes Everest. Before my eyes, everything we've worked for could be wiped clean, erased, in an instant. All my pre-planned moments of joy and pain slipping through the cracks. Because of homesickness? My anger is a switchblade waiting to open. I've seen this over and over. People giving up. I've done it too. Given up on myself so many times. Tried getting sober and gave that up too. We all left home to come to Mount Everest, and I know leaving doesn't fix things, but this hike was supposed to be different. I imagined us running high the first few days on adrenaline and the glory of the Himalayas. If Jimena would just keep walking, we might get somewhere.

All of us might get somewhere.

"Listen," I say slowly. "Turning around is an option, but we haven't even gotten to the magical part. Trust me. If you can give me one more day, there is something incredibly powerful awaiting us. You've got to see the view from Hotel Everest. Tomorrow. When we were training, you remember what you told me?"

"What?"

"About this trip, what Everest meant to you?"

"Ya," Jimena says, shrugging.

"Right before we left, you said that Everest meant you could touch the sky. Literally touch the sky. Who can do that? It's wild, it's spiritual, it's unheard of. You said Everest would force you to trust yourself and that it would mark a new chapter in your life. I want you to live that chapter, Jimena."

"I know, but I also said shit like 'Everest means that happiness can be a reality, not just a hope.' I know what I said. I said some quotable things. But you know I'm working on my mental health too. Shit's tenuous. Making goals? For someone like me, it's not just marking shit off a checklist. It's tears, anger, anxiety. It's even being able to have a goal. And I had one and I made it. I came."

"You said you could never trust yourself to build for the future. Or even believe that there would be one. I know what it's like to be on the move, running, trying to survive. I do. Look, you can go down, for sure, but it's going be a whole thing. Why don't you just sleep on it?"

Now that everyone is struggling, I wonder if I've made the right choice.

Not only for them, but for me. For my chance at Everest.

* * *

The next morning when I come down for breakfast, Lucy has her makeup bag at the breakfast table and is drawing on eyeliner.

"It's too dark in the room," she snaps but with a grin.

This is a good sign.

Shreya squats down next to Lucy, leaning in to watch in the tiny compact mirror as Lucy pulls liquid kohl over her lids in long, swift strokes.

"Perfect! How do you do it? Show me?"

"Sit here." Lucy pats the bench next to her.

Water and laptop in hand, I move to a corner table at the far end of the dining hall and open Excel. I start shifting the whole itinerary down by two days, calculating the delays and imagining the worst possible outcomes. What is my plan A and B and C? Putting things into boxes helps soothe me. Especially since I'm not drinking. Microsoft Excel is my sanctuary. An ordered world where boundaries are not only clear, but I can bold them, dash them, and put fresh new columns between them. Here, there's a formula for everything.

I turn to find Jimena walking toward me.

"I'm gonna go," they say.

"Oh?"

"To the hotel. I came all this way. I should at least see the Himalayas."

My grin is a mile wide. "Yes, my dear. Yes you should."

It's an acclimatizing day, and we'd planned to hike to Hotel Everest, the highest elevation hotel in the world, for a fancy lunch and our first clear view of the mountain. While Lucy stays at the lodge with Shailee, the rest of us walk and walk and walk as the beating sun turns again to wind. The girls move easily together, their friendship blossoming. As we round the final bend, the Himalayas rocket into view, Everest a tremendous snow-capped tooth at their center. Jimena freezes and stares wide-eyed. It's like watching myself in this exact spot a decade ago. The first view of Everest had set something unstoppable in motion for me. I see it swelling in them.

Jimena doesn't say a word, just stares, their mouth hanging open.

"What do you think?" I say softly.

"It's cold and proud and powerful."

We both stare for a few more seconds in silence.

"It's like my mother," Jimena whispers.

I know why Jimena whispers when they see Everest.

It's awe.

It's that sense of being both small and a part of something so much bigger than our smallness.

Awe is the gateway drug to healing trauma through nature.

Awe must be experienced. And trauma isn't something you scoop out with a spoon. It has a home in you, and in that home, it lives, often comfortably, sometimes quietly, but always ready to trash the place at a moment's notice. As we head back to Namche, Jimena scans the horizon, walking ahead of the group in their own reverie. Jimena moves at a bright clip that I hope means they are recommitted to the hike. Each girl has to find their own inner compass for this journey, I realize. We're navigating foreign terrain, and everyone's healing is their own. A unique algorithm of sorrow and mercy. Their story arcs will not manifest according to my plan, no matter how much I want this for them. I can only stand witness. God knows my path hasn't been neat.

When I was Jimena's age, I hadn't even started to look at my trauma.

Chapter 6

LANCASTER 90210

The summer before I started high school, I cut off all my hair. Not a cute impish pixie, but a blunt bowl cut, which, true to its name, looked like I'd plopped a salad bowl on my head and sheared right around it. It was ugly and crude and perfect. Ugly was exactly the point. I wanted to be unseen, and the only way to do that as a girl in Lima was to become unattractive.

We still wore the uniforme único for our five years of high school—the crisp starched shirts, the long, heavy-duty, rat-gray skirts. I hated those skirts. Any skirt, really. Even at school, under the Catholic halo, a long skirt could be flipped up. How easy a girl's uniform made it for men to do what they wanted.

As I walked between school and home, construction workers catcalled after me. Even when I looked away, refusing to make eye contact, they whistled. Not the way J had exactly, but by then all whistles were the same to me. A command to call a dog home, an order to obey.

"Mira, mamacita, que rica, voltea acá," they'd shout, their laughter trailing me.

Ay mamacita, how delicious, turn around.

Could they smell it on me?

Could all men?

Did they know what J had done?

And if so, did that make me public property?

My body, it seemed, no longer belonged to me.

But then, maybe it never had. Maybe it was like the woman on *The 700*

Club said—that I was trash—and maybe that's why they hollered freely even as I tried desperately to hide everything womanly about me.

Sendero Luminoso had escalated. Chopping up civilians with machetes. Abducting people off the streets and holding them for ransom. But I had already been taken by Peru. By its men. My father's best belt lashing my bare legs. J's hands running up my skirt. Body snatched in my own home. And I hadn't stopped them. Now, walking down the street, whispering a Hail Mary under my breath to drown out the catcalls, I wondered if it was always going to be so hard to say no.

Every day after school, I stripped down immediately, adopting an off-duty ensemble of high-waisted jeans, polo shirts buttoned to the top, and baggy '80s track jackets. At first Mom didn't say much about it, or my hair. Anything that meant less work for her. Eventually, she started to slip in little comments here and there about lesbians.

"Gay men I can accept, but two women together?" She'd let loose a little shiver. "Gives me the heebie-jeebies." Or "Your smile is so pretty, hija. You should share it more."

I did not share my smile more. At school, things got worse when a group of boys started to taunt and bully me relentlessly, making fun of my deep voice and boyish look. What little was left of my spirit was snuffed out. I stopped speaking almost entirely.

Instead, I started listening to American heavy metal. AC/DC, Poison, Ozzy Osbourne, Skid Row, all the greats. I could barely understand the lyrics, but the emotion was visceral, and it surged through my veins like shadowy medicine. Heavy metal was a language no one else in my family understood, and its orchestrations of misery comforted me.

* * *

Slouched at the kitchen table one Saturday during my junior year, I watched my mother bustle around the kitchen, seasoning the arroz con pollo to my father's precise palate. As she watched him take his first bite, it hit me. My mother was too weak to order J's abuse and too fragile to stand up to my father. Look at all she'd given up, how he'd controlled her. It wasn't a plan for my future that went awry by J getting married. It'd been an explicit intent of my father's to destroy me.

"Oye, imbécil, sit up straight," he barked at me.

A beastly growl rose in my throat: "You," I said, through clenched teeth, suddenly fearless. It was the voice of a stranger. "You did this." All the years I knew what J did was wrong, knew the commandments were being broken, but I kept it in for him. For my father. All those years of shouldering his contempt, all the bullying and beatings and half-truths and whole lies, to honor him. But no more. "You are the most despised man who ever lived. I hate you." My stool clattered to the floor as I jumped back from the table and charged out of the kitchen. I ran into the hallway where I'd slit the throat of Tía Emerita's birthday chicken and, panting and crying, raced up the stairs. At the top, I stopped to catch my breath. To my left, down a long corridor, was the door to the third-floor apartment where J used to take me. His whistle still haunted the hallway.

I ran past the hallway and stumbled onto the azotea, where I crumbled into a heap. Above, white shirts strung like birds on the line flapped in the warm afternoon wind. I could see into the first-floor window of my father's office, with a small desk lamp still on. I envisioned him there, long, late nights, scribbling columns of numbers with red pencils, clacking away at his adding machine.

Always with his back to us. To me.

I heard the urgent thwack of chancletas hitting stone steps, and then my mother was next to me. "Silvia," she dropped down and draped herself over me like a blanket. "Oh mi hijita, my daughter, ven acá, calmate."

"He did this," I repeated.

"What is it, hijita?" She pulled me to my feet. "What are you going on about?"

"He wants to destroy me. That's why J did those things," I cried, gagging on the tangle of words and phlegm rising in my throat. "My father told him to do it."

"Que cosa?"

"It's his fault I'm damaged. That I'm trash. Garbage. Just like the prostitutes from *The 700 Club*!" I grew more hysterical with each word. "That's how much he hates me! That's why J hurt me. Why he got on top of me. Because my father asked for it. Asked him to touch me. To abuse me. Because he hated me. But why? I want to know why, please, Mamita."

I was now on my knees.

My mother clasped my hands in hers and shook them. "What are you saying?" she screamed.

"So many years. For so many years, J came to my room. He brought me there," I said, pointing to the third-floor apartment. "Right in there, he rubbed himself on me. Put his mouth on me."

"Stop!" she slapped her palm over my mouth.

One by one, I peeled her fingers away, and as the wind slammed the door to the azotea against its frame, everything I could remember poured out, a litany of abuses in chaotic, unstoppable bursts. I could feel the trauma ooze out of me like a wound. "He did all that," I declared in one final breath, exhausted. "And he told me he had permission."

"No, mi hijita." My mother's voice was a deflated balloon. Her umber eyes wild. "Que cosa. Nooooo, nooooo. You're wrong. He's hard. But my God, Silvia. Silvita. Your father wouldn't do this."

Her voice trembled, but she didn't break down. She cradled and rocked me like she hadn't done since I was small, as I sobbed into the crook of her arm. She kissed my forehead, whispering, "It's okay, my beautiful, sweet daughter. It's okay. I love you. It's okay. Let's go down to your room."

I felt protected.

When all my tears were dry, I fell into a deep sleep.

A couple hours later, she woke me up, cuddling me. "My cholita berrinchosa," she hummed. "Let's go for a sandwich." We did, and while I ate, she told me not to worry. That we would get through this together. And as she said it, I realized that was all I'd ever wanted. I'd waited ten years for a conversation with my parents that had never come. But I'd never really been waiting for my father—it was always her. I never saw her cry that day, and in my family, that was a good thing. It meant she was sturdy and strong, ready to stand up for me.

But soon after, she went dark. She didn't get out of bed for weeks.

"Estás segura, Silvita?" she'd ask at random. "Are you sure this happened?"

"Absolutamente, Mama. I can tell you how it was here and here . . ."

"But I'm the godmother to his kids. How could he have done that?"

It took little Eduardo, who was in kindergarten, asking if she was going to die, to snap her back to life and into fix-it mode. She asked if I wanted to press charges against J, but I didn't. As much as I loathed him, I couldn't picture myself testifying, shaking like a leaf as an audience watched, their eyes in disbelief. In the news, on all the shows, in the mythology of early 1990s Lima, women were the ones who created havoc. Modern Eves paying for original sin, victims were attacked and blamed for the actions of "innocent men." If a man whipped himself into a violent rage, a woman had always "driven" him to it. I imagined the headline for my case:

6-YEAR-OLD SPOILED CHILD LURED OLDER YOUNG MAN FOR SEXUAL PLEASURES; RESPONSIBLE FATHER OF THREE BATTLING FOR HIS LIFE

No, I did not want to press charges. To be blamed when I'd already blamed myself for so long.

"Well," my mother said. "We should at least go see a doctor."

There were two appointments with a psychologist, who asked endless questions, ran a round of intelligence tests on me, which were actually sort of fun, and then concluded that I should leave Peru.

Politics in Lima were seismic. It was scary how fast we had adapted to the violent undercurrent. The bombings and kidnappings that started when I was a child had escalated into a full-blown war between the Peruvian government and the Shining Path, who were officially designated a terrorist organization. I'd started to read the paper for myself and learned that they were communists fighting to destabilize and replace what they called a corrupt government. But they also were killing civilians. And a new faction of the movement had surfaced—the Túpac Amaru Revolutionary Movement, or MRTA, inspired by an eighteenth-century Andean revolutionary who fought against Spanish colonialists. MRTA fighters wanted to distribute property ownership and wealth equally throughout the nation, and their attacks focused on the very rich. My father, a man born in the very mountains that birthed the ethos of the movement, a man who'd built his wealth from nothing, was furious at the idea that someone thought they were entitled to what he had built.

People were migrating to the United States in droves. My sister, Marianela, had already gone to San Francisco, and Rolando and Ramiro had followed.

So, when the therapist recommended that I apply to college in the United States, we agreed.

I never told my father about J, and I don't think my mother did either.

Or if she did, he never said he was sorry. Part of me still felt my father had something to do with it.

But I was no longer waiting for him.

My mother found out about a scholarship that would cover a four-year university if I maintained a B average and majored in a STEM subject. So for the next two years, I focused at school and worked to polish my application. I'd never imagined leaving Peru, but suddenly it was all I could think about. The United States. *Full House. Beverly Hills, 90210.* A place where problems were glossy and fixed by fast cars and money. A place where the laugh track was not at the expense of women. Where I could start a new life without anyone knowing my past.

It would be better there. It had to be.

* * *

The day I was supposed to fly into Miami—August 24, 1992—Hurricane Andrew hit. I'd been accepted to Millersville University in a town called Millersville outside of Lancaster in the state of Pennsylvania. The school had originally arranged for someone to meet me at the airport in Philadelphia, but because of the hurricane delay, I'd have to make my way from the airport to Millersville on my own. It'd be fine, the Fulbright staff assured us. I spoke fluent English—at least that's what we'd told them.

Almost twenty-four hours after leaving my family in Lima, I arrived. As the wheels touched down on the runway, I gulped my first breath of American air. "Ah, FILADELFIA!" I cried to no one in particular. At the baggage claim, I pulled my two clunky suitcases from the conveyor belt and looked around to see families greeting each other and chauffeurs picking up businesspeople. I found a reception desk and introduced myself.

"Hello," I said, clearing my throat. "I am Silvia from Peru and I am going to Millersville University of Pennsylvania."

A Black woman looked at me, surprised. "Say what?" she asked. "Millville?"

"No, I am going to go to Millersville University of Pennsylvania. Can you please help me with the directions to go to the university?"

"Roger," she said. "Can you help this young lady?"

An older white man got out of his chair and walked up to the counter.

"Where you going?"

"Millersville University of Pennsylvania," I replied, proud to be a new student of a prestigious university. I had heard of the University of Pennsylvania and thought that maybe Millersville was an extension of it.

"Millersville. Millersville?" His face was blank. "Sorry. Never heard of it."

When it came to picking the college, I'd left that to my mother, trusting she'd only choose the best. We'd received offers from Pomona College, Pepperdine University, Ithaca College, and Wesleyan. I pulled out my welcome letter from the school and handed it to Roger. He snapped his fingers. "Oh, Lancaster!" he said.

"Yes, Lancaster, yes," I echoed with a cheerful nod.

"Nobody's here to greet you?"

"No, sir, I do not see anybody from Millersville University of Pennsylvania."

"Right. Okay. So you're gonna take a taxi to the Amtrak station and buy a ticket to Lancaster."

"Very good," I said. "Thank you very much, mister."

Está bien Silvia, todo va a salir bien, I chanted to calm my nerves. Head held high, I wheeled my suitcases out the airport door and hit a wall of humidity so thick that sweat streamed down my back and armpits, soaking the white cotton cafarena, or turtleneck, as it was called in the U.S., and alpaca sweater my mother had insisted I wear for the plane ride.

"With the hurricane, the weather up north must be out of hand," she had said as we packed. "I wouldn't be surprised if they have snow there!"

It was winter in Peru.

"You'll never be cold with alpaca, though." She packed two fluffy alpaca blankets into my suitcases, with a bunch of cafarenas, two pairs of jeans, three pairs of shoes, and a traditional Andean costume I'd never worn a day in my life. "You need to share your heritage proudly," she said when she caught me rolling my eyes.

Outside the baggage claim, a dozen identical taxis were lined up. Banana yellow and gleaming, they were nothing like the informal cabs in Lima, which could be anyone's beat-up old car. No one even shouted for my business.

"Hello, sir," I spoke slowly to the first driver in line—there was *a line?!*—translating each word from Spanish to English first in my mind. "I am going to the Amtrak station, please?"

"Thirtieth Street station?"

"I am going to the Amtrak station, please."

"All right, Thirtieth Street. Get in."

As we approached the city, the freeway paralleled a glistening river. I was giddy as we flew past glassy skyscrapers and sparkling steel buildings. It was just how I'd imagined the United States. So slick. So modern. Like stepping inside *The Jetsons*. Into a new future that I was going to be part of. I couldn't wait to start my new cosmopolitan life.

We pulled up to Thirtieth Street station, a regal white-stone building with Roman columns. It was like something from a history book. I paid my fare with a crisp twenty-dollar bill, feeling extremely sophisticated. Slung over my shoulder was my high school backpack, holding a math encyclopedia, and tucked inside was a fanny pack with my birth certificate, passport, a rosary from the Virgen del Carmen, and $6,000. Enough money to pay the remainder of my tuition after the scholarship and any other necessary expenses. For my family, credit cards didn't exist; it was all cash.

Inside, the station was a scene from a classic Hollywood movie. The marble floors. The polished wooden seats. In my country, train stations were poorly kept. There was little tourism. The Shining Path had kept even the most adventurous foreigners away, and the government was on the verge of collapse. There was no money for things like beautiful train stations.

At the ticket counter, I asked for a ticket to Millersville University of Pennsylvania at Lancaster.

"Oh, Lancaster," said the ticket agent. "Yeah, Harrisburg."

"Hamburger," I replied.

"No." She stood and shouted slowly, "YOU HAVE TO BUY A TICKET ON THE COUNTER FOR LANCASTER; IT IS ON THE HARRIS-BURG LINE. SEE THAT C-O-U-N-T-E-R. GO OVER THERE."

"Ah. Thank you very much, misses, thank you very much. I really appreciate it."

I proceeded to the next ticket counter.

"Hello, I need one ticket to Lancaster to go to Millersville University of Pennsylvania."

"One way or round trip?" asked the woman.

"Excuse me. I need one ticket to go to Lancaster for Millersville University of Pennsylvania."

"Do you want a ROUND TRIP? Are you coming back?"

I still didn't understand, so I just nodded yes and smiled.

"Here's your ticket. Board the train for Harrisburg. NEXT!"

In the center of the station, there was a grand clock, and next to that a central board with little tiles that continuously clicked over showing the next arrivals and departures. I was mesmerized at all the names of places I'd never heard of. Then I saw the big ones—New York, Washington, D.C.—oh, and Harrisburg! Track Nine. Wow, maybe Harrisburg was important too.

To me, the USA was a vague glamorous mass with two major cities: New York and Los Angeles. San Francisco I only knew because my sister, Marianela, was there, and my mother had gone to visit her.

As I boarded the train, yanking my wheel-less suitcases up the platform stairs, a luxurious whisper of cold air swept past. In Peru, we didn't have air conditioning inside cars or homes. I settled into my seat and pressed my forehead against the chilly glass of the window. The train started rolling, and within ten minutes, the conductor called the first stop. *Ardmore!* The landscape was beautiful: lush groves of oak trees dotted with old stone buildings. The streets were tidy and free of trash. There was no honking, and traffic ran neatly between yellow and white lines, everyone stopping before the red light and only moving again at the green. Buses with scrolling neon signs rode peacefully down the streets with all the passengers inside. No one hung out the doors hollering, like in Lima. There wasn't even a ticket taker. And no smog. That was the strangest thing. No smog anywhere.

So this was the American suburbs.

Only a few more stops left before Lancaster. Perched at the edge of my seat, I was ready to hop off as soon as I heard the call.

The conductor came by and punched my ticket.

"Lancaster?"

"Yes, sir. I am Silvia from Peru, and I am going to Millersville University of Pennsylvania." I repeated my line for the twelfth time that day, grateful for once that my father had instilled such manners.

The conductor flashed a little smirk.

"Well, you got a ways, so settle in. Probably another hour or so."

An hour? The first stop had been only ten minutes. Maybe it was now rush hour and the train would need to stop for traffic. I leaned back and watched as the horizon of strip malls and diners began to thin out. My smile drooped as the towns grew smaller. A cluster of houses along one main road. A gas station. A corner store. Then they faded away entirely, becoming grass, yellowed at the tips, corn maybe, yes, endless fields of corn, the sun glinting off the road in great silver patches. The sky sewn to the horizon as far as I could see.

Anxiety overrode my excitement. My heart was palpitating. Why were we so far from the city? I'd always lived in the city, and this looked like a place for cows. Was this Millersville University—Millersville University of Pennsylvania?

This could not be right.

My second suitcase was wedged into the seat next to me, and I curled up against it. A surge of hunger hit. A craving for steamed buns. For lomo. For home. I'd been awake for almost twenty-four hours, running on adrenaline and one meal on the plane from Miami. Inside my suitcase, between the blankets, my mother had tucked a packet of dried aji peppers, yellow and red, and the bible of Peruvian cooking, *¿Qué Cocinaré Hoy?*, full of the best recipes for ceviches, lomos, stews, and my favorite, chifa. I closed my eyes and tried to dream of her cooking.

"You can cook for all your friends and share the deliciousness of our food," she'd said. "Okay, Mamita," I said, humoring her.

She'd kissed me softly on the head, and as she pulled away, I'd seen a glimpse of sadness. Three years had passed since I'd told her about J, and once she overcame her depression, she kept her emotions bottled up. But I knew she was torn up watching me leave. "Each of my kids is an extension of my fingers," she used to say. "Of my own hand."

Now four of us had left Peru.

"Look, look, look, there they are!" cried the couple in the seat behind me.

I rubbed the sleep from my eyes and looked back to the road. Instead of cars, there was an old buggy, one of the horse-drawn carriages from American Westerns, trotting down the middle of the street.

Then there were two more. One driven by a serious-looking man with a long pointy beard and a flat straw hat, wearing a long dark coat buttoned up to the neck. Huddled behind him in the carriage was a woman and three children, all draped in long black capes and funny little bonnets that reminded me of what Father Pedro wore for Sunday Mass. God, I'd thought I was overdressed. They must have been dying in that heat.

"The Amish Country!" said the woman behind me.

"Amish Country?" I whispered to myself, incredulous. What America was this? Did my mother know where she'd sent me? She must have made a mistake. My stomach somersaulted. I looked around the train car for the conductor.

"Lancaster, next stop! Lancaster, PA," bellowed his voice over the intercom as the train slowed to a halt.

I lugged my twin suitcases onto the platform and crossed a low ramp toward a flickering red exit sign. I was sweaty and hungry and on the brink. But as I approached the taxi stand, I saw a friendly face. A Latin-looking man.

"Taxi?" he said with an accent I couldn't place.

"Yes, I need a taxi. I am Silvia from Peru, and I am going to Millersville University of Pennsylvania."

"Habla Español?"

"Sí!" I was so happy I could have collapsed onto the sidewalk and cried. If it wasn't for my father's voice in the back of my mind—*Being polite doesn't cost a thing*—I would have.

"Hola. Sí, soy Rafael."

"De donde es usted?"

"Boricua."

"Perdón, Boricua?" I'd never heard the word before.

"De Puerto Rico." He smiled.

"Ah, hola, que tal, como está?"

I knew Puerto Rico was an island off the coast of the United States, but nothing about the relationship between Boricua and the United States. All I knew was that Rafael was an angel, a gift sent from above to meet me. After thirty hours of travel, his Spanish was a salve. As he drove toward Millersville, Rafael told me that his family had fled New York City for Lancaster several years ago, because where he lived in the Bronx had gotten too dangerous. I didn't tell him that I was fleeing too, but it was strangely comforting to have that in common. Rafael clearly loved his job and played tour guide as he drove, telling me about the history of the area and who the Mennonites and the Amish were—how they still lived with no electricity. I thought of the rolling blackouts in Lima and wondered who the hell in America, the land of the free, would live like that on purpose.

As we drove through the heart of Lancaster, there was a pulse again. Rich redbrick buildings and a shiny clock tower. Manicured parks and cobblestone streets and quaint little cafés. Rafael assured me that even though it was

Amish Country, Lancaster's international community was growing. *Maybe it won't be so bad here*, I thought. But then it was all cows and corn again, occasional houses dotting wide-open plains, all very *Little House on the Prairie*, or as we knew it in Peru, *La Familia Ingalls*.

Was I going to be churning butter? Wearing bonnets to study molecular biology?

This was crazy.

When Rafael dropped me off, I gave him our customary right-cheek kiss, and he handed me a card.

"You call me when you need a ride!"

I'd made my first official friend in the United States.

The following Monday, as I was leaving the university bookstore with a shopping bag full of science books, I saw a photo of Rafael smiling on the front cover of the *Intelligencer Journal*, Lancaster's leading newspaper.

"Hey! There's my friend," I shouted to no one. As I stepped closer, the headline came into focus.

SLAIN TAXI DRIVER WAS FATHER OF FOUR

Slain? I didn't know the word, so I skimmed the article, picking out the English I knew to try to piece it together. Saturday evening, right after he dropped me off, Rafael had been the victim of a murder-suicide by a passenger. I gasped. Things like this happened in Peru, not here. Not in America. Not in Amish Country. How could Rafael have left the Bronx only to be murdered here?

Nothing made sense. Nothing at all.

* * *

On my scholarship application, we'd marked fluent, and technically, I was. I'd studied English for years in Peru, but always with Peruvian teachers who'd learned the language from other Peruvian teachers. I could read and write, but once my Millersville professors moved from introductions to the heart of a course, I floundered. My classmates spoke so fast that all I could do was nod and smile. I spent most of my first year treading water.

The summer after classes ended, I received a message from my mother. "Silvita, please call us, it's urgent." Terrified that something bad had happened, I called back immediately.

My mother's voice wavered as she answered the phone.

"Mama, que pasó?!"

"I can't speak, hija. It's a tragedy."

"Mom! What is it?"

"CLAE," she paused. "CLAE, Silvia. It went bust."

CLAE was an investment bank that had made a splash in Peru by promising a 20 percent interest return on investments. What seemed impossible at first had been making many people filthy rich. And fast. So fast that even my father, an incredibly conservative investor, had been riled with jealousy. Tempted by CLAE's success, he'd decided, unknown to me, to invest his entire savings, including the funds for our college educations.

"I'm so sorry, Silvita," my mother sniffled. "We've lost it all."

"Mama, it's okay," I said. "It's okay." I'd always had my needs provided for and naïvely figured that we'd work it out. I didn't have the specter of poverty hanging over me like she had.

"I'll get a job here," I said. "No problem. I'll figure it out."

Most of my classes were paid for by the scholarship, but I'd need money for food and essentials. A student visa limited me to working ten hours a week. But if I could show proof of increased financial hardship, the school would waive the restriction. With certified letters from my parents and their bank, I was granted permission to work twenty hours a week.

My mother said she was going to ask my aunt Flor to help me with money for a while. Flor was from Trujillo, the small northern city in Peru where my father had been sent to live after his mother passed away. Tía Flor had immigrated to the United States four years earlier, but I had never known where. Mom said she was living in New York and had a Peruvian restaurant. I was thrilled. I'd always dreamt of visiting New York City. Maybe I could even transfer to a university there. My mother gave me the address—123 Main Street in Port Chester—and told me Tía Flor would be waiting. With little more than my aunt's telephone number tucked into my pocket, I set out on the train from Lancaster.

As the Amtrak approached Manhattan, I was embarrassed for the girl who thought Philadelphia was cosmopolitan. She'd been naïve. Had seen so little of the world. New York was my new horizon. One tiny island holding so much of the world's power. The sheen of wealth, the energy, the vertiginous topography. A skyline of slick skyscrapers and gritty graffitied brick. I figured I'd just hop on the subway to 123 Main Street, but after lots of pantomimed conversations with friendly New Yorkers in Grand Central Station, I found out that Port Chester wasn't in Manhattan at all, but in a county called Westchester outside the city. I didn't care. I was brushing up against the Big Apple, marveling at buildings I'd only seen in movies and on television. I spun circles under the celestial ceiling in the train station's main concourse, tilting my head up to take in the gold zodiac constellations against a navy sky. Even though my parents had lost everything and were now technically broke, the stars were aligning for me. I'm sure I was the only person on the Metro-North grinning through the hourlong ride.

In Port Chester, I jumped into a taxi. The driver took one look at me and spoke in perfect Spanish.

I thought of Rafael.

"A dónde va?"

"El Norteño," I said. *The one from the North.*

"It's over there." He pointed to a bright neon sign on a corner several blocks away.

It was a Friday around nine p.m. when I stepped into the elongated entryway of El Norteño. Tía Flor stood smiling behind the bar. She was beautiful, with her mother's fair skin and dark brown eyes.

"Silvita! You made it," she said, her smile kind but her words measured. "Welcome."

Tío Jorge made his way out of the kitchen. He was tall for a Peruvian, around five feet ten, with fair skin and naturally pouty lips. Almost Betty Boop–like. Jorge had worked with Tía Flor's family business in Trujillo for years. He had a wife in Peru but had jumped at the opportunity to work in the United States.

He was Tía Flor's business partner and something like her boyfriend.

"Hello!" he boomed, pulling me in for a hug, which, to my surprise, felt instantly safe. His jovial warmth put me at ease. Tía Flor was more reserved. I told them about my trip, and he seemed shocked that I'd maneuvered New York City with no fear. "I've met your mother," he said. "Always on the move, she is. I nicknamed her Coca-Cola! You must take after her, so we'll call you Coca-Cola Jr."

Tío pointed me to a table, and just as I pulled out my chair, a waitress in a tight white shirt and miniskirt set a steaming lomo saltado in front of me. One of my favorites. Lomo saltado—beef stir-fry with tomato, onion, and

French fries in a soy-and-red-wine sauce served with white rice—was one of our national dishes. Like the burger for Americans, it was the litmus test of any Peruvian restaurant. If you could nail a lomo, we'd trust you with the rest. Tío's lomo was the best I'd ever eaten. And outside of Peru. I was shocked.

I stayed with my tíos through the weekend, and El Norteño never slowed down. The dozen diner-style tables were always full, and the line for take-out ebbed and flowed out the door. Most of the clientele were Peruvian, but there were also Colombians, Salvadorians, Guatemalans, and Mexicans, with the occasional Ecuadorian and a couple of Brazilians. I was surprised to see so many Peruvians in New York. Only later I learned that the largest concentration of Peruvians in the United States was in Paterson, New Jersey—dubbed Little Lima. With its stucco storefronts caked in decades of grime and colorful awnings announcing chicken shops and pupuserías, Port Chester reminded me of the working-class barrios in Lima. Specifically, La Victoria, where my half brothers had grown up.

In Lima, we'd come to expect poverty and violence; even if it wasn't in our everyday lives, it was in the fabric. But America was all glittering cities and glamorous teen dramas—a place of abundance and freedom and security. During that weekend in Port Chester, I started to understand why my parents had chosen Millersville. American life was harsh. Even there, in a rural utopia, people who looked like me, like Rafael, could be murdered while doing their jobs.

Most of the immigrant community in Port Chester worked several jobs, many without papers, for minimum wage just to support their families back in their countries and eat or drink at El Norteño on the weekends. I was here on a student visa and had been supported my first year. But now, I too was an immigrant, only I'd been living a weird Amish fairy tale. With the cushion of my father's wealth gone, I saw what coming to America really meant.

* * *

That Sunday, in the middle of the tamale brunch rush, I watched Roxana, a beautiful Colombian waitress, become flustered while serving a table of white customers. Although Port Chester was mostly immigrants, it bordered Connecticut, and one of the most affluent towns on the East Coast, Greenwich, was just over the bridge. On weekends, its more adventurous residents came into town to dabble in cheap, international cuisine.

"Silvia, mi amor," Roxana said, running over to me. "Can you help me? I can't understand what they're trying to order. Please, I'm desperate."

"Of course," I said. I was having a blast eating delicious free food all weekend. The least I could do was help out.

Pretending to be a waitress, I politely approached the table and took my time explaining the dishes with flair, relishing the descriptions of foods I loved. My English wasn't perfect, but my conversational speech had seriously improved since I'd first blundered my way through the *Filadelfia* airport.

After the table of guests had eaten and paid the bill, Roxana beamed as she cleared the plates.

"I love serving the gringos," she said, carrying a stack of dishes to the kitchen. "They're so generous. More than Latinos. They left me a twenty percent tip!"

Twenty percent? For a tip? I was stunned. In Peru, tipping meant pocket change, a sol or two at a mom-and-pop restaurant like El Norteño. I did the math. If I could work weekends, tips alone could cover the expenses my parents had been taking care of.

Plus, I might have the chance to explore New York City.

When I proposed the idea to my aunt and uncle, Tío's eyes narrowed. "What about the outfits?" he asked in a fatherly tone. Tío had three waitresses on staff, all in heavy makeup, short skirts, and tight white shirts. I saw how the skimpy outfits drew the attention (and return business) of Tío's male clients, and how as they got drunker, they grew more insistent. Sometimes, a waitress left to dance and drink with a customer. Growing up, Peruvian shows cast women in two roles—young, ditzy eye candy or a washed-up nagging wife. I swore to God I'd be neither. I wondered if Tío had asked the other waitresses how they felt, or if he saw me differently because I was family or because my style was so tomboyish—I'd never even worn a skirt as short and tight as Roxana's.

But to make good money, I convinced myself I could play sexy. Plus, I felt safe around Tío Jorge.

"You know, most immigrants here are not going to university, Silvita," Tío said. "I'm concerned you'll get tempted. And if you were to drop out, your father would do something nasty to me."

I didn't tell him there was no temptation here for me. There never had been with any men really.

"No problem," I said, nodding to Tío Jorge. "I'll stay in school and only work weekends. And I'll wear whatever I need to."

I was surprised at my ease waiting tables. All the English-speaking customers were seated in my section, but I treated everyone equally, as my mother had hammered into us. Even the typical Peruvians, who after a long dinner, folded one dollar bill into four to make it seem like four times as much, or other times left nothing. Everyone came to El Norteño for the food, but the real value for me, and I think for many of them, was the community. Tío was the "Godfather" without the crime, leveraging killer ceviche and saltados instead of cocaine. Of course, he knew people in the trade. Pablo Escobar was at the height of his power, and over long meals with wine—Tío had gotten me a fake ID—at fancy New York City restaurants after busy weekends, Tío would tell me wild, boisterous stories, whispering them like secrets.

"Did I tell you the one about my old bartender? Took a shark-loan from some local dealers and they shoved him into a dryer when he didn't pay on time. Those ones at the laundromat that run on quarters!" He'd laugh and pour more wine.

He had a running list of restaurants he'd been dying to try, but he was shy about his broken English. I translated the menu for him, and while we ate, he'd close his eyes and savor the food, rattling off each ingredient. Later, he'd have me check his guesses with the waiter. He was right so often that I began to trust everything else he said too. His palate was instinctual, and his instincts precise. He loved food like my mother did, and for that I loved him.

When Tía Flor wasn't there, sometimes he'd tell me about other women he'd "gotten to know" in New York City. "What can I say?" he'd shrug. "They flock to me." And they did. As much as I wanted to hold against him all the stereotypical things he embodied that I hated in Latin men, I couldn't. Because he was also all the best parts of them. Unlike my father, he was tender, generous, hilarious, and, most of all, paternal, and for that I forgave him everything.

I didn't even mind the four-hour drive between Millersville and Port Chester.

Tío Jorge helped me buy my first car: a used 1987 Nissan 200SX coupe with a sunroof and headlights that automatically flipped up and down. I'd make it to New York City by six p.m., then drive into Manhattan, taking wrong turns and running red lights while I stared up at the buildings, my mouth agape, wowed by the immensity. From inside the grid, the city was colossal. I was just a tiny ant. Insignificant. Which was thrilling in a way I didn't yet understand. There was always dinner waiting for me at El Norteño, but most nights I'd stop and wander into cheap Chinatown restaurants to savor dim sum. Steamed buns. Dumplings and shrimp cakes. Some things I'd loved in Lima, others new. I'd wander through the streets of Lower Manhattan, past glamorous clubs like Limelight and Palladium and the Tunnel, where snaking lines of club kids in foot-high platform boots and giant checkered blouses waited to get in. With neon hair teased high and operatic makeup, everyone was loud and free, and I wondered what that was like.

I was Alice in Wonderland. Looking for a hole to fall down. I didn't go into the clubs then. I didn't feel trendy enough. But just walking past was an aphrodisiac. My teen years had been sad and serious and scared without flying high on the giddy wings of first love or the intoxication of sweaty all-night dance parties. None of the ecstatic release of drugs I'm sure all the club kids were on. As I lurked on the corner, watching bands of them filter into the club or get rejected and holler at the bouncer, I realized my body had never been that free.

Chapter 7

⚉⚉⚉

RIDUM

Morning brings the rich funk of melting yak butter. The clatter of tin pots streams from the teahouse kitchen as the cook prepares our morning meal. A string of prayer flags winds and tangles around me as I perch on a stiff wooden chair scrawling the names of our donors onto white tabs that I had sewn onto each flag back in Kathmandu. The list of donors who helped fund some of this trip is over a hundred people long. I told them we'd leave their names at Base Camp, but I've been procrastinating. I wasn't sure we were going to make it.

But it's day six in the wild, and we have settled into a rhythm. No internet. No distractions. None of the drama that creeps into everyday life. We've settled. It's like a detox. The first day or two are okay, then you scramble for a fix, and finally you just surrender. Last night, we made it to Deboche from Namche, and with Dr. Jackie along, I'm feeling confident.

I try to stay present, pausing for a moment of gratitude as I scribble each donor's name, but I'm distracted by the huge panoramic photo of Everest hanging over the table. Her summit is ominous. It taunts me.

Shreya lingers in the kitchen doorway, pointing and speaking to the cooks in Nepali. Dining on the hike is informal. Often teahouse cooks will invite you to wait in the kitchen and watch them prepare the meal. The rest of the group comes clamoring in, bowing to the teahouse owner.

"Namaste, namaste."

"Come on, breakfast time, Silvia," says Shailee. "Do you ever sleep?"

"I'll sleep in my next life," I say, laughing and shooing away the gnawing feeling that it may come sooner than later.

I set aside the flags and follow them to the dining table, sliding onto the long wooden bench between Lucy and Rubina.

Shreya arrives, gripping a steaming tureen of garlic soup, the Himalayan preventative for altitude sickness. I push garlic soup on the group at every meal, ladling up pungent bowlfuls and staring the girls down as they sip the cloudy green broth. Especially the Americans.

"At least we don't have to worry about Himalayan vampires," mumbles Lucy.

The wiseass is officially back. *Thank God.*

At the end of the table, Dr. Jackie, Shailee, and Ehani are deep in conversation. Dr. Jackie is shining a light in Ehani's eyes.

"They've been failing her," Shailee says to Dr. Jackie. "She's never seen an eye doctor. But she visited a medical post in Kathmandu, and they said she might need surgery."

"Hold your eye open wider," says Shailee, demonstrating. "Yes, yes, like that."

Dr. Jackie pulls up an online test and holds her phone at Ehani's eye level. "Okay, now cover your right eye," she says. "Is slide one or two clearer, one or two?"

"Mmmmm," Ehani hesitates.

The girls chatter. "Testing her eyes right here?"

"Over omelets, what's better?" says Dr. Jackie.

Shreya shuttles between the kitchen and the table, balancing plates of curry and omelets arranged around a dome of rice with poppadums wedged onto the side.

"Thank you so much, my little Shreya," Jimena coos sweetly.

"The diagnosis, I'm afraid"—Dr. Jackie says as Ehani holds her breath—"is a bit simpler than surgery. Turns out, what you need, ma'am, is a good old pair of glasses."

We roar as Ehani grins, ducking her head in embarrassment.

Jimena points to their rectangular purple frames. "Hey. Nerds are in."

Shailee and I gesture to each other to follow up with Ehani about arranging glasses.

"Wait," says Jimena, jumping up just as we are digging into the food.

"This is a great picture." Jimena grabs their phone and wiggles onto a bench across the room, turning the phone a few times to find the best frame. "I just love all the colors."

I'm bleary-eyed this morning, my mind already racing with the day's itinerary—nuns, Lama Geshe, Periche—I hadn't even noticed the room. I take a long sip of ginger tea, the spicy steam clearing my nostrils, and look around through Jimena's eyes. They are right. The teahouse is an explosion of color. Blooming flowers and fruit fill every corner—bold mismatched floral textiles drape the walls and benches and tables. A teal curtain with lush fuchsia and orange roses is our backdrop. The bench we're sitting on is wrapped in a scarlet shawl with Tibetan-style blue and pink flowers. And the dining table, a wooden slab no more than a foot wide, is covered in turquoise oilcloth with a border of wild tropical fruits so vivid they're almost edible.

"My God," says Jimena. "This reminds me—in a really good way—of the twelve apostles sitting at the table."

The Last Supper.

Through Jimena's eyes, it's easy to see art. Our plates and cups arranged in a modern still life. Nine in a row, we sit side by side on the long bench, looking not at each other, but out toward the horizon together. For a moment, it's as if we've already arrived. We are regal and royal and bold. We are spilling over with fruit and flower. In a small teahouse in the Himalayas, surrounded by monasteries, we are rewriting the old stories, painting our own versions of sisterhood onto them. Connecting to sacred womanhood, but with sporty mountaineering gear instead of ancient cloaks.

The highlight of my Holy Week as a child were the marathon replays of *The Ten Commandments* and the *Jesus of Nazareth* miniseries. I was mesmerized by their force and realism. Every single time I watched the Last Supper scene, I hoped that Jesus would meet a different fate. But he always knew what was going to happen.

And still, they dined.

No matter what happened, he wanted his people, the apostles, to come together in unity and know they would be forgiven their trespasses and betrayals. Even those they didn't know they were going to make.

"Get my good side," Lucy calls, smoothing down her hair. Shreya laughs and turns to the same side as Lucy. My buff is pulled up over my head like an old man's nightcap, and Asha yanks it down. Glamour shots are not my thing.

"Smile," says Jimena, and everyone holds up their ginger tea.

Ehani is distracted on her phone.

"Ehani!" Jimena calls. "Look at me."

Jimena snaps a few, then jumps down. "Okay," they call, signaling to one of the teahouse staff to take our photo. "I need to be in one too!" Their face is bright, their brow unfurrowed. It's hard to imagine just forty-eight hours ago Jimena was ready to quit.

I say a silent *thank you* that they didn't.

I watch the sweet faces of all the girls.

"Beneath the surface of the protective parts of trauma survivors there exists an undamaged essence," writes psychiatrist Bessel van der Kolk in *The Body Keeps the Score*. "A Self that is confident, curious, and calm, a Self that has been sheltered from destruction by the various protectors that have emerged in their efforts to ensure survival."

While the Last Supper was a moment of grief, it was also one of reckoning. Betrayal and death led to resurrection, and, ultimately, forgiveness.

I know that all of us at this table will need to find a way to forgive ourselves too.

* * *

After we take a short walk through a thick rhododendron forest, the stone pathway opens up to a wide dirt courtyard with a long row of brass prayer wheels. We turn the wooden dowels at their base and set the wheels into motion, spurring a sound of creaking metal. Underneath the spinning, I hear a cough. Dr. Jackie. She's been coughing all morning.

Across the courtyard and through a stone gateway, Ani Chockle, the head nun, greets us. Behind her are the half-crumbled stone remnants of the Deboche nunnery, parts of which were destroyed in the 2015 earthquake. Ani Chockle, bald and draped in a maroon cloak, bows in greeting, giving me an extra nod. When I first met the nuns last year in Kathmandu, one of the other ani was wearing a donated cheetah-print coat and laughed about how it was wrong for her sacred calling. After that, I was determined to get them more dignified coats and spent two days in Kathmandu hunting down maroon winter jackets and gloves. Vendors in Thamel thought I was just another picky foreigner who wouldn't settle for just any color. But I needed that signature Deboche maroon, and I needed twenty of them, quick. Finally, I found a shop that sewed jackets in-house and ordered them with matching gloves to be delivered to the nuns before deep winter hit. I understood the necessity of the right uniform.

Deboche is Nepal's oldest Buddhist nunnery, but the nuns aren't trained as teachers or meditators as are the nuns at many monasteries. They're ceremonial nuns who travel throughout the Khumbu region performing pujas. Although Deboche is often overshadowed by nearby Tengboche Monastery, one of the tallest on earth, I find the beauty of Deboche quieter and the nuns' origin story more kick-ass. It's said that their leader, Ani Ngawang Pema, was a beautiful young girl with many men fighting for her hand in marriage, but she didn't want to be married and escaped by slipping through a hole in a cliffside bathroom. She then fled to Deboche, where she lived in isolation in a stone hut for fifty-one years, eating two simple meals and praying every morning to relieve the suffering of all living creatures. After the Chinese occupied Tibet in 1950, a group of Tibetan nuns determined to preserve their religious beliefs sought asylum with her, trekking together over Nangpa La, a treacherous mountain pass, to land in Deboche.

Their sisterhood was born there.

It's a humble life. One I've been excited for the girls to see. I expected a brief hello and we'd be on our way. So I'm surprised when Ani Chockle guides us into their makeshift temple, a low stone building, and drapes yellow silk khatas around our shoulders as we enter. Asha reminds her I'm attempting the summit, and she murmurs and pulls out a white khata instead. White for extra blessings. I bow, grateful.

In the center of the room, three bald ani sit cross-legged, swaddled in maroon cloaks, one in gold wire-frame Dolce & Gabbana lookalike glasses. Slivers of dusty light fall across a colorful altar, and small bowls of incense line a long table that cuts the room in two. Another table along the back wall holds a string of Buddha statues and candles and a simple red wood box with "Donations" handwritten in white paint. And another statue: Miyolangsangma. The goddess riding a red tiger at the entrance to Sagarmatha Park. One of the Tibetan five sisters of Long Life, Miyolangsangma began as a demoness and was converted by Guru Rinpoche, one of the founders of Tibetan Buddhism. The valleys and peaks of Everest are her playground, and it's only with her blessing that a climber can reach the top. She is the Goddess of Inexhaustible Giving. I hope her giving extends long enough to get me to the summit.

We mill around the room, uncertain about the protocol.

Shailee is telling Ani Chockle our intentions for the trip, but in the middle of a sentence, one of the nuns begins to chant, low and quick, and then the other two join in turns, until they're all chanting in unison. The sound is rolling and propulsive—less singing and more a litany, like how I used to pray the Rosary.

We drop to our knees side by side along the back wall and bow our heads. Candles flicker low in polished brass votives as the sound slowly fills the room. Its soft lapping closes around me until I hear nothing else. Not my own breath, no birds or chatter from outside. The chant becomes a closed circle. Its end and beginning fuse until it's no longer a string of words but a constant thrumming.

It travels into my ears and down my throat, washing me with sound, and just as it seeps into my chest, it splinters into light—a million tiny beams diffusing through my veins. My eyes spring open and I'm holding my breath. *Holy God.* I glance down the row to Rubina, Shreya, and Ehani, but they seem unfazed, composed even, hands folded in their laps. Jimena's brow is furrowed in reverence, and Lucy's fluttering lids and serene smile give her a cherubic glow. Everyone nods their heads in rhythm with the chanting.

In a test run on trauma survivors, Bessel van der Kolk found that it was almost impossible for them to physically relax. During a yoga session, he monitored the participants while in Shavasana—Corpse Pose—which is supposed to be the final relaxation portion of the class. When told to "totally relax" and let go, their muscle activity increased. "Rather than going into a state of quiet repose, our students' muscles often continue to prepare them to fight unseen enemies," he writes. One of the major challenges when recovering from trauma, says Bessel, is being able to achieve total relaxation and safe surrender.

Being soft is dangerous, too dangerous for some of us. But the small stone room cradles us, and the girls sit at peace, eyes closed, in the dark. It's only my mind, I realize, that's trying to run, darting a million miles an hour, looking for a way out.

By their age, I'd lost faith in anything sacred.

Lucy's eyes open, and she meets my gaze. She smiles and quickly looks away, her fingers absently stroking the silk khata at her shoulder.

I take a deep breath and close my eyes again. The sound swallows me. The nuns' voices become wind, divorced from any person or object. It moves freely, abundant and available for us to receive, like the Buddhists say about the value of prayer. It is unconditional. Untethered to any judgment or performance. All I have to do is be and I will be loved. I don't know where this thought comes from, but it's so radical, so foreign to everything I've ever known, that the simplicity of it almost crushes me. I feel a physical twang in my heart.

As the song fades to silence, I open my eyes to find the girls looking at me. The faces of the women in the room are warm and tender. I'm not sure how much time has passed. A minute. Ten. An hour. I realize I've been sobbing. My face is soaked with tears, and little rivulets of snot run down my chin. Embarrassed, I smile and quickly wipe my nose on my sleeve.

"Thank you." I bow to the nuns. "Thank you so much. I swear I wasn't planning to cry today."

Laughter ripples through the room, but the nuns seem to know exactly what I mean. They bow to bid us good-bye—they've got another blessing to do in Pangboche—and their smiles are joyful. Shreya and Ehani reach out their hands to pull me up and embrace me in a hug.

"It's okay, Silvia," says Ehani.

"I know," I say. "They're happy tears! I promise."

I had no idea the nuns were going to do a full puja. I'd never experienced anything like that. Maybe the Nepali girls had.

As we leave, the nuns promise to pray for us every day, and to keep praying for me until I reach the summit. "But send us a message when you get to the top," calls Ani Chockle in a serious tone. "So we can stop praying!"

I laugh. I guess even unconditional love has its limits.

* * *

We're high on blessings as Rubina sets off in the lead. Next stop: Pangboche. To visit the famous Lama Geshe, the highest-ranking lama in the Khumbu region. During my first trip to Everest, I didn't pay enough attention to the traditions or religion of the Himalayas. I was too hungry for answers, for an explanation, for insight. On a roller coaster of self-destructive behavior, I was in pain and seeking some sort of instant spiritual benediction. I figured that if Everest was a grand transformative experience, then the faster I got to Base Camp, the more quickly my realizations and healing—whatever vague concept of healing I grasped at the time—would come.

I was looking for a logical solution to a spiritual problem.

And I was still drinking then.

I was still drinking until two months ago.

Our trail chatter dies down quickly. At 12,500 feet, our every step takes more energy than yesterday. The air is cold and dry. Desert like. Even in the blazing sun, we're bundled in fleece and beanies. It's April, but it doesn't look like spring here. No blooming wildflowers. The hillside is scabbed. Scrubby brown grass with an occasional tree clinging on. The palette dusted. Dried ashy browns. Dull yellows and beige. Slate blue. Gray. So many grays. I'm no artist, but even I see that gray is its own universe here. The mountains in the distance expand and unfold into dimensions of ash and dove, of stone gray and smoke gray and steel gray. Lead and flint and pewter and cloud. Graphite and pebble and smoke. In our slick mountaineering gear, we're the most colorful thing in sight—a string of parkas in fuchsia and teal and tangerine, almost slapstick against the ancient tones of these geological beasts. This is the point on the trail where you really understand that mountains are rocks. Fossils anchored to the earth.

We march along a narrow path—a pencil line drawn into the steep mountainside. Tawny sand crunches under our feet. Our boots leave impressions like dust on the moon. We are moon women. Earth astronauts. Explorers. The mountains are our frontier.

Far below, the river runs seafoam green. It's thinned out a bit, shallower, revealing banks of chalky rock in some places. Instead of thick churning or sloping graceful arcs, the river here is a necklace tossed onto a dresser, lying wherever it lands. Perched high up on the hillside above us are the monopoly houses again. But gone are the bright primaries of the hike's beginning, when the landscape was verdant and the river full and rushing. Here the buildings are washed denims and hospital greens.

We're deep in the High Himalayas now. Life is sparse here.

Numbness nips at the tips of my fingers.

"Rubina," I say softly, jogging to catch up with her. "How did you find today's ceremonies?"

"Nice, very nice," she says.

"Those nuns are so pure and full of love," I say.

"Yes, most definitely," says Rubina.

As we left the nunnery, the rest of the group seemed misty-eyed and soft, clearly touched by the ceremony, but Rubina was almost stoic. Ehani is quiet because of the language gap, and maybe a bit of natural shyness, but Rubina's silence strikes me as different. I wonder how much to push. Everyone is treading a fine line between pushing our bodies and pushing our minds. I don't know where the edge is. Healing, like high-altitude hiking, is often tenuous—even dangerous.

Before I can say anything else, a string of children come out of nowhere and run alongside us, their laughter like the clattering of little spoons. Two young girls with shoulder-length black hair in baggy American T-shirts and worn sandals dart past. Three boys all in a row by height huff and puff as they walk. The little-kid wheeze at the end of each breath makes me chuckle.

"Are you Korean?" a girl in highwater jeans and torn sandals asks, pointing to Shreya. "An actress?"

"Ohhh!" giggles Shreya, clearly thrilled. She pouts her lips and tilts down her movie-star glasses to look at her.

"No, she's a fashion model," Rubina says.

"Come on Ms. Model!" Lucy cries.

"I wish!" says Shreya, grabbing Lucy's hand. "If you teach me all your makeup tricks."

Rubina and Shreya are cousins. Over the last five days, I've watched a fire rise in Shreya. She seems bolder and bubblier, while Rubina remains measured. They carry their histories so differently, but their stories are woven together.

During harvest season in Sindhupalchok, the homes of Rubina's neighbors were full of food—baskets of rice and millet and maize—while hers sat empty. Her grandfather was wealthy but wouldn't help Rubina and her siblings because they were all girls. Daughters were considered less valuable because they didn't work or earn money. Their only value was in marriage.

Her grandfather used to say: "With girls, when others find gold, you will find shit."

But Rubina's mother was determined to get her daughters into school and out of poverty. She worked in the fields several days a week with the men and made enough to enroll the girls in school. Then, in a freak accident, Rubina's older sister was attacked by a leopard roaming the village, and her parents had to take out a huge loan to cover the treatment. There were no savings left, and villagers wouldn't barter with the family. "Your daughters are going to elope anyway," they'd say. "You'll never be able to pay us back. So why should we give you meat?" Her family had to scavenge leftovers from the fields just to survive.

It was a close relative who first told the family about India.

If they sent Rubina away, she'd have a job and an education.

It was an easy yes.

Rubina won't speak about her time in India or what it was like to see her little cousin, Shreya, arrive there, or what the two of them went through before they ended up here today, on the mountain with us.

Shreya was young when Rubina left their hometown. When her parents heard how well Rubina was doing, they decided to send Shreya too. She was twelve when she arrived in India. It was like no school she'd ever seen. She kept waiting for schoolwork, but instead she was kept in a dark room, new clothing and fresh food delivered to her each morning by another young woman. She rarely got to see her cousin and never heard her passing by, like she would have on the way to school.

She couldn't see much from her room at all, so she learned to listen well.

One day, she overheard the man she'd traveled with to India speaking in a hushed voice to the old woman who roamed the halls with a big set of keys clanking at her waist.

"We're moving her now, the new one," he said. "Yes, yes, a better spot. Virgins pull a higher price there."

Her mind quickly puzzled it together. She was being plumped and primed, cared for like a sacred cow, so that she would grow shiny and healthy and strong, and like livestock be sold to the highest bidder. There was no school. She was the virgin.

Rubina had done this. Her own cousin had lied to the family and betrayed her. How could she? And why? For days, Shreya was desperate to reach Rubina. She tried sending messages through the girls who shuffled past her door late at night, cryptic notes begging Rubina to come talk to her. Then one night she heard a tapping against wood and woke to her cousin's whisper. Through the door, they argued quietly.

"How could you do this?" Shreya cried.

"It wasn't me," said Rubina. "I didn't know either."

"Where are we now? What is this place?"

But she already knew the answer. She'd heard the stories of girls disappearing, especially from their home region, but still she needed to hear her cousin say it aloud.

"We're in a brothel here. I'm so sorry."

"How do I get out? We have to go. We have to get away from here."

"No, no," Rubina said. "If you get out to the road and get caught, you'll be chopped into pieces." Her voice dropped. "It's happened before."

"Ma timilaai maya garchu," said Shreya. *I love you.* "But if you're not coming, I don't care. If I can get to Nepal, I'll get our families and come back for you. If I don't make it, then you die here, and I'll die outside. I'd rather die on that road. Then at least I tried. We have to try."

* * *

Making our way down to a ravine, we pass a long wall of mani stones. At the end of the trail, we enter the gorge of the Imja Khola, a tributary of the Dudh Koshi, and are pulled along by the fierce sound of the water rushing through the valley. A broken bridge lays next to the new crossing, its metal rails bent and smashed, left to decay beside the river.

Two Sherpas tromp up behind us, carrying superhuman loads strapped to their foreheads with fabric bands. One is in a hoodie, and the other, in a T-shirt, has an entire wooden table strapped to his back. As we step aside to let them pass, I see many packs are roped to the board like a stretcher, and he uses his body as a fulcrum to pick it up or set it down.

We start up a grueling hill, scaling a path artfully carved into the rock face. "Oh my God, of course. We're going up again," cries Lucy. She's getting hammered by the altitude but pushes on like a tank. Ehani is glued to her side, tugging a water bottle from her pack every so often and forcing Lucy to drink. Shreya puts on her movie-star sunglasses and charges ahead, a sly grin on her face. And Dr. Jackie's cough sounds worse.

Jimena walks slightly ahead of the group—fully on their own path now.

As we round a bend, the Himalayas open up to us, their granite teeth rising from a thick blanket of fluffy clouds, ancient streams of sediment cascading down their faces like waterfalls. Closest is Ama Dablam, one of the most majestic-looking mountains. It resembles the Matterhorn in Switzerland. Some say it looks like the arm of a mother protecting a child on each side.

"I'm going to climb that!" Shreya points to the furthest peak. Everest. It's an arrowhead. Rounded to a point of pure, clean white. "Someday," she says.

Being sandwiched between the Himalayas on either side feels like being held by the mountains. Nothing has ever made me feel so safe and so terrified at the same time.

* * *

At the top of the grueling hill we arrive in Pangboche and climb yet another grueling hill to the house of Lama Geshe, the reigning lama and the official priest for anyone attempting to summit. It's quite an operation. A woman leads us to a low-lit room, where incense smoke slithers past shelves crammed with trinkets and stacks of red ribbons and envelopes. It's like a sacred office supply closet, a hilarious blend of the commercial and spiritual, which describes so much of trekking on Everest. Behind a desk sits an old man in thick black glasses. Lama Geshe. His face is leathered and dotted with tiny growths, his shoulders permanently hunched under a red robe. He's wearing a smirk that says he just pulled a prank and is waiting for us all to find out. Through the translators, he kindly agrees to give us each an individual blessing, a short grumbling ceremony no one seems to understand, while he chuckles and talks to the women running things the whole time.

We are more reverent than the lama has time for.

Lucy kneels in front of his desk, bowing her head low, and he breaks into a snickering laugh, demanding in mumbled Nepali that she get up. "Up, up!" I imagine him saying. "Off your knees, woman. What's all this fuss?"

When my turn comes, I look around at the walls crammed with pictures of climbers from around the world. Many standing on the summit. I try not to think about those who stood where I am now for a blessing and never made it back. My Base Camp puja is in four days, and the ticking clock at the back of my mind has quieted a bit. I hand the lama my money and khata, which he mumbles over, and then he motions to me to bend toward him. He tries to tie a red string, a sungdi, around my neck, but it gets tangled in the necklaces I'm already wearing—my mother's rosary and two with images of La Virgencita del Carmen. The Virgencita has promised that anyone wearing her image when they die will be granted secure passage from purgatory to heaven. After I fell climbing up a cliff on Mont Blanc and lost my necklace, I wear two just in case. I'm not taking chances on a speedy entrance to heaven. Only the Virgin herself knows what my purgatory wait time would look like.

I'm holding up the line while Lama Geshe, a wildly revered monk, is trying to painstakingly untangle all my religious trappings and tie a simple string. I'm already bringing my spiritual baggage to the mountain.

"Bahh," he says, flapping his hand, finally giving up, and finishes the ceremony by tossing a fistful of rice over my head. I laugh as it rains down on me. I had to trek all the way to the Himalayas to get my good Catholic wedding.

"Om bolo sat gurubhagavan ki jai!" He locks eyes with me and grumbles a chant. "Om bolo sat gurubhagavan ki jai! Om bolo sat gurubhagavan ki jai!"

His voice grows louder, insistent, as he repeats the chant, bobbing his head toward me until I catch on and repeat it. This is what I should take with me. I understand. He hands me a picture in an envelope, and his assistant translates that I should take a photo at the top of Everest and send it back to him.

I'm touched by his confidence in me. It makes the dream seem more possible.

* * *

The light on the trail has shifted. Distant bells chime as the temperature drops and the sky around Everest fades to a chilly pale pink. The tingle is totally gone from my fingers, as if the day's blessings gave me a shot of oxygen.

I think about Rubina and her story. I've never known poverty like hers, or like the poverty that pushed Shreya and Ehani's parents to send their kids away for a chance at a better life. But I do understand what it feels like when the people who hurt you are the ones you must depend on to live. There's a schism. A mental break. Trust becomes an impossible loop. A snake eating its own tail. A part of me still feels like I earned what J did to me. That bad things happen to bad people and good things to the good. I know it isn't true and sounds juvenile to say, but shame is illogical.

It is a heavy, hungry cloak.

The umbilical cord that connects us all on the trek.

I think about Rubina's grandfather and how he basically said that women are useless. It's a story I wish I didn't understand so well. That we all didn't know so well. The more I learn of everyone's stories, the more I see that each of them has pieces of the others, chunks of the same sea glass washed up on distant shores. We've survived atrocities committed by men and weren't the first in our family lines to do so.

We lose sight of Everest and the landscape morphs from pine-covered hillsides to a barren wintery terrain as we descend into a valley called Heaven, home to the Rai people, a small indigenous Nepali population and one of the country's oldest ethnolinguistic groups. The Rai don't have gods or temples or books or idols. Their religion is based on the worship of ancestors, and the central practice and idea is *ridum*. Each area and group has its own collective ridum, not only in the people, but in the stones and trees, objects alive and inanimate. And each of those things carries the story of a lineage from the beginning of time to today.

Ridum is less a faith than an act of storytelling. An inheritance. The Rai both *tell* and *do* ridum. Everything we are contains our ancestral lineage, and by *telling* the stories or *doing* the rituals that nod to or reenact those stories, the Rai are remembering where they came from and becoming who they are meant to be. It's only by telling the stories that they know who they are.

If we all inherit the stories of our ancestors, then maybe all of this is not mine to carry. Maybe Miyolangsangma's inexhaustible giving is not martyrdom. It's not wringing ourselves out to be proven worthy. It is inexhaustible because the source is all of us.

The sun is dipping fast behind the horizon. "I'll go ahead, then," Asha says, striking out ahead. "And book the teahouse!"

"Me too," calls Jimena. "Wait!" They seem distracted, anxious, even.

"What's that?" Asha is already a hundred feet down the trail.

"She wants to go with you!" calls Shreya. "Wait."

"They." Jimena turns to Shreya. They repeat firmly. "They."

"What?"

"I go by *they*," Jimena repeats.

"They? Uh, oh, yes. You are they." Shreya laughs nervously and I know she's worried that she's hurt Jimena's feelings.

Everyone is silent for a moment.

"It's okay," says Jimena, grabbing Shreya by her arm. "We are going to keep learning together."

Asha rejoins the group and links arms with Jimena. Shreya hooks her arm in Jimena's other arm, and the three of them march down the trail together toward Periche, the highest point of our journey. Even as the wind begins to howl around us, there is a brightness and bounce to their step.

"Shailee," I ask, "what was that chant the nuns did?"

"A chant for compassion."

"Compassion for who?"

Shailee stares at me deadpan. "Why, the yaks of course."

I must have given her a confused grin because she bursts into laughter. "What do you think? Compassion for yourself, of course. Only then can you have it for others."

Laughing, I nod as if to say, "Of course. Of course, I knew that."

Compassion, I'll learn later, is what allows pain and love to sit next to each other. It means allowing ourselves to actually receive the love and protection showered on us in these Himalayan blessings. Shouldering the trauma of my abuse and the moral responsibility of stopping it left little space for compassion in my life.

Not for others or myself.

We're rolling nine women deep as we leave the paradisal valley of Heaven. I feel Miyolangsangma listening. All our blessings and conversations and the land we are traversing have a singular message: You are not alone. Your ancestors are here—for better or worse. The only way to undo what has been done is to keep telling the stories and righting them as we go. To trust others and ourselves even after we've been betrayed and hurt. And to accept people regardless of our own ideas and limitations.

Compassion means respecting each other's experiences even if we do not understand or relate. I, we, don't have to understand Jimena's experience to respect and have compassion for it. We just have to allow her—*them*—to be.

Chapter 8

༼༽

TOP SHELF

At a party during my senior year at Millersville, a new student named Yoshiko, a half-Japanese, half-German woman, approached me and told me she was wildly attracted to me. I was slack-jawed—less stunned at what she'd said than by the fact that she didn't burst into flames right there. In my world, gayness was a capital-*S* sin.

I was going out with men. I had had one serious college boyfriend, Huib, but after him it was just little party flings. I found men attractive enough. They were fine. But I'd never considered dating women. I didn't even know how gay people got together. But Yoshiko was so bold, expressing her desire for me loud and proud, where others might hesitate.

And as I stood next to her, close enough that I could feel her warmth, I let the words settle in. Something deep and true rattled inside me. Something that I grew desperate to explore. But neither of us felt truly comfortable experimenting in Millersville, and I wasn't ready for anything physical anyway, so over the next year Yoshiko and I developed an intense romantic friendship. We never touched, but it was intimate and emotional. I didn't know what to call the relationship, but it felt different from anything I'd ever known. We made plans to move to New York after college. There we could be anonymous. Stand in line with the club kids. We could figure out what this was.

Just before the move, I flew to California to spend the summer with my half siblings, Marianela, Ramiro, and Rolando, who were all living in San

Francisco by then. Rolando was dating a Colombian woman, Caleña, whose best friend, Tony, was a flamboyant Latino gay man.

"Call me Tony, preciosa," he introduced himself.

"No, his name is To-to-to-to-ny." Rolando mocked him.

Tony was hyped about something called Gay Pride.

"It's the biggest inclusive festival, Silvita, come! It's like a massive carnival."

My feelings for Yoshiko were strong, but we still hadn't kissed. Did Tony smell something on me? Had my brothers?

"I'll skip it," said Rolando. "There is no way I'm gonna be groped by a bunch of gay men."

"Aye. You're crazy," said Tony. "San Francisco gays have better taste than to go after you."

That Sunday, Caleña, Tony, and I took the BART to San Francisco. By the time the train passed through Oakland, our car was packed with people in shimmering hot pants, feather boas, and chunky glittery platforms. Rainbows were everywhere. Their colors familiar—the rainbows of Tahuantinsuyo. The Inca Empire.

Were the Incas gay?

Was everyone gay?

Woo-hoo! people shouted as they squeezed onto the train.

Happy Pride, everyone!

Carnival whistles punctuated the cheerful commotion.

"What's Happy Pride?" I asked.

"It's a saying for Gay Pride," said Tony. "A celebration of being gay and being open."

I wasn't ready to be gay or open.

We filed off the train and into Montgomery station, which was more crowded than the procession of El Señor de los Milagros in Lima. I'd never seen that many people in one place. That summer, I often took the morning BART from my sister's house into the city, watching the commuters in trench coats and briefcases looking serious yet fashionable. I was reminded of my father's suits.

Part of me wanted to follow that tradition.

But as we stepped out onto Market Street, confetti shot through the air, tumbling and bouncing down around us, and the trill of whistles and the rattle of maracas flooded me with joy. We wriggled through the crowd and found a spot behind one of the steel barricades blocking off the street. Leaning against the cold steel, I watched in awe as floats with DJs blaring techno roared past. On one float, dancing drag queens with big purple hair; on another, chiseled men in whips and chains and topless women in rainbow body paint openly kissing each other. Fighting against control, my hips swayed to the beat, my shoulders swiveling and shaking loose something long stuck in me. We were all one organism, everyone dancing and hollering, radiating an unbridled freedom and ferocity of acceptance that I'd never dreamt possible. The streets were euphoric.

Even the San Francisco mayor, Willie Brown, drove by, waving from his car.

Wow, I thought. *Even the mayor is okay with this?*

My faith, my parents, and much of my country called this lifestyle sinful. But the defiant joy of the parade was intoxicating. It seemed to me that being gay meant being happy. I understood what Tony had been trying to say.

Pride was the opposite of shame.

"Ay Dios, que bendición!" my mother exclaimed when I told her I'd be moving to San Francisco after graduation. Nothing made her happier than her kids being together, finally. Little did she know what was to come.

Yoshiko was still set on New York.

We said a tearful good-bye without ever having touched each other.

* * *

"Can I help you?" asked the pretty blonde receptionist whose name tag read MARIKKA.

"I am here for an interview with Mr. Mitch," I replied shyly.

"Ha! Mr. Mitch. Sure, honey. Take a seat on that sofa there. I'll call *Mr. Mitch*." She chuckled, pointing to a waiting area with a glass ceiling and modern white leather couches. On every surface sat artfully arranged clusters of royal-blue glass bottles with shimmering gold print spelling out "SKYY."

SKYY Vodka had been started by the eccentric genius and inventor Maurice Kanbar, who got rich in the 1970s by inventing the D-Fuzz-It, a lint comb for sweaters. He held dozens of other patents—everything from a varicose-vein stripper to the Tangoes puzzle game. The story goes that Maurice wasn't a big drinker, but after a couple vodka cocktails one night he woke up with a terrible hangover. A chemist friend told him hangovers were caused by chemicals called congeners. Vodka typically goes through a three-step distillation process to reduce congeners, but Maurice figured if he added an extra distillation process, he could make a "hangover-free" vodka.

Of course, I didn't know any of that as I sat in the SKYY offices at the end of Van Ness Avenue, perched as delicately as I could manage in the too-tight navy blue Lord and Taylor suit I'd panic-purchased the day before at Ross Dress for Less. I pulled out my notes and added an extra *y* to "SKY." The *sky's the limit*, I thought. Three months out of college, I'd just moved to San Francisco and was desperate for a job. There was one year left on my international student visa, a post-university period they called "practical training." In order to stay in the United States after that, I would have to find a job willing to sponsor me for an H-1B, the three-year program for international workers. Many of my international friends from Millersville hadn't made it past practical training. With my business degree in accounting, I'd applied to every single dot-com, then moved on to accounting firms, but the rejection letters had piled up. My carelessness during those first college years had consequences. The job at SKYY was the two hundredth I had applied for.

If no one sponsored me, I'd have to go back to Peru.

That was not going to happen.

The United States had become home. I was safe here. Far enough from Peru that the pain had faded into the distance. I remembered it like a sad story that had happened to someone else, somewhere else, a long time ago. But I couldn't stay in the United States undocumented. It was too tenuous. I had to be able to get home if my family needed me. When I worked for Tío Jorge, he'd admired my intense drive and work ethic. It was rare, he said. He didn't know I was fighting to survive.

"Mr. Mitch will see you now, honey," said the receptionist, pointing toward an open door at the end of the hall.

"So, Silvia," asked Mitch, the curly-haired CFO, as I settled in. "Have you ever heard of SKYY?" He smiled from behind his desk. His nerdy wire-framed glasses and tidy demeanor eased my jangly nerves.

"Yes, I have," I said, surprised at how easily the lie slipped out. As Mitch launched into a speech about the company history, I nodded along pleasantly, scribbling incomprehensible notes.

When I looked up, Mitch was watching me expectantly.

"I'm . . . I'm sorry?" I stumbled.

"I said have you heard of MENSA?"

I had no idea that MENSA was the oldest high IQ society in the world or that he had just told me that he and Maurice were both members and that was how they'd met.

The back of my knees sweated against the plush office chair.

"Of course," I lied again. "MENSA!"

According to Rolando and Ramiro, pretty much everyone in San Francisco was gay. MENSA sounded like "men," so it must have been some kind of acronym for a gay men's club. Was Mitch gay? I eyed his pin-striped button-up shirt and khaki pants, scanning his gentle face for a giveaway.

My father had always worn a suit. Men in suits weren't gay.

But what did gay look like exactly?

"So Millersville," he said, peering over his glasses at my resume. "Franklin and Marshall is close, isn't it?"

"Oh yes," I nodded vigorously. "We have many F and M teachers at Millersville as well."

Another white lie. Franklin and Marshall was a highly ranked private university, the pride of Lancaster County. Occasionally, their teachers had given guest lectures at Millersville.

"We're a small team," he said. "Only twelve of us in the whole company. But the product is taking off. We're sort of like a start-up without the dot-com. That's to say, everyone does a bit of everything. Think you can handle that?"

I was already starry-eyed. *A dot-com without the dot-com.* Whatever that meant, it was music to my code-loving ears. The Bay Area was the dot-com frontier. It felt like I was witnessing the dawn of a new world that my peers in Lima had hardly begun to imagine. Working for a company that operated as a dot-com, whatever that meant, was as good as the real thing for me. If I couldn't work in computers, at least I could work around them. The longer I sat in Mitch's office, the more desperate I was to get the job.

The two-hour interview ended around six p.m. on a Friday with him offering me a position as an entry-level accounts receivable specialist. I tried not to cry. I tried. I'd been rejected from every other job, but Mitch took a chance on me, not pointing out the obvious—that I was a mediocre student from a small state college in the middle of Amish Country. I vowed to prove that hiring me was the best decision he'd ever made.

After we shook on it like real American businessmen—I fought my urge to hug him—Mitch wanted to show me the "fun room." He led me down a dark hallway and opened a door to what looked like a walk-in closet. We ducked down and stepped inside. Every inch of wall space was covered with shelves, and on those shelves in orderly rows were bottles of SKYY vodka in every size imaginable—from airplane bottles to gallon jugs with handles. All the blue glass cast a somber underwater shadow in the room. Gold letters— S-K-Y-Y—sparkled like sea gems, and I was nine again, under the stairs in my parents' liquor cave, enchanted by a menagerie of strange and glamorous bottles. Underneath the generic floral air freshener, there was a faint musty tang I'd smelled before. Astringent.

"You get two liters every month as an employee bonus," Mitch said with a little snap of his head.

"Wow," I replied. "That's so generous."

I did the math. Two 1-liter bottles was 2,000 milliliters, or basically three normal-sized 750-milliliter bottles. Who drank that much vodka in one month? I shrugged and took my first allowance with pride, waving good-bye to Mitch, cradling my bottles in each arm like newborns.

"Thank you," I shouted as I stepped out the door. "Thank you again. See you Monday!"

* * *

Not having a permanent place in the United States seeded a particular sense of angst in me. Every day I was twenty-four hours closer to the day my papers expired. All my fears and confusion were soothed by becoming a disciple of SKYY. I arrived at the office every morning by seven a.m., and I was usually one of the last to leave. It helped that we weren't just any alcohol company. We were a top-shelf brand.

Dave, our sleek blonde salesperson, had explained it to me.

"When you walk up to a bar, you see only the fanciest booze up top," he said. "The cheap stuff is hidden, stuck in the well. You never want to be at the bottom. Don't forget that."

I nodded enthusiastically.

When I called my parents to share the news, my father skipped the congratulations and started right in on accounting jargon.

"I'm curious about the ledger and structure that North Americans use," he said. "This is a good theoretical discussion for us to have in the future."

"Ughhh," I groaned. I wasn't ready for a theoretical discussion of SKYY's accounting. After eighteen months as a molecular biology major at Millersville, I was having a hard time grasping the science. My childhood love for computers resurfaced, but when I told my father I was going to switch to computer science, he threatened to bring me back to Peru. He didn't take computers seriously. Called them a fad. "Nothing changes with the calculator," he'd say. "With the abacus. Computers are a technical career. You need something reliable." So I pursued accounting. I never thought of this as following in his footsteps, exactly. More like just doing what I needed to do to stay in the United States. But I'm sure he saw things otherwise.

"You must be ready to take notes at all times!" he hammered on. "Every single concept is priceless at first. Be ready with your pen and paper. The worst thing you can do is to inconvenience them by asking for a pen or paper."

"Yes, sir," I replied. "You are absolutely right."

My mother was focused on the money.

"Your father and I have worked hard to make sure you received an education," she said slowly. "We sacrificed so much for you, Silvita. Avoiding expensive holidays so that we could provide for you and your brothers. Soon it will be your turn to help us."

"Of course, Mamita. I could never forget. Let me just get on my feet here and I'll send money down." It was strange having my parents ask me for money. All my father had ever cared about was work, and if everything my father had built could be gone in a day, then nothing was safe.

* * *

SKYY sponsored my immigration classification, getting me one step closer to a forever life in the United States. It was a boutique company, still very new, which catered to hip, artsy VIPs. The aficionados. We sponsored extravagant fashion shows and gallery openings and even the San Francisco Film Festival—Maurice was a huge movie buff. He had helped finance a couple of Hollywood films.

I was rubbing elbows with the sleek, sexy Americans I'd always imagined. The 90210 crowd. The dot.commers and waifish models and fast-talking entrepreneurs. I was twenty-three years old and living the high life in one of the world's best cities in the late '90s. It was the Wild West. The digital frontier. Everyone was turned on and turned up. SKYY employees went to only the hippest, high-end places. I learned to wine and dine clients, quickly becoming a connoisseur of not only vodka, but all liquor. From the finest burgundies to bourbons, I learned to mimic the talk of the who's who and the it crowd, adopting their all-American mantra of work hard, play hard.

I was learning to party professionally.

Shuffling into the office with a hangover every morning was almost expected. And because we were dining—not eating—on the most expensive food and getting sloshed on the finest booze, our lifestyle was elite, not shameful.

Even outside of work, going to the hippest bars was de rigueur. After events, my coworkers and I strolled into the bar at Boulevard or Jardinière or whatever the new spot was. Bartenders sent over rounds of free drinks. After the third or fourth cocktail, fancy hors d'oeuvres—oysters, fried calamari, prosciutto-wrapped dates—arrived in waves. It was a win-win. All the bartenders wanted SKYY swag. Those fancy sky-blue cocktail shakers and perfectly designed cocktail kits. I festooned my apartment with company paraphernalia until my roommate finally said enough.

I crammed my suitcases full of swag to visit Peru. My mother had never been a heavy drinker. She'd have one drink, a drink and a half tops, but stopped when her cheeks went rosy. My pride must have been contagious, though, because she spoke endlessly to friends, neighbors, anyone who would listen, about her daughter's position at a prestigious liquor company, as if we were bottling holy water instead of grain alcohol. During my first visit back home, she arranged a one-liter bottle of SKYY on the mantle next to our framed portrait like it was the newest member of the family.

Even my father, a sucker for prestige, took pride in SKYY. It didn't matter that our product was bottled at Frank-Lin Distillers in San Jose, the same distiller who made the cheap well vodka Dave had warned me about. We had the extra distillation process.

We were special; we were different.

We were *top-shelf.*

A year later, I was living a double life.

* * *

Fluorescent light flooded my eyes. I blinked, then blinked again. Above was white. White so bright I had to squint to take it in. From every direction, there were chirps and hums, a low whooshing of air, a series of long beeps, then shorter beeps, then long again. Everything was so white. My limbs were cement. Maybe I was dreaming. I closed my eyes and tried to wake up again, but all I saw was the same white nothing. A constant skittering beep nearby. My tongue was sandpaper.

"Where *am* I?" I croaked.

My head was a bag of straw as I looked down at my hands. On the top of the left one was a butterfly bandage holding down a thin clear tube. I followed the tube slowly up my forearm and over my shoulder to where a long silver pole draped over me, with a nearly empty bag of clear fluid hanging from a little hook. An IV line. My mind started spinning. I looked down at my legs. I was lying on a hospital gurney. I closed and opened my eyes again. Still there. Was this an insanely realistic nightmare? Maybe I could just walk out of it. That used to work sometimes when I was a kid.

I felt like the room might flip upside down at any moment. I gripped the handrails to stop it from spinning.

Just then, a nurse walked in.

"Wow," she said, whistling. "You're finally up."

Silent, I pointed to my arm.

She stood over me, pulled off the butterfly bandage, yanked out the IV, and covered the spot with a small Band-Aid.

"How are you feeling?" she said, more softly. I wasn't ready to talk.

She shrugged and left the room. I rolled off the gurney and looked around for the nearest exit sign. No one said anything as I ducked past the nurse's desk. Maybe it was a dream. Once I was outside, I'd wake up . . .

It was daylight on the street. The same flat white as the hospital room.

A sign at the corner. Sacramento and Buchanan.

Another sign.

In red.

EMERGENCY.

What happened?

I had no wallet. Where was my wallet?

I had on washed black jeans and a tight cropped white T-shirt with some yellowish dry spots.

My keys. I dug into the pockets of my jeans. Nothing.

I remembered that Sacramento Street was a couple blocks parallel to Bush, where I lived. I'd walk home and see if my roommate was there. Luckily, she'd just finished her shift at a luxury linen store on Union Square and buzzed me in. I told her I'd left my key at home, then beelined for my room, where I pulled back the covers, climbed into bed, and fell into a deep sleep, hoping that when I woke up again, this dream would finally be over.

Dusk was falling when I woke.

I was still wearing the same stained clothes.

I tried putting the pieces together. First it was a void. Nothing.

And then in little snippets it came through. A slideshow. Black-and-white images of someone else's life. All out of order. No captions. No context.

Waiting. Dancing. Thumping bass and bodies. Lights—purples and greens, swirling pinks. Cocktails. Laughter. Smoking. Smoking. Smoking. Bodies again. Sweating and grinding. Hands and breasts. Mine. Others. Women everywhere.

Club Q.

Today was Saturday, so yesterday had been Friday. The first Friday of the month. The legendary girl party. In a huge warehouse on Townsend in SoMa, Club Q was the hottest lesbian night on the West Coast. Started by prominent DJ Page Hodel, Club Q was a once-a-month party. Women drove from all over the Bay Area and stood in line for an hour just for the chance to get inside.

I'd crunched the numbers and figured that statistically it was my best odds of meeting a woman, though I still wasn't sure what I'd do with her when I met her. Waiting alone in line with fifteen hundred other people, I tried to make small talk, but everyone seemed glued to their own crews and cliques.

I was too naïve about the scene to even be embarrassed.

After my coworkers and I shut down the straight bars and they'd turned in for the night, I'd go back out. Alone. To gay bars. I always went alone. I didn't dare to go to a straight club alone, but at places like Club Q, I felt safe disappearing into a crowd, slipping nameless through sweaty, drunken women, trying to find my way to something like belonging. Trying to see myself reflected in them. At first, I was a bewildered girl wandering a strange new land. A gay Shangri-la with a range of women, some who looked more feminine, some more butch, and some who looked like me—in the middle of the spectrum. Janet Jackson and P. Diddy thumped through the speakers as Black and Asian women, Latinas, and a scattering of white women all came together in what felt like a wild family party. Neon-lit bodies slick with sweat and glitter. Go-go dancers in leather writhed on stages and scaffolding. Acrobats twirled in silver rings hung from the ceiling. It was like MTVs *The Grind* meets Cirque du Soleil, with all the safety and freedom I'd felt during that first Pride parade, but now I was inside instead of in the crowd watching.

Maybe one day I'll be here with a posse all my own, I thought, wandering the massive warehouse to take in each room, catching glimpses of WNBA and soccer players I'd seen on TV in the VIP section. My SKYY VIP status didn't translate here. Little from my outside life did.

I didn't know how to make a move. So I wandered from room to room hoping to get lucky and stumble upon a beautiful woman open to teaching me the ropes. Some nights at Club Q I thought about what would happen if I actually met someone I wanted to date. What sort of life would that be? Whenever I tried to visualize the future, I saw a husband and child by my side. My parents beaming in the background, proud. I couldn't revise the picture. There was too much at stake.

How the hell had I wound up in the ER? Slowly, I remembered getting ready the night before, arriving around ten-thirty and hyping myself up. *This is gonna be my lucky night. Tonight is the night.* Inside Club Q I didn't hit on anyone and nobody hit on me, but I drank and drank until I couldn't see straight. I was so used to drowning my shame.

I remembered the midnight performance—thirty dancers in harnesses and cherry-red lipstick dancing to Missy Elliott's newest single, "The Rain." With the liquor, my body loosened. Hopping onto the stage, I shook a life of stiffness from my limbs, swinging my body to the beat, sweat dripping, shirt clinging to my chest, both hoping someone was watching and terrified that they were.

After that it was blank.

Quickly, I showered, dressed in fresh clothes, and went back to the club. All traces of Club Q were gone, and the venue was back to being a regular straight club. A bouncer I recognized was taking IDs outside for the early afternoon drinkers. A tall Black man with a no-bullshit grin.

"Well, well, look who's back for more."

"Hello, sir," I said, sheepishly, shifting into the oddly formal language I used when ashamed. As if civility could counteract any nasty image someone had of me. In this case, I didn't know exactly what I'd done, but I had a feeling it couldn't be good.

"Actually, I was hoping you could help me piece together what happened last night. I woke up in the ER, and I'm still confused."

"Confused?" he exclaimed. "I'm just happy you're alive!"

I stared blankly.

"Really? Okay."

He shook his head in disbelief, then went on to tell me that after last call I'd been one of the few still on the dance floor, and that he had watched me leave with two beautiful women.

"Wow," I said, juiced on my own game. I must have been on a roll. "Two beautiful women? Do you happen to remember what the women looked like?"

Maybe I still had a chance with one of them.

"Focus, woman! Damn," he shook his head. "You left with them. Climbed into a car, stumbling and slurring. Five minutes later, car comes squealing back and they open the door, dump you out on that curb right there, then peel off."

"What? Wowww."

"Yea. They were shouting about you throwing up in the car. Shit was pretty cold to toss you out like that, though. I tried to wake you, but no dice, so I called the paramedics. Hence the ER."

I was stunned. My fairy-tale club ending—a girl on each arm—had been a disgusting, embarrassing nightmare.

"I'm sorry for the inconvenience," I muttered. "Truly. I'm sorry. Thanks for watching out for me."

"I'm glad you're alive. Get some rest. You'll feel better by Monday. And I'm sure I'll be seeing you next month."

Not a chance. I'm done.

"Oh, one more thing. Did you see my wallet?"

"Yep. Paramedics took it. You should go back to the ER."

An hour later at the hospital reception desk, a woman handed over my wallet, and again I apologized profusely and formally as if she'd been the one to pump my stomach. She didn't register a word and returned to her paper-work. All day people had been looking at me with a combination of exasper-ation and pity. Apologies flowed out of me, and I was desperate for someone to receive them. To assign my penance. I pulled out my driver's license and stared at the picture in disgust. That smile. I hated that smile. Could anyone see the mountain of shame under that smile?

Idiot. Idiot!

I repeated it over and over, flagellating myself.

Imagine if someone at work found out. You'd be sent back to Peru.

SKYY has been so good to you, and you're going to destroy it.

This country is your lifeline. You want to ruin everything, you piece of shit?

Pedazo de mierda. My father's voice echoed.

You'll become nothing. A bum. A drunk. Trash waiting to be taken to the curb.

Each criticism was a lashing with his best Pedro P. Diaz belt. There was no one else to scold me or hold me accountable because no one knew where I'd been. My only friends were my coworkers—my drinking buddies and hang-over comrades—but I played straight with them. They knew nothing about Club Q. And I still hadn't made my own gay friends in the city.

Waking up in the hospital shocked me sober for a while. But as my mother always said, "Borron y cuenta nueva."

Kiss and start new.

So I did.

* * *

My brother's girlfriend Caleña hooked me up with a local soccer club, Las Atrevidas. *The Daring Ones.* Part of the Golden Gate Women's Soccer League, we were in the lowest division and played a game every Saturday. Soccer transported me back to the driveway with Miguel. To running track during gym at school. To the sports and motion I'd been hungry for but that my family saw little value in. My mother too distracted, my father focused on practicality over recreation. Athleticism wasn't prized, especially not in a young girl. When I did run track for a while in high school, he never came to events or offered pointers like the other fathers.

But I was built to run. And with Las Atrevidas, I was fearless. My drib-bling techniques were self-taught, but my sprint was unstoppable. I didn't care about getting injured. I had a killer instinct. It was a thrill to be on the lookout for a loose ball. To catch it between my feet and run it down the field, leaving everyone behind. Even outrunning my own shame.

"Run, Forrest, run!" My teammates screamed from the sidelines, and I was never happier than when doing just that.

I became the top scorer for our division, averaging three to four goals a game.

With Las Atrevidas I found the sort of community I'd never had. Most of the players were queer, and two-thirds were dating each other, which made for some, well, complex game calls when arguments from home spilled onto the field.

"Carol, pass the ball to Yana!" I'd scream.

"Oh, hell no," Carol would shout back, dribbling down the field. "Not talking to her! She's a lying bitch and a cheater."

"I wasn't looking at her that way," Yana would cry from center field. "She was just serving me coffee!"

After games, we went to someone's house to barbeque and dance. It didn't matter what time it was, barbeque was mandatory, and with it came free-flowing Coronas. If the game started at ten a.m., we'd be drinking by noon and dancing until long after the sun went down. Being with Las Atrevidas gave me a chance not only to explore queerness in daylight hours but to soak up the Latino culture I was missing. With them, I could be all of who I was becoming.

Still, there was the drinking. The only spaces where I was exploring out-ness were also places where I was constantly getting wasted.

But we were a crew—a dysfunctional, passionate, drunken family. Even off the field. We rolled deep to the weekly Latino night at Bench and Bar in Oakland, where I danced to salsa and cumbia, my body awakening to the joy and safety of dancing with a same-sex partner. Singing lyrics to the music I grew up with—Alejandra Guzmán, Maná, Shakira—in Spanish at the top of my lungs. In some ways I felt more connected to my culture than I had been in Peru. The parts that I loved had always been dampened by the misogyny, by the restriction and abuse inflicted upon my body. Fear does not move to the beat. But the beat was finally pouring out of me. I was unlearning the idea of home, or maybe I was just starting to learn that for me, home might mean something else altogether.

Nobody at work knew about Las Atrevidas.

Secrets were so natural for me that keeping the parts of my life separate was not only protective, but intuitive. With my sexuality, I maintained tight control. Exploring on my own terms.

My drinking, on the other hand, had slipped out of my control.

Marianela and her Peruvian husband, Beto, bought their first house and baptized it the way we knew best. A massive party. I brought my standard liter-bottle of SKYY for the christening and quickly became the default bartender, shaking batches of cosmopolitans, which were very chic at the time. Even as we blew past the limit without slowing, drinking cosmos lent a classy aura to the night. Also, Peruvians have this theory that dancing feverishly all night balances out the booze.

We were fine. We were sober enough.

As the crowd thinned out, the "drunks," as Marianela called us affectionately, stayed up for one last drink. I was crashing at her place, so I'd been keeping pace with the older men, matching them beer for beer. We'd moved on from frilly cocktails by then. Marianela, who wasn't a big drinker, went to bed. The others dropped too, and finally my brother-in-law, Beto, and I were the last men standing, chugging "just one more" at the kitchen counter. Suddenly we were kissing.

My sister came shuffling down the hall in her pajamas and flipped on the light.

"Beto!" she screamed.

I was instantly sober.

The next morning, she sat me down and asked calmly if I was interested in her husband.

"Marianela," I said. "No. Absolutely not. Please listen. I was beyond drunk and don't even know how we ended up kissing each other. Please! It had no meaning whatsoever. Zero."

I was torn apart. I remembered nothing about the night before or who'd kissed whom. Tío Jorge had been right. When I was working in Port Chester, he issued a warning I never forgot.

"Mujer borracha hasta el perro se la cacha," he said. I'd gasped.

A drunk woman could end up easily fucked by any animal.

We hadn't grown up together, but Marianela had taken me in like a true sister and helped me land in San Francisco. I was desperate not to lose her.

But I'd crossed a line. Her eyes were guarded. I knew it didn't matter what I remembered.

The only thing left to do was drop my cover.

"Marianela," I said, taking her hand in mind. "I promise you I'm not after him. I promise you because . . . I'm gay."

That's how I officially came out.

For the first time. Not because I wanted to share who I was with my family. But because I loved my sister and my drinking had hurt her. And even as I said the words, I didn't know how true they were. Yes, I counted down the days to Club Q every month and spent my free time running down a field with queer Latinas, but for some reason, I still never thought it'd be necessary to say the words aloud. I'd still never touched a woman. My soccer crushes didn't give me the time of day. I was attracted enough to men that I figured I'd eventually settle down with one. Maybe I could be with women on the side. For me, I hoped gayness was a choice. I could decide when to turn it off and on. I could please my family and still find love, I reasoned.

I wrote my first rule that day.

Rule #1: Never drink in front of my sister. Not even at family gatherings.

Drinking in San Francisco was still allowed, of course. It was practically a job requirement. But I'd skip the booze during family gatherings if it would repair my relationship with Marianela.

Within months, even though she forgave me and supported my coming out, I was skipping family gatherings.

Chapter 9

⊗⊗⊗

NOTHING WE DO IS SMALL

In the movie of my mind, we've been hiking toward a crescendo. Arriving not just at Base Camp, but at a moment of catharsis. A time when we sit down, dirt caked and muscles worked, and reflect on how this journey has empowered us. I imagine it happening naturally. All part of the script. But we're still three days from Base Camp, and it hasn't happened yet. At the end of the day, there's little energy left for dealing with the weight of the past. And that's sort of the point, I see. To be here now. To be present with each other. With our bodies and how they move up the mountain.

But there's something else.

A gnawing anxiety that I've been burying with majestic views and daily itineraries. With blessings on blessings. Nuns and lamas and prayer wheels and katas. With dinners around yak-dung stoves. I appointed myself the leader of these young survivors, so if I don't teach them something, if they don't feel changed or split open the way I did when I first experienced Everest, then what is my worth? If we don't have a grand moment, have I failed them?

Between Dr. Jackie's worsening altitude sickness and the brutal climb, we barely made it to Periche last night. We marched straight to the medical outpost when we arrived.

"Your last name?" the doctor asked, scribbling on a clipboard. She was a young, fit, and hip-looking doctor. If it wasn't for the stethoscope on her neck, I would have thought she was just another climber on the trek.

"Vasquez-Lavado."

"Lavado! Habla español?"

"Sí! Soy Peruana. Y tú?"

"My name is Isabel and this"—she pointed to a woman in a slouchy beanie and flannel shirt hunched over a book behind us—"is my girlfriend Raidi."

Raidi waved and returned to reading.

"It's just," I say. "It's so cool to meet you here. I'm usually, well . . ."

"The only one?" Isabel laughed.

"I wasn't going to put it that way. But now that you did . . . yes!"

"Is there any other way to put it?"

She was right.

I've gotten so used to being Brown in a white space, being a woman in a male space, that I'd never even imagined what it might be like to see more of myself in the mountains. When traveling, I often lied when asked about a partner, or I answered in a way that made people think I was talking about a husband unable to join me because of work. Being a woman alone in much of the world, especially a woman who loved other women, had been its own kind of challenge. Seeing Isabel and Raidi together here in the mountains gave me hope that things were changing for the better, and that maybe I would someday travel this path openly with a partner.

As the girls lined up to get their vitals checked, Raidi walked past with an armful of papers, stopping to peck Isabel on the cheek. "Nice to meet you!" she said, waving. I wondered what it would be like to have a partner here. Someone to climb with.

Dr. Isabel cleared everyone to finish the hike but ordered us to take an extra rest day in Periche.

"I don't know," I said, stalling. "We have a timeline. I think we can make it."

We were behind schedule, and taking another rest day would mean we wouldn't make it to Base Camp together in time for my Everest puja.

"Listen," Dr. Isabel said. "Even your team doctor is sick. Take the hint. There's no playing wonder women up here. You should know that. You rest or you fail. That's it."

Her sternness sent a little zing up my spine. I needed a firm voice. The mountains had sent me a sign through Isabel. My job was to listen.

"Yes, Doctor," I said. "You're right. Alright, team, we're going to get some extra rest."

"Thank God!" said Lucy, punctuating a chorus of sighs from the group. Had they all been struggling? Even the Nepali crew? Rubina and Ehani seemed so sturdy. Shreya never complained. I scanned their faces for signs of fatigue. Water. Food. Altitude. Those things I monitored constantly. But how were they really doing? I didn't want to invade anyone's privacy or pry. But it was time to find out.

Instead of using the entire next day for rest, I called a meeting for the next afternoon.

Just a quick check-in, I told them, already plotting an agenda like a corporate summit.

How's everybody feeling? I would say.

Oh, I'm really liking x about the hike, they would say. *This is what I've learned, what I want to improve. I found new strengths like XYZ, etc.* Everyone would say maybe three, *yes three, that's good,* three things that they've learned, then, as a group, we'd come up with goals and objectives for the final days of our hike. I figured we'd get it done in forty-five minutes, an hour tops, then everyone could rest in their rooms.

The next afternoon, we meet in Asha and Shailee's room all bundled in our fleece and down coats, carrying armfuls of blankets from our own rooms. The higher we climb, the weaker the heat in the teahouses gets. We push their two twin beds together against a wall to make one king bed, then layer all the blankets into a giant parachute of a comforter. We crawl onto the bed and nestle shoulder-to-shoulder under the blanket in a big semicircle, close enough to feel the rise and fall of each other's breath, our toes touching at the center. I'm on one end next to Shailee and directly across from Rubina. Dr. Jackie is resting in her room.

"Everyone comfortable?" I say.

A murmured chorus of *yes, mm-hmm, good, fine.*

"Sooooo," I say. "I wanted to take this time and check in with you all. How's everyone feeling, overall?"

"Fine."

"Okay."

"Hungry."

"Tired."

"Okay, for sure, of course, yes. Sounds about right. But . . . mmm, what else?" I flinch at the leading tone in my voice. I thought this would come more naturally. "Anyone want to share part of their hike experience?"

Scanning the group, I meet blank stares and shrugs, averted eyes, like I'm the teacher and they didn't do the homework. I gnaw at the nubs of my nails.

"What's your favorite moment on the hike so far?" Shailee breaks in.

Bless you, Shailee.

"Hotel Everest," says Jimena, with a firm nod. "My first sight of the Himalayas."

"The nuns," says Rubina, and I'm surprised to hear it. All I remember is her stoicism during the puja. Her silence the rest of that afternoon.

As the group calls out their highlights, I reassess my approach. I pull a photo from the front pouch of my bag and prop it up on the blanket in front of me.

"Some of you know parts of my story," I say. "But I want to share a bit more about my background and how I came to climbing and organizing this trip."

I wait as Shailee quickly translates.

"From the age of six to the age of ten," I say, "my parents regularly left me with a family friend who did work around our house. He sexually abused me and convinced me that my parents knew what he was doing."

I pause to catch my breath as Shailee translates.

"I waited years for them to tell me why they wanted him to do it," I go on. "I waited years for it to stop. But I never said anything, and all the pain I swallowed grew into a darkness so big that it cast a shadow over everything. I was a walking shadow. But when I first came to Everest and hiked to Base Camp, I felt I could breathe easier."

"Bah!" Lucy lets out a sarcastic cackle.

"I know! Too weird—but I found I could breathe more where there was less oxygen. The shadow of the mountain was the only thing big enough to swallow my shadow. I didn't know what that meant then, but I trusted it in a way I've never trusted another person. This mountain, Mother Everest, is so sturdy. Eons of rock. Nothing could shake her."

Shreya nods and presses her hands into prayer. "Thank you," she says shyly in English. "For bringing us here."

"Thank *you*," I say, checking my watch. We've got a good forty-five minutes. Plenty of time for everyone to share.

Rubina is sitting directly across from me. I give her a little bow. She clears
her throat and speaks quickly in Nepali.

Shailee laughs and tells us that Rubina has given her a direct order.

"She said, 'Shailee, make sure your translation is flawless for this!'"

Everyone but Rubina starts cracking up. Straight-faced, she draws in a
deep breath and starts speaking quickly again in Nepali.

Shailee listens attentively, nodding along, letting out a small "uhu, uhu"
every once in a while to acknowledge what Rubina is saying. Lucy and
Jimena watch Shreya and Ehani's faces for an immediate reaction. But their
expressions are puzzled.

We look expectantly to Shailee.

"She says that usually she doesn't watch movies. They stir up too many
emotions and ideas. But this year she has already watched four. Something
is changing for her."

Rubina goes on, her voice lower, more methodical than I remember.
She pauses after each passage to let Shailee translate, which Shailee does
swiftly. She tells us that Rubina's parents made a deal with a family friend
who turned out to be a trafficker. Like most parents of trafficked daughters, they had no idea what was happening. They were deeply in debt after
her sister's surgeries from the leopard attack, and the friend told them
that by studying and working in India, Rubina could quickly pay off the
family debt.

During my first trip to Kathmandu, I learned that most sex trafficking in
Nepal is based on debt bondage, a form of modern-day slavery outlawed officially in Nepal in 2002, but which continues in different forms. In agricultural areas like Sindhupalchok, where Rubina, Shreya, and Ehani are from,
poor, landless families often have to borrow money from landowners. When
someone can't pay off their own debt or has inherited debt from ancestors,
sending a family member to work in a city outside Nepal with more a robust
economy is seen as a way to begin to settle the debt. But the people who
arrange the travel, and in some cases, legitimate jobs, often charge high interest and take steep wage deductions for room and board and airline tickets,
which means the workers accumulate more debt by the time they arrive. It's
a cycle that can go on indefinitely for some. And those who wind up doing

sex work are often stigmatized by their communities even after they pay off the debt and try to return home.

Every year, between twelve thousand and fifteen thousand Nepali girls between the ages of six and sixteen are trafficked to India, where they work off their family's debts one customer at a time. Some girls see as many as four men a day. Taxi drivers. College students. Restaurant owners. Tourists. Married men. Even police in exchange for letting business go on.

Most of these debts amount to less than 80 US dollars.

By the time Rubina arrived in India, her family's debt was so high that the traffickers essentially owned her. While she was in India, Shailee explains, her minders forced her to call her parents to check in, holding a knife to her throat while she lied to her parents, saying how well she was doing in school and at work. So well, in fact, that Shreya's parents were excited to send her to join her cousin.

"When my cousin Shreya showed up in India," says Rubina, "I was heart-broken. I tried to make a deal with the trafficker. I told him I would take on more debt if he let her go. But he refused. He said my debt was already so big I'd never be able to pay it back in this lifetime. I was ashamed because Shreya was so young, just twelve, and living there alone, locked in a stone room like this." She gestures to the room around us. "But dirty and cold and with nothing. There was nothing I could do to protect her."

I look at Shreya, who's sitting across from me, her long face, high cheek-bones, eyebrows finely shaped like calligraphic flourishes. I try to imagine her with all her spunk and glamour drained, curled into a ball in the corner of a dark stone room. A slat of wood for a bed, one stained pillow, no blanket. Bars on the window. I imagine someone feeding her well so her coat grows shiny, like an animal being prepared for market, only to break her later.

It's excruciating to picture.

"She was determined to escape," says Rubina. "I knew Shreya, and I knew that if anyone could do it, she would do it. I couldn't let her go alone. But while we were busy making our plan, two other girls tried to do the same. We never saw them again in the brothel. We didn't know if they made it or if something worse happened. Still, Shreya was set, so we kept thinking and thinking about what to do."

I picture the cousins planning their escape in stolen whispers. Aunty, the brothel madam, ready to slap suspicious words from their mouths. How they must have created a secret language to talk to each other at the dinner table or in line for the bathroom or during rare outings through the crowded streets of Sonagachi, one of India's largest red-light districts, where rickshaws splash through muddy puddles, vendors hawk hot chai, and men leer from storefronts and street corners, full of both lust and disdain for the young girls.

Rubina continues: "The main thing was the gate."

"Ughhh," Shreya groans.

"There was this huge iron gate with a giant lock in front of the house," says Rubina. "It was too heavy for us to even shake. For four days, during our daily walks, we snuck away and tried everything we could think of to open the lock. Nothing worked, but on the fourth day, everyone left the house to attend a funeral, even the security guard. We knew this was our only chance. It was eleven a.m. when we ran to the gate. I shoved and shoved it, as hard as I could, but it wouldn't budge. Then Shreya turned to me, and do you remember what you said? She told me: 'Connect to God. You don't have to be in a temple. You don't have to give offerings. Just connect to God.'"

"Yes," says Shreya, squinting out the window toward the Himalayas as if trying to conjure that night. She's dropping into the story. "I said, 'If you pray hard, if you really pray from the inside—it works.'"

"And just at that moment," says Rubina, "I gave another great shove and the gate shot open with such force it practically blew me to the ground. The steps down to the street—I remember, they were huge, purposely built wide so people couldn't easily run up and down. We were out of the gate, but every single step to the street was still a challenge. I could hardly breathe from the fear at my back."

"When we got to the main road," Shreya breaks in, "we ran barefoot. We ran barefoot down the dirty streets as fast as we could, cow dung squishing between our toes, little rocks and bugs sticking to them. We ran through a maze of alleys, our feet caked in cow shit, but all we could do was keep going."

"We never looked back," says Rubina.

"When we reached the other side of the red-light district, there was a group of taxi drivers standing around," says Shreya. "Indian. Rubina approached them. She knew the local language by then."

"I told them I was the daughter of an army man and needed to catch the bus toward Nepal," says Rubina. "I knew Indians were afraid of the army, and that was my one chance to get them to listen."

"And they did!" says Shreya. "They listened."

They're talking faster now, splicing each other's sentences, as if reliving the escape in real time.

This is the first time I've heard their story in such detail, and my heart is thumping, shattering. For a minute, my corporate brain kicks back in, and I wonder if Rubina is going to talk about the hike. If I should steer her back to the prompt and ask her to share what she's learned along the way. But I violently shake the thought away. My exercise is absurd in the face of what they've lived through. Every face in the room is rapt. Imagining the ingenuity it took them to escape. The confidence and fight it took to get back to Nepal.

To hell with the goals and objectives.

"When we climbed on that bus," Shreya is saying, "we were scared. We figured if we fell asleep, the driver might sell us off too. He was so old, he had hair growing out his ears." She starts to laugh. Tears rain down her face.

Is it joy? I can't tell.

"It took two days to reach the Nepali border," says Rubina. "We had nothing to eat or drink. Then just before we crossed into Nepal, the bus stopped. The driver said we had only paid to go this far, and we had to get out. We begged him to let us sleep in the bus overnight. If not, we were sure to be discovered and taken by the cops. He grunted and walked away. He let us stay. Neither of us slept, of course, and early the next morning we snuck off the bus and walked across the border together. Just as we stepped over the border into Nepal, I was stopped by the cops. Shreya still looked like a little kid," Rubina says. "So they paid her no mind."

Shreya flashes a jokey duck-lip pout.

"I kept walking," she says. "I didn't even look back. I didn't want to leave my cousin, but if neither of us made it home, that was it for good. There were buses scattered about, and while Rubina was being interrogated, I slipped onto one headed for Kathmandu."

"Finally the cops who were questioning me said, 'Go get your sister!'" says Rubina. "I said I would look for her. I found Shreya's bus and just as I stepped on, the door closed and it pulled away, leaving the cops behind and taking us to Kathmandu."

Shailee translates the final words to Lucy, Jimena, and me, and we sit stunned, speechless. It's so quiet that I can hear the breeze scratching over sun-bleached grass just outside the window. Rubina looks up and her eyes are glowing, as if they've captured all the light in the room.

From the outside, they look untouched. Their faces so young and fresh.

But when I look more closely, I see it's not youth written into their features but resilience. At every step, their story was precarious. If the gate hadn't opened. If the cabbies hadn't believed Rubina's bluff. If the bus hadn't pulled away at that exact moment. If all the things had gone wrong that go so devastatingly wrong for most women who don't make it out . . .

But they had not.

Rubina's silence, her stoicism, makes more sense.

"I can't believe you made it," says Jimena, pursing their lips together thoughtfully and raising up a fist of solidarity to Rubina.

"Our parents couldn't either," says Shreya, flashing a tender look at her cousin. "They didn't even know what had been happening."

The one time I visited Sindhupalchok, I met Rubina's family. Her mother, father, one of her younger sisters, and her grandpa. They insisted on having us for tea in their home, a ten-by-twenty-foot shed that the whole family shared with a stable of goats. Her mother must have been in such pain hearing the girls' story.

My mother hadn't known either. What J was doing to me. So many mothers don't. And what pain that must bring them. I taste a hint of that motherly rage as I think about how the girls were punished for wanting more. How they were deceived with so many false promises. How their dreams of school and supporting their family were distorted and exploited. Used against them. I let out a big buffalo of a sigh, and Lucy jumps. "Ahh!" she says. "You scared me. Dang. You're like one of those yaks."

We all laugh, and through it Ehani begins to speak.

"When I came home, no one even cared," she whispers in Nepali. She's speaking so low that Shailee hushes us to hear her.

"I was gone for two years."

We all lean closer.

"No one would accept me after that. After what had been done to me. I was marked. You know? Wasted. I simply wanted to die."

Shailee translates, and we all nod in agreement. We all know what Ehani means. Whatever the details of our stories, we've all lived with that feeling.

"I was fifteen when I was taken away to India, and like Shreya and Rubina I was placed in a brothel. But after six months, the police raided the place and we all got thrown in jail. There, the water was so cloudy I could never see the bottom of the cup. We ate bits of leftover rice infested with worms and stones. At every meal, we had to comb our food with bare hands to pull out what was edible. When we finally got released a year later, maybe a year and a half, the police sent us right back to the brothel. I was moved to another location, and that one was even worse because it was run by the wife of a policeman."

"Oh, God," Jimena and Lucy whisper in tandem as Shailee completes the translation.

"Under her eye," says Ehani, "there was no way out. Those who tried to run, we heard, were chopped into pieces. But I made friends with an older woman who had access to the keys. And there was a man, a customer, who loved her so much that he agreed to help us escape. We planned to bring another friend too, a woman whose legs were always swollen. She had a sickness of some kind. I remember just as we were planning to leave, she tells me, 'Leave me behind.' She was afraid she'd hold us up. 'I won't leave you,' I told her. 'I won't do it.'

Ehani pauses, gulping down air like it's water.

As Shailee translates, we all hold our breath.

"One morning," Ehani goes on, "before dawn, the man who loved the woman with the keys arrived in a cab, and the three of us ran out the front door. We ran into the cab. We ran for our lives. For a while, we traveled through another part of India to avoid the cops and border patrol. The woman with the keys and the man who loved her got married. And after some time, I found my own way back to Kathmandu."

We stare riveted, mouths slack as Shailee relays this unlikely love story in the middle of a tragic escape. There are a thousand questions on the tip of my tongue. How did she get back to Kathmandu with no money? How long did they travel in India? Were they dressed in disguise? Where did the couple get married? The couple got married?! What happened to the woman with the swollen legs?

But this isn't the sort of story whose spell you shatter with logistical questions and nosy curiosities.

None of them are.

Out of respect, I don't want to press for further details. Nepali people are gracious yet private. What they choose to share here must be enough. And it is. More than enough. Their stories are complete however they come out.

"From our region, hundreds of girls, thousands maybe, were trafficked," says Rubina. "Of those, just six of us started the case. The three of us here, today, and three others. Powerful people wanted us to be quiet. My own family was threatened many times. Offered loads of money to settle. But they wanted justice for me more than anything."

She turns to look directly at Shreya. "And that's why I only worship them now, Shreya." Her eyes narrow. "I no longer believe in God," she says.

The pressure in the room drops. Everyone's attention expands.

"God opened the gate!" cries Shreya. "You know it was."

"Not that God, Shreya," says Rubina. "I don't believe it anymore. Where was God when we suffered? Only my family was there for me."

"No one stood up for me at all," says Ehani. "In my family, not one single person stood up for me. When I went to the court to file my case, the clerks badgered me. 'If I was your sister,' I said to them, 'would you be asking the same questions?' In that moment I knew I couldn't let anyone intimidate me no matter how powerful they were. Not for the rest of my life. My family was weak, see, but I'd already come so far alone that I knew I could do it. And I had Shakti Samuha. They were the only ones who cared."

"Shakti is never afraid," says Shreya.

I watch Lucy's perfectly lined eyes brimming over. Wordless tears roll down Jimena's face. I've been softly crying too, wiping tears away without noticing.

"The men also tried to bribe me to drop the case," Ehani says, whispering again. "I told them, 'If you can return what we lost, then we'll talk.'"

* * *

This is the most I've ever heard Ehani talk. She is blazing. I'm floored. At her age, I was drinking my story down. Starting my climb up the corporate ladder. Convinced that achievement was my ticket out of trauma. I've had to climb the world's highest mountains, five of them so far, just to find a modicum of the vulnerability and honesty on display in this room. Our conversation is not the tidy healing montage that I imagined. I'm so embarrassed at my impulse to lead the group through some corny checklist of strengths and weaknesses. For assuming they needed me to teach them. I try to surrender to the moment. To tamp down the urge to contain, to control. My mind is a white board. Deadlines and spreadsheets zing past. Heat radiates from the center of the blankets. My underarms are soaked.

"Crack the window, will you please, Jimena?" I ask. "Wow. I mean. Just wow. Thank you so much for sharing these incredibly powerful and painful stories. I just . . . should we take a little break?"

I'm not sure if I'm asking for them or myself. My stomach grumbles, and I glance at my watch again. Two hours have passed. I pull a bag of almonds from the pocket of my fleece and offer them around.

Everyone nods a polite no. No to the almonds. No to the break.

No one even moves or takes a sip of water.

Something has been let loose, and it's unfolding on its own time. Our bodies have formed a mass, our breath rising and falling in tandem, one voice speaking at a time. We are distinct yet collective.

It's a shape I can't quite make out. A circle that I am certainly not in charge of.

"It hurts me to hear your stories," says Lucy. We all turn to face her. Her full cheeks are pinker than usual. She's been unusually quiet today, curled between Rubina and Jimena like a cat. She closes her eyes now as a cool breeze waves through the room.

"I was held captive too," she says. "By someone I knew and trusted."

Shailee starts to translate again, now from English to Nepali.

"I was too trusting, maybe," says Lucy.

"You were only sixteen," says Jimena.

"My little sister had an older boyfriend. One day one of his friends told her that he'd take me and my younger brother to school. He dropped my brother at middle school but then took me to a strange house somewhere and raped me. He kept me there overnight. It was so dark I couldn't tell where I was. He told me that he'd kill me if I tried to run or if I ever told my family. Then the next day he took me home like he was the one who had found me. Everyone was there waiting with the police. They were all worried to death, but I told on him. After that, my family sent me back home to Mexico to get therapy. When I returned to the States—my mom was still living in San Francisco—she and I did not get along. We fought all the time because I felt like she chose boyfriends over my siblings and me. Sometimes she left for long periods of time. So I started to leave too. When I was in high school, before I dropped out, I lived between her house, shelters, and the streets."

She stops to draw a long breath, and Shailee launches into translation for the Nepali girls, who sit with arms crossed, waiting patiently.

"Shailee!" I hold up my Nalgene. "You need water?"

"I'm okay."

"You sure?" asks Lucy.

"Sure," says Shailee. "You should know by now I'm part camel. Makes me excellent at my job."

"That explains it," Lucy quips dryly.

"Go on, go on," says Shailee. Even after epically long passages, she seems to catch it all. I wonder how she can carry so many words in her head all at once.

"Okay," says Lucy. "So after that, I'm living on the streets back and forth, you know. One day, walking to a friend's house to pick up some clothes, I pass a gas station, and suddenly everything goes black. I wake up in the back of a car and realize I'm in a garage. It's like two a.m. There's a clock on the wall. The same man, my sister's boyfriend's friend is there, and he keeps me in the garage for a week with no food or bathroom. Instead of figuring out an escape plan, like you all did"—she gestures to Rubina and Shreya—"I kept trying to understand why this was happening to me."

Jimena drapes an arm around Lucy's shoulder.

"I knew that week was my brother's birthday, and I asked the man if I could use his phone to text him happy birthday. Instead, I texted my friend and told her to call the police. I deleted the message, but when the man took the phone back, he saw my friend answer *"WHAT?!"* He beat me so hard that when the cops showed up, I was crumpled and bloody on the ground. But still alive. I was alive. He got deported back to Mexico for what he did, but they never charged him. Then a couple years ago I found out he's back in San Francisco. It's scary to live in the same city as him. To know he's out there. But he's not taking my life away from me. I'm the oldest of three, and I have to be a role model for my younger sister and brother. I lived on the street all through my teen years, you know, but now I have my own place and just signed up for community college. I'm doing justice work. *Social justice entrepreneur.* That's my destiny."

"And you're going to do it," says Jimena. "You already are."

"I wanted to come on this trip because Everest sounded epic," says Lucy. "Magical. Just the training to get here was the hardest thing I've ever done. Well, the hardest thing, physically. But I haven't given up. And that's because of you all."

Tears roll down her cheeks as Rubina wraps her in a hug. Shailee translates the rest of the story for the Nepali girls, and as she finishes, I see Ehani is crying and Shreya is sniffling, trying to keep her composure.

From our first meeting, Lucy and I had bonded instantly. We were both immigrants and understood something unspoken about each other's stubbornness, about talking smack to mask the pain, but Lucy had never shared her story in full detail with me. I'm stunned. Even while she complained and struggled, her jovial nature has been a bright light on the trip—her quick wit and boisterous sarcasm, her warmth, her endless grab bag of one-liners. Hearing her story now, my affection for her blooms into something fully maternal. I want to mother her through and after this. I want to be by her side after the trek is over.

Ehani looks thoughtful. "We have power to hold people accountable," she says. "Our case showed me that. The man who we charged, he was evil and feared everywhere. He ran one of the biggest trafficking rings in Nepal. Hundreds of thousands of women. But with Shakti's help, us six young women got him sentenced to 170 years in prison. No one in Nepali history ever heard of a sentence like that. Back home, in our region, the people still talk, you know. They'll call us *stupid girls*. Say we'll be killed."

"But the ringleader died already," says Rubina. "In jail. His partner escaped, though, and they still haven't found him."

"We don't worry about him anymore," says Shreya.

"Nope," Rubina says, shrugging and stone-faced. "If we find him, we'll just beat him to death."

Jimena starts to laugh.

"I'm sorry," Jimena says. "Holy shit. I'm sorry. I'm still trying to process it all. What incredible stories, wow. I just, I was laughing because I was part of a radical feminist group in college that did that. A group of Black and Brown women, a few Asian women—none of us had been believed about our assaults so we all banded together. We knew a girl who was raped, and we literally went to the guy's house and beat his ass."

"Hoooo!" says Shreya, nodding her approval. "Queens."

"Have you heard of the Gulabi Gang?" asks Jimena.

"Gulabi?" Ehani speaks to Shreya in Nepali.

"They fight all in pink?" asks Shreya.

"Yes, yeah," says Jimena. "Over in India. Anyhow, that reminds me of them. What you said reminds me of them. We protect us."

"We protect us," repeats Shreya.

The charge in the room is palpable.

"As for my story," says Jimena, a faraway look on their face. "Sometimes it's hard for me to remember what's real and what's not. Because it happened for so long. It happened for a long time . . . I tried to speak up. But in my world, male comfort was valued above the safety of women."

The circle is a chorus of nods and murmurs of *yessss*.

The price women pay for male comfort is not confined to one country or culture.

"I was raised by two mothers," Jimena goes on. "Lesbians. One of them, my bio mom, the one who gave birth to me—that's what they call it, a bio mom—was disowned by her own mother for being gay. My grandmother, a staunch Catholic Mexicana, didn't talk to her for like twenty-five years. You'd think after going through that, my mom would be more caring. You would think she would have listened more. But you know, trauma begets trauma begets trauma."

As Shailee translates that last part, Ehani's eyebrows lift and she nods slowly, emphatically, in agreement.

"My mothers split when I was eight. My bio mom moved us back into my grandmother's house. The one she hadn't talked to in twenty-five years. There were nine of us kids: my mom had foster kids—not sure what you call that in Nepal? And we were all living in a two-bedroom mobile home in a Latino neighborhood in Southern California. The first time my step-grandfather abused me, I told my mother, who told my abuela, and they were both like *shh shh shh*. They hushed me because they didn't want to make any problems. He would come to me while my little sister was sleeping right next to me. I was terrified. When I was younger, I remember being able to easily disassociate—to really detach and float away from my own body."

I shiver. I remember that feeling too.

The feeling of being both the balloon floating away and the little girl crying as the balloon slips out of her hands.

"One day," Jimena continues, "we were having a yard sale, and my mom sold all my stuffed animals because she needed money. She told me to go inside and get change for a customer. My step-grandfather was in there, and he pulled me to a corner and abused me right there, in the middle of the day, while everyone was outside slinging old T-shirts and toys. I didn't get the change for my mom, but something did change. Afterward, I burst out of the trailer and started to run, screaming out to my mom. In front of me there was a white light, and I ran toward it and saw my mother fly past in the other direction. She ran back into the house, grabbed a knife, and went after him, while I fell to the ground crying. All I could think was, 'I'm responsible for this. For all this chaos.'"

Jimena told us that when the cops came later, two white men, Jimena's mother was nowhere to be found. Left alone to answer leading questions from the police, Jimena was so clear and succinct about what had happened that the police didn't believe the story.

"I've always been too articulate to be believed," says Jimena, their face hardening.

Ehani turns to Shailee and whispers in Nepali before looking back to Jimena.

"Ehani says it's incredible that these same problems happen in America," says Shailee.

"We thought everyone there was blonde and beautiful and happy," Shreya adds, laughing.

Jimena and Lucy cackle, shaking their heads. "Not at all."

"You know, Ehani," I say, smiling to myself, "I used to think the same thing."

"After I let go of my body for so long," says Jimena, "I had to bring it back. It's a process of resensitizing. Now, sometimes I'm extra sensitive to everyone in the room. That's why you might notice I get real quiet. I don't like to say I'm healing because that would mean I've been broken. And I'm not. I'm trying to transcend the trauma. For a long time, I trashed my body. Treated it like I'd been treated. But this trip is changing things for me," says Jimena. "Breaking down some barriers. Like Lucy said, I've been through so much worse mentally, emotionally, even physically, than this." Jimena looks at me accusingly. "But this—this trip right here—is the hardest thing I ever *chose* to do physically."

I grin.

"And I think there's something to that," says Jimena. "Those other things happened to my body. I didn't get to choose them."

Ehani gestures to Shailee to translate as she starts to speak in Nepali.

"When I was living at Shakti and trying to go back to school, I had this friend at work," says Ehani. "He was the only one who helped me. He became the brother that my blood brother no longer wanted to be. We used to listen to this popular Thursday radio show. The host always said: 'Nothing you do is small. Everything begins from there.'"

"Ah!" says Shailee. "I love that." She slowly repeats in English: "Nothing we do is small!"

"That's it!" I say, throwing back my covers and pumping my fists into the air like we just discovered the cure for cancer. Ehani has said exactly what I couldn't find the words for.

Nothing we do is small.

At the beginning of our trip, back at Shakti, Jimena said sisterhood isn't an idea. It's an action.

A force created by everyone in the room.

Now I know what they meant.

We fall into a huddle and repeat it aloud together—*Nothing we do is small!*—a tangle of voices and laughter, tears streaming down our faces, until it becomes a chant, a battle cry.

The room is purified. Like freshly washed air after a violent storm.

I exhale all my deadline stress and gulp down this new air. I glance at my watch. *Wow.* Five hours have passed. Dr. Jackie will be waiting for us.

"Dinnertime?" I say.

Everyone nods, then slowly slips out of the cocoon, shakes out their legs, and gathers their water bottles and coats. The girls shuffle out of the room arm in arm, and I hang back to close the windows. As I linger at the window, I take in the landscape. Periche sits at the flat bottom of a great bowl, a frozen lunar tundra surrounded by a ring of serrated peaks. Outside, smoke slithers from the chimneys of municipal-looking stone buildings and hangs there like skywriting, like a half-formed message. The Himalayas are no longer distant. We're inside of them. The sun is just starting to set in a way that backlights Lobuche's profile in the window frame, and beyond that, Everest. I realize that she has been there the whole time. Watching through the window, quietly listening to our stories, absorbing the shadows of our lives. Chomolungma is a part of our circle.

The Mother of the World stands witness where our own mothers could not. A huge smile creeps over my face, and I feel a jolt of confidence.

We're all going to be okay. We're all going to make it.

* * *

I have to get to the Everest puja. It's a mandatory ceremony for everyone attempting the summit. A lama will guide the ceremony, asking the mountain for permission to climb and giving offerings in exchange for her blessing and protection. My whole team is already at Base Camp, getting to know each other and the other teams attempting Everest this season.

I didn't think my hike with the girls would overlap with my summit bid. We were supposed to be done already. Resting easy at Base Camp. I imagined bringing them with me to witness the epic puja before their hike back. But if this trip has taught me anything, it's that everyone moves at their own pace, and we are still two days away from Base Camp. For me, today, that means double time, whatever-it-takes-to-make-the-puja time. The girls encourage me to go on ahead and promise to make their way slowly with Shailee and Asha leading them to our next stop at Gorak Shep only a mile away, while I trek the five hours to Base Camp in time for the puja. Afterward I'll hike back to meet them in Gorak Shep so we can hike the final stretch to Base Camp together.

I figure it'll be easy to spot the puja ceremony, but when I come huffing up the final hill, sweaty and panicked, I'm stunned. Base Camp is enormous. I've never seen it during summit season when all the climber camps and service tents are set up. It's the size of a small shantytown, like one of the settlements up in the cerros surrounding Lima.

"You'll see us," Anthea, the Adventure Consultants Base Camp manager, had told me. "We'll have a large blue tarp and five yellow tents clustered together."

There are blue tarps everywhere.

And at the edge of the rocky barren landscape, hundreds of bright-yellow tents swarm together like bees.

In the center of the small village, wide snowy lanes are lined with house-shaped tents marked "Dining" and "Technology." There are toilet tents and recreation tents, long tubular red-and-white ER tents, and geodesic-dome tents, for what, I'm not sure. A thousand people set up temporary homes here, training, ascending, descending, and waiting for their perfect summit window. As I look around, what I'm about to do finally hits me.

This is going to be my home for the next six weeks.

I shake the thought away.

First things first. Find the puja.

I rush toward the center of the makeshift village and ask climbers in slick North Face coats if they know where the main puja is, but all I get are confused looks. A helicopter hovers over the helipad, its propellers slicing the air, whipping my hair across my face. Everything is so high-tech and outfitted. It's a shock after hiking with our low-key group eating simple meals focused on healing and connection, on putting one foot in front of the other. Finally a guide stops and explains that each expedition team has their own puja, and I have to find my group. He points out the Adventure Consultants camp.

"Wayyyy back there," he says. "Just follow the trail for another thirty minutes or so."

Shit.

I hoped our camp would be close to the main entrance. Half running down the trail, I'm annoyed, more at myself than anything. I hopscotch over an icy rock and topple to the right, catching my balance just in time but tweaking my ankle a bit. My anger drains as I force myself to slow down. Weaving my way through the sea of yellow, I jump carefully from rock to rock, focused on staying upright and ignoring the hulking glaciers in my peripheral vision. I still can't see the end of camp.

But just ahead I see a perimeter of men.

I trudge forward. When I get closer, ten look-alike Western climbers outfitted in Patagonia and North Face sit on a neon orange tarp in front of a stone altar draped with silken images of Buddhist gods. And beyond that, a shimmering glacial bowl rises from the valley into a piercingly clear blue sky. In front of the altar, Ang Dorjee stands center stage next to the lama, who's already in the middle of a chant. Standing next to him is a tall white man in Ray-Bans. It's Mike—the leader of my expedition. Tibetan prayer flags flap in the wind above them. A semicircle of about fifty Sherpas and Nepali men stand surrounding the seated group. Besides Anthea and Lydia and a couple of other Western-looking women sitting in chairs behind the tarp, the Sherpas, kitchen staff, rope staff, climbers, and doctors are mostly men. There must be eighty people in the Adventure Consultants expedition team, all here to attend the puja.

I feel their eyes on me—the disrespectfully late foreigner—as I try to sneak in silently, but still panting after my marathon trek.

There's an empty cushion one row behind Anthea. As I sit, the chill of the frozen ground underneath the cushion seeps through my pants. A young Sherpa brings over a small blue stool and motions for me to sit.

It's kind, but I don't want any attention or special treatment. I just got here, and you're giving me a chair? Just because I'm a woman, I'm sure. I don't need a chair.

I smile politely, mouth *namaste*, and set the chair next to me.

At the center of the altar is a stone firepit full of fresh pine branches. As they burn, thick clouds of herbal smoke whip around our heads. The Sherpas chant, scooping handfuls of dry rice from a plate to throw into the fire. Looking around, I see some buff-looking white guys sitting on stools, and I decide if they can do it, then I won't look weak if I also take a seat for a bit.

For the next ninety minutes, I'm lost. I chant along and follow orders to *eat this* or *drink that*, consuming a wild mix of tea, cookies, butter, chocolate, and Sprite. It's like a college-kids Eucharist. I'm so wired and blissed out that when the man sitting next to me passes the final offering, I almost take it down immediately. But then I look down into a container of amber liquid. Its sweet, oaky smell unmistakable. Whiskey. I haven't had a drink in two months, but I'm afraid to skip any of the blessings. I need Mother Everest 100 percent on my side, and if the lama tells me I need this to get my blessing, who am I to argue? If it's for sacred purposes, it doesn't count. I chug down a fiery shot before I can think anymore. The familiar burn sears my throat. The tips of my ears tingle. A flush of liquid bliss.

Flour begins to rain down from the sky. Sherpas are winding through the crowd scooping it into the hands of all the climbers. I cup my hands together ready to receive communion. A weathered man fills them. I toss the flour into the air, and the wind whips it back into my jacket. Sherpas and climbers start to hug their neighbors and smear flour over each other's faces, a Sherpa tradition to express hope that we would live until our hair and beards turn white.

Holy water, Ash Wednesday, the offerings of peace to the neighbor.

Peace be with you.

Ghost faced with flour, I rush over to introduce myself to Mike, then try to namaste my way out of there. As I'm walking away, I hear Mike call over the chatter, "Okay everyone, dinner in an hour." My head snaps back, but no one's watching me go. Instead, they linger near Mike, chatting easily like old friends.

As I hike back down the rocky trail, golden moonlight creeps up the face of Nuptse. Tonight is my last night with our little family—the eve of fulfilling the promise I made to the mountain ten years ago—and the taste is bittersweet. On one hand, I'm filled with joy about the fierce team of young warriors who trusted me enough to come on this journey with me, and I can't wait to see their faces when they reach Base Camp. For Ehani, Shreya, and Rubina, it's a pilgrimage. Like Peruvians going to Machu Picchu.

On the other hand, I'm devastated that I have to let them go, passing the baton to Shailee and Asha to get the girls back down the mountain. I assumed that if I kept my part of the bargain and got everyone to the mountain, somehow Everest would take care of the healing. But listening to them air the most painful and shameful parts of their stories, not in the dark corner of a club, or at the bottom of a bottle, but in the light of day, was humbling. That they could sit in the truth of each other and themselves and not try to pretty it up or hurry it up or drink it down or work it away, it was clear they already had the power I dreamt this hike would instill.

Their stories showed me how small and tidy my conception of healing had been.

This whole time I've been preaching the gospel of matriarchy, of women power, but at some point I'd stopped seeing myself as a fellow survivor. Managing the group instead as an outside force, making sure we met our hiking goals, strong-arming us into catharsis. I pushed them in the way that I've pushed myself. Like a father might.

All I know is how to push.

It's how I've survived, and I always thought that surviving was the point.

If I survive, then I've conquered my past.

If I could live through J, make it to America, and become successful there, then I was fine. But surviving doesn't mean you're okay. It doesn't mean you're better. It just means you're alive. Functioning, even functioning well, is not healing, just like hoarding blessings and calling this hike a healing journey doesn't make it one.

It was they—the courageous girls—doing the vulnerable work of telling their stories that made it true. The vulnerability they displayed is something I didn't have at their age.

Maybe I still don't.

Suddenly, I feel a sharp rumble in my gut. A familiar ominous gurgle.

No, no, no, no. Not now, please! Not now.

My stomach has been so well behaved this entire hike. But now it's churning with Sprite and whiskey and tea. As I run down the trail, looking for a tucked-away spot to squat, I give thanks to my father, Segundo, who, if nothing else, taught me to always carry a roll of toilet paper.

In Peru, toilet paper was seen as a Western luxury, which my father was committed to aligning himself with. He kept a roll in his car at all times. I still keep one in all my bags, a tic I'm grateful for as I'm forced, after all the blessings and breakthroughs of the last day, to run to the side of the mountain and deal with my shit.

Chapter 10

⬦⬦⬦⬦

PERUVIAN COWGIRL
WITH NO PAST

It was the summer of 2002, and I was fishing. My early days of not knowing how to make a move were over. The catch of the day varied. Preferably she was tall and uber-feminine—everything I was not—but the specs went down as the night went on.

Club Q had shut down the year before, but hip new higher-end spots were opening all the time. Powerful art-and-tech-world lesbians were flocking to Mecca, a chic new restaurant on the corner of Market Street and Dolores that drew a lot of buzz for its grandeur. Betty Sullivan, a prominent LGBTQ+ entrepreneur, launched Ladies Night on Thursdays as a social gathering for gay professional women. It was the perfect pilgrimage for my conquests.

Mecca had a swanky circular bar that was always packed by eight p.m. It had a tucked-away lounge area with buttery brown leather booths—the perfect low-lit nook to exercise my newfound bravado. Thursdays not only guaranteed a catch but often set me up to eat all weekend.

I rarely brought them back to my apartment. Staying at theirs contained any morning-after disasters. When hungover and disoriented in a strange bed, I'd run through my own version of a Byron Katie checklist.

a) *Am I dead?* No, next.
b) *Am I in a hospital?* If so, where are my clothes? If no, next.

c) *Am I in my own bed?* If so, you struck out, loser. If no, next.

d) *Whose bed* am *I in?* Doesn't matter. Get up, get your shit, and get out.

In the harsh light of day, the smoky eye and red lip had all worn off, and the carnal desire that drove a night of already forgotten passion was replaced by the awkwardness of smelling a stranger's morning breath. Our clothes, stripped off in a fury, sat crumpled in a sad pile on the floor, and I'd feel desperate and dingy as I hopped up and pulled my jeans on.

"I have to run, but I'll see you around," I'd say, pulling a crumpled shirt over my head and darting out the front door before she could rope me in with breakfast or questions about my childhood.

Vulnerability, it turned out, was highly overrated. I'd shed my past like a snakeskin and become someone new once again. Someone stoic and sexy. Someone impossible to know.

The Peruvian cowgirl with no past.

Back home, I'd strip down and hop in the shower for my morning-after ablutions, scrubbing every inch of sin from my body and washing my hair twice for good measure. I was working incredibly long hours on the new merger between SKYY and Campari when the strangest thing started to happen. My hair, which had always been thick and straight, started to grow out in ringlets. Not just waves, but Shirley Temple curls. And with them came an unexplainable sense of virility.

A modern-day Samson, I discovered new strength in my hair, letting my curls grow and making note to avoid any woman named Delilah.

Everyone else, though, was fair game. I was out every weekend, sleeping with someone new each night. If I didn't, I had failed.

My plan was to sleep with a hundred people. I didn't fail.

I had threesomes.

I slept with a former boss.

I slept with straight women and gay women.

If a woman told me she was straight, I'd think to myself, "Yeah, straight to bed."

I topped everyone.

I respected no boundary. Relationships became suggestions. Permeable walls. Mine or others', it didn't matter. I slept with the partners of friends who were out of town caring for ailing parents. *Twice.*

Friends became former friends, but I marched on, chalking up the loss to well, nothing, really. I wasn't looking for answers or life lessons.

I was hunting oblivion.

And the more I hooked up, the more I wanted. I wanted to see where the edge was. I think part of me hoped I would fall right off.

* * *

My mom came to visit my half siblings and me whenever she could. My life hadn't gone like she had expected when she put me on that plane to Millersville, but she didn't know that. I hid who I had become because I knew it would disappoint her.

Secrets had become home—a warm, dark cave I could duck into, a comfortable cloak I donned to protect others. At least, that's what I told myself. But little by little, life was chipping away at my tolerance for silence.

For lies and secrets.

On my last trip to Peru, I had decided it was time to be honest with her, so I sat her down and took her hands in mine.

My plan was to tell her and then run to the airport.

"Mamita, listen to me," I said. "I know you won't approve, but I need to tell you something. I have a girlfriend." I didn't have a girlfriend, so I guess I wasn't completely done with lies, but I figured that was easier than telling her I had committed to sleeping with a hundred women.

She stared into my eyes for what felt like forever and then slowly shook her head no.

"But there are so many good men. You will find a nice man."

I had loved men back when I didn't know that loving women was an option—when I still believed that being gay was a choice.

Tears pooled along the rims of her eyes, but she didn't let them fall. Not yet.

"You're killing me, my daughter. No tengo palabras."

Her eyes were heavy with disappointment.

"It's not a choice, Mamita." I could hear my voice break.

We'd lost so much; we couldn't lose each other.

"Oh, Silvita. It's me who has no choice, you see? How can I make you see that what you are doing is wrong? I took care of J so you could have your life back. You don't have to make this choice."

"What are you saying?"

"You know, I called J to the house, and Meche and I, she helped me, we tied him to a chair. Then I filled the big pot with water and set it to heat. And when it was boiling over, I carried it to J and poured it over him, nice and slow."

I was shocked. Why had she never told me this?

"You see, J has no more power over you," she said. "You don't have to be afraid of men." The tears she had been holding back rolled slowly down her cheeks.

It was true that I was terrified of men. My father, J, the Latin machismo I'd watched squash so many of the women in my family. Memories of men hurting me were in my earliest consciousness, but that's not why I loved who I loved.

I didn't love women because of J.

I loved women in spite of J.

"I'm sorry, Mamita, that doesn't change anything."

She gasped at the strength in my voice and then stared into my eyes for a long time, saying nothing. Finally she pulled her hands out of mine and used them to smooth down her hair and wipe her eyes.

"I have to accept you as you are because you're my daughter." She pulled me in for a hug, her perfume flooding my senses. "And I love you."

"I love you too, Mamita."

Her voice dropped to a whisper. "Please, hijita, just don't tell anyone else. Especially your father."

* * *

After coming out to my mom, I moved to the Marina District in San Francisco to be closer to work. While unpacking at my new place, I came across a picture of me in my first-grade classroom at María Reina school.

In the photo I'm wearing an ill-fitting turquoise Lycra tracksuit, which meant it was sports day. A Thursday. I remembered that day well. It was the day of our annual Christmas picture, and preparations for our annual nativity scene were in full swing. All the first graders were assigned to a table group with twenty other kids—my table was 1B. We sprinkled crayon homes with imagined snowflakes and turned strips of red velvet into crooked top hats. I hummed with holiday cheer as I cut rectangles of blue construction paper into clouds and piled gluey balls of cotton into the shape of a snowman. We were crafting a Christmas we'd never seen. One from American movies; one of reindeer and snowmen and the characters from *White Christmas*; of Santa Claus on a sleigh with his big belly bringing joy to all the good kids. We went to Mass and hung sparkling decorations and sang and chomped on Lentejas, Peruvian M&Ms, but snow was something we could only imagine.

Christmas in Peru, in the Southern Hemisphere, was always sunny.

We'd never even seen snow.

My mother came early to make sure the photos went well.

"Look at the camera and smile," cooed the photographer. But I didn't want to smile. I was missing my front teeth, and plus, what did I have to smile about? I was uncomfortable in my own body. The Lycra felt slimy against my skin. The top was just a little too tight and short.

And how could I smile when I never knew what was waiting for me at home?

All I could manage was a weak smirk. The beginning of putting on a happy face.

"Next!" called the photographer.

Alone in my empty apartment in San Francisco, surrounded by boxes and half-empty bottles of SKYY, I turned the photo over and saw the date written in my mother's loopy handwriting: October 1981.

God, I hated that tracksuit. That stupid smirk on my face. That little girl was weak. Afraid of everything. Powerless. Pathetic. I wanted to shred the picture, but I couldn't bring myself to tear her face in two. So I buried her instead. Deep in a box in a dark corner on the top shelf of the hall closet.

I buried her again and again, night after night, in a coffin made of SKYY blue bottles.

* * *

I woke to a banging at the door. Sun spilled in from the bay window. My head throbbed. Those last three shots of 1800 tequila hadn't settled well. My stomach cramped with hunger pains. I'd come home ravenous the night before. Oh, I made chicken! Maybe there were leftovers. Did I make the chicken? I remembered the icy breath of the freezer as I opened it to pull out a bag of frozen thighs. I set them in the sink to defrost. Turned on the stove. But I didn't remember eating them.

"SILVIA!" Fists pounded hard against my front door. The inside of my skull was a throbbing cavern. Every sound a terror train. "Open the fucking door!"

Oh shit. Shit.

When I stood, the pain throttled me so hard I almost collapsed. I stumbled toward the front door, passing through the kitchen. Something smelled off. Scorched. A rotten, ashy scent. Long splinters of wood hung from the doorjamb, as if it had been busted open. I braced against the frame to guard myself from a flying fist, a boot, an arrest warrant. The morning after, I never knew what was coming for me. I tried to run through the highlights, but it was all a blur.

I turned the handle, praying for salvation, which would have been a gallon of water and a quick slip to my death off the fire escape out back. Standing in the hall, his teeth clenched so tight it looked like he was fighting off a smile, was Sy, my second floor neighbor.

"What the hell happened," screamed Sy.

I drew a blank.

His face was terrifying.

"You should be ashamed of yourself," he yelled. "You could have killed us all. You could have killed Mrs. Lueck." Mrs. Lueck owned the building's three units, but I never saw her because she was in her early nineties. Sy and his wife owned an Italian restaurant in North Beach and managed the apartments for her.

He handed me a folded piece of paper with EVICTION stamped in red at the top.

"The firefighters had to break down the door because they couldn't wake you up," he said. Somewhere in the foggy recesses of my memory I saw a man checking my pulse, trying to hold me upright, and me falling back into bed. "You have forty-five days."

"Sy!" I called, but he was already gone.

This was my third eviction.

Clasping the notice in my hands, I walked toward the scene of the crime. The hood above the stove was coated with an oily black residue. In the pot, the chicken had gone charcoal. Coughing, I tossed the whole thing in the trash, then sank down to the floor, the linoleum cool against my feverish skin.

I didn't have a drinking problem.

It was just that drinking sometimes caused problems.

I would cut back. Steer clear of hard liquor. That's where the real issues came in. No more shots or cocktails. Just a few beers here and there. A nice glass of red.

* * *

SKYY's annual sales meeting was scheduled for mid-July. We'd added more brands to our portfolio, and this year was going to be our biggest yet. Teams flew in from around the country, and after long days of meetings in our flashy new conference rooms, we'd gather for a pre-toast. After dinner, the late-night crew would regroup for a stop at AsiaSF, or the Gold Club, San Francisco's infamous strip bar. Finally, we'd close out the evening with a nightcap back at the office bar or at the Marriott Fisherman's Wharf, where most of the out-of-towners were staying.

My libido had gotten out of control. Getting wasted no longer fed the beast; it wanted more. I had to get laid every night. I was like a just-add-water sex fiend. But my water was booze, and the more I drank, the hornier I got, and the more sex I had, the more I needed. It was just a phase, I told myself. A delayed adolescence. A sexual coming-out. The more sex I had, the more validated I felt. I was living out the male energy inside me. The machismo. The conqueror.

No one can take anything from you if you take it first.

After three drinks, I was reckless. As people paired off for the night, I'd panic, scanning the club, bar, dinner table, whatever, for someone to leave with. By the time last call came and my drink was empty, it didn't matter who it was.

SKYY's sales and marketing reps were gorgeous. Models hired from promo firms, they used their sex appeal to get our products the best placements. All the sloppy straight guys hit on them relentlessly, but I didn't have the guts, so I drooled in secret. My San Francisco team finally knew I was gay, but I'd never been with a woman in front of them. The national team in town were mostly Republican men from the Midwest who were incredibly vocal about their conservative views. A real "family values" crew.

My job was the only thing going right, and I was determined to keep climbing the chain of command. I wasn't going to do anything to give them something to use against me. Besides, I didn't want to make the women uncomfortable. Men ogling them was one thing, but I wasn't about to be branded the lesbian creep.

The last night of the sales conference we were back at the Marriott. Everyone was sloppy drunk. Diehards lined up at the bar bellowing for one final shot. Others flashed not-so-subtle looks at each other and slipped away to their rooms. My last-call panic button had activated, and for some reason it pushed me toward Nick, a senior executive. Nick often brought his girlfriend along to company events. But she wasn't there that night. As a group of us left the bar, swerving down the thick carpeted hallway, I hung back and whispered into his ear: "Nick, I want one last drink in your room."

He looked at me, his blue eyes wide with surprise. "Sure," he said, a smirk growing on his face. "Come on."

Inside his master suite, the bar was stacked. We pounded a couple of twenty-dollar tequila shots and I transformed. In seduction mode, I became someone else entirely. A serpentine force guided my hands over his body, our mouths to each other, forked tongues lapping. All the restraint I exercised in my work life was obliterated when desire took over. I craved something rough, and I thought Nick would give it to me.

That night, though, my fantasy didn't play out as erotic and rowdy as I'd hoped. Between Nick's out-of-shape body and our excessive drinking, we fondled each other for a bit before passing out naked under the crisp white duvet. The coolness of the sheets soothed the heat of my skin enough for me to sleep.

When I woke, the duvet was still covering the lower part of my face, but I felt a strange ache between my legs like the dull pressure of pushing in a small, dry tampon. My eyes were gluey, heavy. Breathing slowly to steady my heart rate, I ran through my usual post-drinking checklist.

Dead? *Nope.* Hospital? *Too quiet.* My own bed? I ran my hands over the sheets. *No, too crisp.* Whose bed? *Time to go.*

I wrenched my eyes open, and the room swiveled as I peered out through lowered lids. Light flashed and beamed through the bare window. The blinds had never been drawn. Woozy, I blinked the sun away, and as I looked back to the bed, I was startled to see Nick on top of me. *Nick?* Nick! Shit. What was happening? He was rocking slowly and moaning. He'd pushed the duvet up from the bottom of the bed just enough to enter me. "Urghhhh, urghh, uhh," he grunted, as if trying to set the mood. It took a while to figure out what was happening, because even though it looked like he was having sex with me, I could hardly feel him. My body was numb, still half-dead from the night before. But I didn't remember Nick beginning to kiss me or trying to seduce me into morning sex. I guess he figured last night's *yes* was enough.

Oh God, was he using protection?

Clenching my fists, I choked down a scream. I wanted to slap him away, but it was Nick, the executive Nick, the senior executive Nick, so I lay there, praying for it to stop. Waiting for the sound of the garage door opening. Waiting to hear my mother's shoes tapping against the glossy wooden floors of home. Waiting for him to jump off me as she called out, "Silvia! I brought something home for you. Silvita!"

"Silvia? Silvia!"

"Huh? What?!" Nick was sitting next to me, looking sated. His bloodshot eyes scanned my face.

"I said, 'Can I do anything for you?'"

His raspy post-drinking voice grated across my skin. "Can I get you anything?" He winked.

"A new life!" I wanted to scream.

All the times I'd had sex, which by then was more than I could count or remember, there had always been consent. Even during my two years running around town like some sort of sexual conquistadora, there had always been consent. I'd wanted to be topped, but my fantasy of a lusty, passionate affair had turned into a nightmare, a one-night stand gone all wrong.

Nick was untouchable; I was replaceable.

The shame descended on me like a storm cloud.

I'd put myself in this situation, after all. What did I expect? I thought again about the woman from *The 700 Club*. *I am trash. I am nothing.* She was right. But this time, my mother wouldn't chase me to the rooftop and hold me tight. I was alone. Again.

Silently, I rolled off the bed. It was Friday morning, and I had to clean up and get back to work. At SKYY, the rule of thumb was they didn't care if you partied with the owls, as long as you showed up with the early-morning chorus of the larks.

Later that day, Nick's secretary asked me if I was free to have dinner with him Friday evening. She'd booked us a great table at a hip steakhouse. Unsure how to decline and keep my job intact, I awkwardly accepted.

When I arrived, still hungover from the night before, Nick had a bottle of vintage sauvignon waiting. A true professional, I got back in the game, ordering myself Campari with a twist of orange to help me swallow the bitterness of being there. Later, I swirled and sipped the luscious red as Nick spent the evening yammering on about the challenges he and his girlfriend were having. Unprompted, he confided that he was considering separating from her, and as I savored my rare filet mignon paired with a very full second glass of wine, it became clear that he expected me to go home with him.

I politely declined.

A month later, the announcement of his engagement spread around the office.

* * *

Within two weeks, Nick was a fading memory. An old boss from SKYY invited me out to A16, a fun Italian restaurant in the Marina. I couldn't turn her down because we'd slept together a couple of months earlier, just before I was evicted. She'd never been with a woman, and I was thrilled when she confessed her attraction. Pulling a straight woman had become the ultimate coup.

As we sat at the bar laughing with the bartender, we moved through a full Italian dinner with all the boozy accoutrements—Prosecco aperitifs, two bottles of wine, a glass of 1974 Porto, and Sambuca digestifs to round out the night. Around midnight, I got a text from a friend reminding me about a new girl party in the Castro, which was just on the other side of the Marina.

We closed down A16 around one in the morning. My old boss hopped into a taxi, waving good-bye as I stumbled confidently toward my black Jetta, grinning to myself the whole way.

At first, I kept myself in check. Hands at ten and two, I came to a complete stop at every stop sign and didn't swerve too badly. But the route with the least streetlights was also the one whose notoriously steep hills were a challenge for any sober, experienced driver. For a drunk one, climbing to the top was like riding a roller-coaster car and just praying it wouldn't slip off track.

After cresting a few hills successfully, I gunned the Jetta up an almost vertical face and lost control, sideswiping a parked Muni, one of San Francisco's public buses. My front left fender smashed against the bus's rear emergency door and cracked in half, throwing me against the steering wheel. From what I could see, the bus wasn't damaged, so I floored it to the top of the hill, dragging along my fender, which was hanging sideways off the car by a thin thread of plastic.

The fender screeched and bumped along the road, but I kept going. There was no stopping now. The Castro was waiting. My catch of the day was ready to be reeled in. If evictions, multiple visits to the ER, innumerable hangovers, and a morning-after encounter that I still couldn't bring myself to call rape hadn't stopped me, a little fender bender sure wasn't going to. I cranked up Guns N' Roses on the radio. I drummed against the steering wheel, singing along through the open windows to "Welcome to the Jungle" as my car swerved and limped along, dragging the fender behind it like an amputated limb.

I slammed on the brakes at a stop sign, toppled out of the car, and ripped the dangling fender off, then sped away without looking back, trying to blend in with the night. I was dragging myself, bloody and bruised, heart numb, to the party, no matter what. But someone in the residential neighborhoods I was barreling through must have seen me, because just as I approached the intersection of Divisadero and Bush Street, spiraling blue and red lights pierced the air. "Pull the car over!" a voice demanded. "This is the San Francisco Police."

Oh God. Oh God. Shit. Fuck! Stay calm, Silvia. This isn't your first rodeo. If you play the flirty card, maybe he'll let you off with a warning.

"Ma'am, do you know you hit a parked Muni bus?" The cop leaned down to eye level, scanning the inside of my car. "That's city property, and it's a hefty crime. Also it seems that you left your fender several streets back . . ."

"Wistt all resshhhpect, zzsir," I slurred, "I don't know whawhaaaat you arrrr stalking about."

"Ma'am, I'm going to need you to step out of the vehicle."

With calculated control, I stepped out of the car and ran through a series of sobriety tests, passing with what I thought were flying colors. My skin was steaming, and I could smell the alcohol, but I grinned to myself, sure I'd outsmarted the cops, until suddenly I was spun around, my arms yanked behind me. My blood alcohol level was 0.28, the officer told me. Almost four times the legal limit.

It'd been a long time, if ever, since I had thought of my life as valuable, but I'd never set out to put others in danger. I'd been so terrified of the melodramatic *700 Club* prophecy that I tried to outrun it, reasoning that if my life looked respectable enough from the outside, it didn't matter what I did behind closed doors or in the smoky corners of clubs or the sanctioned sloppiness of booze-industry events. Even as I spiraled out of control, I clung to my fancy job and flashy life as proof that I'd beat out destiny. But my pain had simply adapted to its environment. I wasn't selling myself for money, but I whored myself each night to the bottle. Somewhere beneath the haze of booze, anger and shame, my shadow had morphed into a snake. And it was eating me from the inside out.

As I felt the cuffs tighten and click shut around my wrists, a sigh of relief slipped out. Finally.

I needed to be stopped.

Chapter 11

❦

WALKING TOGETHER

"Silvia, can I come in?"

"Of course," I say, as Lucy pushes open the door to the room I'm sharing with Shailee. Teahouse rooms are all pretty much the same—plywood walls, wooden twin beds draped in shawl-like blankets. Maybe a small window hung with frilly handmade curtains. This morning, I'm soaking in every detail.

It's my last day in a real room for the next six weeks.

"I want to give you something," says Lucy, pulling out a little fabric doll dressed in indigenous clothing, her hair in two long ponytails. It looks like the dolls sold at Andean craft markets in Peru.

"This is from my town in Mexico," she says. "I've had it since I came to the United States, and it gave me protection. I want you to keep it while you continue your journey."

"Wow, Lucy. Thank you. This means the world to me," I reply, holding back tears as I tuck the doll into the front pouch of my pack next to my pictures and the extra toilet paper.

"We're leaving soon," I say, burying a cascade of emotion with the day's logistics. "Get your things ready. And please, please, before we go, drink at least two liters of lukewarm water. Add the powdered Gatorade for extra hydration. Pass the order along!"

Lucy snickers. "Yes, Mom."

"I'm not kidding," I say, nodding with a grimace. "It's not over yet!"

Today is our shortest hiking day. Yesterday, I had trekked the same route to the puja and was happy to see how short the final stretch was. But it isn't easy or straightforward. It's a pencil-thin rocky trail of constant zigs and zags and switchbacks pushing past screed and up and down hills laced with ice and snow. With the elevation, the icy weather, and the treeless rocky terrain, this is the point of no return. All trappings of permanent civilization are gone.

We're deep in the belly of the wild.

Waiting in front of Buddha Lodge in Gorak Shep, the team is bundled in ski parkas and buffs, beanies and thick gloves, insulated snow pants over layers of long underwear. The thermometer reads –5 degrees Fahrenheit. Rubina's and Ehani's lips are tinted an icy bluish purple. Antarctica must have primed my blood, because I'm surprisingly comfortable. At the end of last year, I spent three weeks climbing Vinson Massif, the continent's tallest mountain. At the summit, the temperature averaged –28 degrees Farenheit with the wind chill. I battled the cold and high winds and faced the steepest ice wall I had ever seen. I'd never been so cold in my life, but all of that prepared me for the summit attempt ahead. I had to believe I was ready.

"Base Camp, here we come!" Asha shouts, taking the lead. Jimena follows, and Shreya keeps pace behind them alongside Dr. Jackie, who's taking it slow. Her altitude sickness is better this morning, but Acute Mountain Sickness is a higher risk at this altitude, and it can kick in suddenly. Sometimes tragically.

Shailee falls into step with Lucy, chatting away, and Ehani and Rubina walk slowly behind them, with me bringing up the rear. We have only two miles left, and I want to savor every step. To commit the swing of their arms and the melodic thud of their steps to memory, so that when they're gone I can remember this moment when we were almost there, but not quite. When the worst was behind us and the peak just ahead. Getting up each day to do nothing but walk has been a special kind of prayer. Gradually, the outside world has slipped away as we settled into rising with the sun, slurping morning mugs of warm water and endless bowls of stinky garlic soup in teahouse dining rooms.

"Take your time," I say. "No rush today!"

They all pivot to look at me like I've grown a third head. Who is this slow-down-and-take-it-easy Silvia?

I'm wondering that myself.

Marching single file in silence, we navigate around boulders in our path as a huge valley opens to the right. It's like a rock quarry on the moon, all dusty and gray and spanning as far as I can see, running up to the base of the Himalayas, whose jagged icy teeth ring the horizon, wisps of clouds licking at their peaks. At 17,000 feet, all flora is stripped from the land. It's a vast, austere cathedral of stone and ice.

There's really no way to apply human scale to the Himalayas.

Zoomed out, we are specks, smaller than ants, marching toward a surreal horizon. The villages are all behind us. Other hikers are few and far between, and livestock is now sparse. Remnants of Tibetan prayer flags litter the landscape. Some are bright and new, draped around the rocks that line the path like garlands on a tree. Others flap around on the ground, sun-faded and long forgotten. The wind is a knife. Its high whistle and the swish-swish of nylon pants are the only sounds as we settle into the last stretch, surrendering ourselves to the satisfying percussion of feet on the ground.

It's taken ten days of this—of walking together, of moving our bodies in tandem, of silly jokes and small talk; of speaking our truth and not shriveling up on the spot—to walk comfortably in silence. A silence that is not lonely or pregnant with tension or fear.

An intimate, satisfied silence.

A safe space.

In the silence, I notice more, like how Rubina has been walking differently since Periche. Her shoulders, which were tucked up to her ears with tension, have dropped and broadened. She now walks with her chest high as if something has been lifted. But when I look more closely, there's something else.

She's also moving more slowly than usual, practically dragging her feet.

We're all tired.

Ehani hooks her arm through Rubina's and matches her pace.

Before we began our hike, I asked everyone to pick a word or words they wanted to carry with them. Rubina's had been "Let go," and watching her lean on Ehani, it seems like she's done that. In Periche, when she and Shreya told us their story in tandem, I saw flashes of shame on Rubina's face. Shame for having drawn her little cousin to India. Shame that was not hers to carry. But shame is strange like that. It is voluminous. It sucks up all the air in the atmosphere, and over time it can become the very column that holds us upright. It's also the dark center that subsumes everything else, as we struggle to regenerate in spite of it, growing like a tree does around anything that cuts into its flesh, until eventually the wire, the stone, the scar, becomes part of us.

Some of us have carried shame so long, we don't know how to stand without it. When deep shame is excised, there's a hole left in its place. A raw, tender pocket that yearns to be filled. But if we can fight the urge—which, for me, is often overpowering—to fill, to bandage, to distract; to drink, smoke, overwork; to declare ourselves immediately strong and healed, then we might be finally getting somewhere.

I hope this is what we're doing for Rubina. For each other. Creating a palisade, a physical barrier with our bodies, all nine torsos, eighteen arms and legs, pushing their muscles to the max, so that she, so that whoever we hold in the center, can be soft. So that we can expose our wounds to the mountain air and let them breathe, knowing we won't be left behind.

Then, we have a chance to become truly free.

Once upon a time, we were free to swing our arms and swivel our hips. To lose our breath and find it again.

Once upon a time, this was not dangerous.

"In order to change, people need to become aware of their sensations and the way that their bodies interact with the world around them," writes van der Kolk. "Physical self-awareness is the first step in releasing the tyranny of the past."

Releasing the tyranny of the past.

I hope that's what we're doing by the simple act of walking.

* * *

Two hours in, we're only at the halfway point of a two-hour trek, but I'm not worried. We stop to regroup in the shadow of a low boulder, and Ehani leans against it, inhaling heavily through her nose and exhaling steady, serene breaths. She presses her hand to her chest as it rises and falls.

"You okay?" asks Shailee, touching her shoulder.

Ehani nods what looks like a *no*, but in Nepali means yes.

I pull out my oximeter and take her reading. Seventy-five percent oxygen saturation. Not great, but normal at this altitude. While I have the machine out, I test everyone. Ehani's is the lowest. Her chronic cough has been a knocking anxiety in the back of my mind, and late last night I heard her coughing in the teahouse. When she showed up this morning cough-free, my whole body relaxed. I didn't realize I'd been holding her like that. That I'd been holding them all, each joy and pain, in my limbs. I'd been worried about whether they'd make it and worried that they wouldn't. Worried I had pushed them too hard. Worried I hadn't pushed them enough.

"Helicopter!" shouts Rubina.

Flying low over the glaciers in the direction of Base Camp, the blades of a six-person chopper slice through the silence. It's jarring to hear a motor in the middle of this moonscape. The reality of what awaits me at Base Camp—hi-tech operating systems, elite climbers from around the world—hasn't fully hit me, and I push it away, savoring my last moments of simplicity.

Lucy pulls out her satchel of spicy Mexican candies, and everyone huddles around, clamoring to look inside and grab their new favorites.

"Pulparindo, por favor!" Jimena puts their hand out.

I stand to the side, chugging down sugary water and sucking on a Peruvian lemon candy.

As we're strapping our packs back on, a group of three older white men hike past. "Hello," they say. "Namaste," we chime, offering the customary Himalayan trail greeting.

One man stops, looking curiously down the row of us as if we're dolls on a shelf.

"Are you in some sort of a sorority?" he asks.

People aren't used to seeing so many women together. Especially not here.

"Something like that," I say, laughing, too tired to explain.

"No," Jimena interjects. "Actually, nothing like that. You ever heard of the Gulabi Gang?"

The man's eyebrows furrow as he tries to place the name.

Rubina stifles a giggle and whispers to Ehani, who clasps her hand over her mouth to stop laughter from erupting.

"What's a sorority?" asks Shreya, as the men wave and turn back to the trail.

"It's sort of a sisterhood," I say. "Some women join in college in the United States. They live together in big houses and have parties."

"Ooooh," coos Shreya. "Sounds nice."

"We're sort of like a sorority," says Lucy.

"But more badass!" says Jimena.

"Yep," says Shailee, flexing her biceps. "We're tough."

"Listen everyone," Lucy says, batting her lashes. "You can still be tough and have fake lashes, okay? That's just feminism."

"I beg your pardon," says Shailee, bowing her head.

Everyone laughs, and Lucy looks pleased with herself, as Jimena and Shreya strap on their packs and march ahead, their steps buoyant as the rest of us fall into line.

I stick to the back, watching them all. They are experienced trekkers now, with backpacks loaded with Nalgene bottles and cans of overpriced Pringles. The path is packed dirt under a thin layer of ice, and Lucy, Rubina, and Ehani struggle to stay upright, digging the points of their hiking poles into the slippery ground to hold steady. Lucy especially flounders, grabbing hold of every big rock with both of her hands. She looks back at me, and our eyes meet. Hers go soft as if to say everything is okay. That her struggle is okay. That I don't have to make it better.

I wonder if it's true. Will she be alright? Will they all?

* * *

Everest is hidden from view, but looming on the horizon are Pumori, Lingtren, and Khumbutse, a monstrous chain of peaks that adjoin it. Nestled into their bases are what look from a distance like bus-sized chunks of dingy roadside snow, all pocked with pebbles and dirt. But as we get closer, they morph from dirty white to an angelic neon blue that glows from the inside out. Glaciers.

Suddenly, we ripple to a stop like dominoes. Jimena is pointing out something in the distance to Shreya.

"What is it?" pants Lucy from the back, propping herself up with a pole.

We follow Jimena's gaze to the face of Nuptse, where two columns of milky smoke rise from the snow. Strange, I think, no one camps on that side. Thunder rumbles, and the whoosh of a jet overhead ricochets through the valley, and then, all in less than sixty seconds, it becomes clear that the columns are not smoke, but snow, and they merge and explode into a wave of white that screams down the mountain, atomic plumes of powder blooming in its wake.

"Holy shit," whispers Jimena.

"The whumpf," I gulp. My fingers go numb.

"What's the whumpf?" hisses Lucy, her chin on my shoulder. "What was that?"

"An avalanche," says Asha, stepping closer. "It's an avalanche."

"That's where you're going?" Lucy squeaks.

"Oh no, don't worry, love," Shailee says, squeezing her shoulder. "She's going somewhere much worse."

Shailee chuckles, and I laugh along, but no one catches the hollow, tinny ring—the echo of my fear.

* * *

Just ahead, a huge boulder marks the end of the trail, or what's called the bare entrance to Base Camp. To the right, over a rocky crest, I can make out the yellow tents of central camp, the bright-blue roofs of the Everest ER and the helipad, and beyond all the human operations, the icy sea of the Khumbu Glacier.

I pass to the front of the line and take the lead, showing everyone how to lean their weight into the slippery gravel hillside and navigate around the boulder to reach the bare entrance, which is pretty anticlimactic.

There's no neon sign that says YOU ARE HERE. YOU HAVE ARRIVED.

The group doesn't even realize we're done. I don't say anything. As they slip around the boulder one by one, I lean back and look up into the sky. It's a cloud dome of dramatic grays and blues. Two Himalayan griffon vultures glide above me, riding the air with little effort, scanning the ground for corpses, bones, anything to scavenge.

It feels like we could fly here, too. Like if I ran right now and launched from the edge of the rocky cliff, I could soar with the griffons.

Shreya reaches me first, and I draw her close. She pulls back, looking around, unsure what's happening, but then her head falls to my shoulder.

"Yes," I say, my voice low. "Yes. We made it."

Jimena understands right away and walks into my arms, their face scrunched with emotion.

"Yes," I repeat, channeling motherly pride.

Rubina is next. She throws her arms around us without a word.

"Yes," I whisper. "*Yes.*"

Then come Ehani and Asha and Shailee and Dr. Jackie, each stretching their arms open as wide as they can and flinging them around us to complete our nine-person hug.

"Yes, yes, YES!" I boom.

Lucy is last to make it, and in the crook of her arm, she's cradling a dark-brown teddy bear with "I Love You" embroidered in red on the belly. It's the bear her younger sister gave her. The one she clung to on our shaky flight into Lukla, while Jimena gazed out the window, their brow furrowed in permanent thought.

The sight of Lucy cradling the bear almost breaks me. She is a little girl again.

We all are.

We are six and nine and twelve and fifteen. We are waiting for a whistle to echo down the hall. We are locked in a dark room plotting our escape. Sorting through broken rice and worms for something to eat. We are floating above our bodies as our own blood betrays us. We are captive in a garage, paralyzed, wondering why—why this, why *us?*

And then—another image shines through. A little girl who clasped my hand and guided me into the mountains, who pushed me to find the others. Others whose innocence had been taken and who were ready to reclaim it.

Lucy reaches the group and flings her free arm around the cluster of bodies.

"Yes," I manage to squeak out one last time as my voice wavers.

We're one, a swaying mass of down and sweat, breathing together in short, cold spurts. I can't tell who's crying, but we all feel it, and for a moment it is all of us. I try to press this memory into me, what it feels like to be this raw, but I can't take it anymore.

"We did it!" I cry out, breaking the huddle.

"Wooo!" come the muffled cheers. "Woohoo!" "Yess!!"

But they haven't let go, and they pull me back into the huddle, holding on tight. My cheek presses against Jimena's beanie, and unplanned words tumble from my mouth.

"This is sacred, what we did," I say. "This was special, you hear me? Ask anything you want now, ask it to the mountain." I cry.

I pull back, wiping tears from my eyes. "Okay, on the count of three. What should we say?"

"Base Camp," says Rubina.

"Okay," I nod, smiling.

"One, two, three: BASE CAAAAAMP!!!"

And with that, the spell is broken. Everyone looks around at the pile of rocks, unsure what to do next. They're exhausted, and they need their energy to get back to Gorak Shep before dark, so I'm not taking them into the heart of camp. We'll say our good-byes here.

"Well, we're here," I say, laughing. "At the base of the world's tallest mountain. Can you believe it?"

"Wait, wait a minute. Pause." Jimena holds up their hand. "This is it? The tallest mountain? Like, in the entire world?"

"Yeeeeeesss?" Shreya says slowly.

"Why, you know one taller?" cracks Shailee.

"I just," says Jimena, quietly. "I don't know. I didn't realize."

"Huh?" teases Rubina. "You've just now learned that?"

"What have you been doing here, hiking to the foot of the mighty Chomolungma?" Shreya chides, playfully bowing to the ground.

Jimena hangs their head, blushing, but it reminds me that there are many ways to climb a mountain, to move through the world. An experience doesn't have to be the biggest or the best for it to change you. In a way, it had never mattered how high the peak was. They were here to traverse not a mountain, but something more abstract. The terrain of the interior.

"What now?"

"Prayer flags!" says Shailee. We dig the flags we bought in Kathmandu from our bags and climb up to a rocky ledge above, where long strands of prayer flags are strung from a boulder in all directions like the spokes of a wheel.

"What you all did was so very hard," I say. "This was not easy."

"I wanted to give up halfway," reflects Lucy. "But you all helped me keep going. I accomplished something super big."

"At the beginning of the trip, I kept saying I can't believe I'm doing this," says Jimena. "But I've stopped saying that. I *can* believe I'm doing this. In a way, I couldn't have done it without the support of you all. But at the end of the day, I got myself here. And I'm proud. I feel so powerful!" Jimena crouches down and starts to scratch something into the stone with a stick.

"I'm carrying all my siblings with me," they say. "I'm saying all their names, individually, in my head."

Gripping the strings of the flags, we begin tying them together one by one, clumsily looping the nubby thread into triple knots with frozen glove-clad fingers and pulling them tight enough to withstand the thwapping wind. "Nothing like the smell of yak poop to bring it all together," Jimena says, sniffling.

Shailee directs us in Nepali, and we all fumble and sniffle, from both tears and the cold and laughter, as we follow the Nepali girls and try to create a shape with the flags. Each of them started out with a unique constellation of pain, but as we tie one prayer flag to the next, that pain is exchanged for strength. Not the strength of muscle and relentless pushing, but the strength of tenderness, of letting go and letting others in. The flags ripple together in the icy wind, carrying our wishes and prayers to the heavens.

"Everyone has a dark room inside of them," says Rubina. "And a lot of our sisters, I see, are still in that room." She gestures to herself, Ehani, and Shreya. "For so many of us who escape, here in Nepal, the tendency is to immediately marry any man who will accept us. Men see what we've suffered as a weakness, and if any man is okay with our scarred past, women think they should just be happy. For me, the question is no more whether a man will accept me, but whether I will accept the man."

Lucy and Jimena snap their fingers, a poet's form of applause, and pat Rubina on the back.

"My past is no longer my weakness," she says.

"We just need to have a dream, and if it comes from the heart, it will happen," says Shreya. "I'm going to lead people here too, like Silvia. And then, someday, that." We turn to look as she points past Khumbutse in the direction of Everest.

That's the spirit that got her out of India. Both she and Rubina.

Rubina's eyes soften as she looks at her cousin.

"And you will, my Shreya. I believe you will."

* * *

Reaching Base Camp means something different for each of us, but for the women from Nepal, it's more than a spiritual healing journey or a test of physical endurance. It's an achievement that most of their peers will never have the chance to pursue.

"I came on this trip because I knew it was a chance for growth," says Ehani. "That's what I want. Always. Just to grow. Last year I got married, and in my prenup I told my future husband this marriage would happen only on one condition: that I can continue to do whatever I want."

In Periche, Jimena said they wanted to transcend trauma, and I remember wondering where they picked up language like that. I'd never been able to put my experience into words so well. But standing at Base Camp now, I wonder if that's what I've been doing, what we've all been doing, in a way.

Instead of ascending, we are transcending. Transcending expectations. Transcending pain. Trauma gets passed on intergenerationally, but the spell can be broken that way as well. We can heal the history of pain for the next generation by making a change for ourselves.

Ehani's word for the hike had been *soft*. She's shown me that strength doesn't have to be loud or domineering. It can be tender and nurturing. It can be an undercurrent. A mountain. An Everest. Ehani's father told her she must become someone "big," but I want to tell her that she already is.

I'm bursting with everything I want to say before they go, but when I open my mouth, the words slip down my throat.

As the flags are tied and strung up with all the others, carrying our secret wishes and dreams to the skies, everyone drifts off for a few minutes alone to stare at the mountains or sit on a rock and soak it all in. Jimena continues to carve and silently mouth each name that they are etching into the mountain. Shailee, Asha, Dr. Jackie, and I start quietly discussing the logistics of getting everyone back down the mountain safely, since Dr. Jackie will be staying in Gorak Shep. I have to leave to join my expedition soon. "Silvia!" Lucy is standing at the rocky ledge overlooking the trail and waves me over. In one hand, she clutches a gingham bundle, in the other, a stick of white sage. She hands me the bundle. Inside is a tiny pile of red dirt.

"Que pasó?"

"This is from Mexico," she says. "From my home. We're going to do an offering, you and I, to the spirit of the mountain, for protecting us on our trip. And for you to make it all the way up the mountain and come back safe."

"Okay," I say, my voice low. I'm touched.

We close our eyes for a minute, then grab handfuls of the dirt and fling it into the air. It sprays down over the rocky earth.

"Can I make an offering too?" I ask.

"Mm-hmm," she says.

I scoop out another tiny fistful of the special dirt.

"This is an offering for all of you to take what you have learned here and just fly," I say. "As high as you can. As tall as this mountain and beyond. This is for you, Lucy."

I toss the dirt to the sky.

Lucy sparks the sage, circling it through the air as it flames, drawing halos around us with the herbal smoke. For a moment I think I understand the bittersweet nostalgia of being a mother.

No one asked me to play mom. It just happened.

During this hike I've seen what sort of mother I'd be. Not as nurturing as I'd imagined or honestly hoped, but fully committed to letting everyone discover and explore their own strength. Even all the times we had been moving aggravatingly slow, something maternal in me battled down daily the aggro climber inside. A mothering force that knew it was necessary. Not only for them, but for me. She knew that we were moving at the pace of pain leaving the body.

* * *

We crowd in for a final selfie, and I hold my arm out to snap the photo.

"On three," I say. "One, two, three . . ."

"BASE CAMP!" we cry again, fingers in peace signs, tongues askew, some smiling, some serious, all staring into the camera for the portrait of a moment that is going to mark them forever. I'm not prepared to say good-bye. Where I come from, crying openly is a display of weakness. My mother rarely broke down in front of us kids. "Una madre nunca debe llorar delante de sus hijos, por más dolor que tenga," she used to advise her friends.

A mother shall never cry in front of her children regardless of the pain she might endure.

But as we fall into one final group hug, and I'm crushed between the warmth of their bodies, the tears roll down.

There is no weakness in tears. My mother may not have taught me that, but the mountain has. These girls have.

Jimena turns to the group. "I just feel so . . . safe."

We break from the hug.

All of us safer because of this perilous journey.

* * *

"Bye!" I call as they turn to walk away.

"Bye!!!" They turn and wave.

"Bye! Good-bye!" I shout as they step around the boulder.

"Byeeeee," they call without turning around.

"Bye!" I yell, running down the path after them as they round the first bend.

"Bye," their voices fade.

"Bye," I say, more quietly, watching my family grow smaller on the horizon.

I thought that by leaving the girls at Base Camp and then trekking to the top of Everest without them, I would be ending one journey and starting another. But as they disappear from my view, I realize our stories do not have a beginning, middle, and end, but are a continuum. Their journey continues with me. I'm taking their resilience and their courage with me, and it's just as important as any of the gear in my pack. I didn't train them; they trained me to summit this mountain. Maybe I'll make it; maybe I'll die trying. I don't know. What I do know is that just as I'm climbing in the steps of all who came before me, I have to leave my own imprint for those who will come after. For those who have been lost and need to find their way.

Nobody climbs a mountain alone.

I take a deep breath and whisper one last good-bye to my courageous girls and then trudge down the hill toward camp.

I have work to do.

Chapter 12

❦❦❦

WHEN THINGS FALL APART

At six a.m. on a Sunday, a white van marked Caltrans stopped in front of the unmarked white building on Morris Street. I was reporting for my community service duties as part of my DUI plea.

The door to the van slid open, and I hopped in fast, heading to the end of the seats.

A woman in a white hoodie in front turned to face me. "Hey!" she said. "So what'd you do?"

"Uhh . . . DUI," I murmured, looking straight ahead.

"My boyfriend got one of those," she said, nodding. "I'm here for shoplifting."

"Shoplifting?" piped up the blonde next to her with racoon eyes. "Me too."

"Insurance fraud," boomed a deep voice from the front. "Allegedly."

I didn't make an effort to see who'd spoken, keeping my gaze fixed on the window and the road ahead, a polite smile plastered on my face. My plan was to do my time and get out. To make no enemies or friends.

"Hey, Michael!" The woman in the white hoodie pointed at me and yelled to the front of the van. "She's here for DUI too!"

I sank lower in my seat.

No one knew about the DUI. Not my friends or family or anyone at SKYY—who, ironically, had a zero-tolerance policy. No one knew that for the last two months I'd spent my Saturday afternoons in a court-ordered alcohol-education class at Fort Mason watching gory videos of people being killed and maimed by drunk drivers. Instead of jail time, the expensive lawyer I hired got me assigned to trash pickup. My Sunday mornings were now spent picking up trash on the side of U.S. Route 101. The driver dropped us off at various spots along the 101, and we did our community service, one piece of litter at a time, in eight-hour shifts.

It was a new spin on the holy day. Sort of like Mass—with none of God's glory, but all of the damnation and penance. Each candy wrapper or cigarette butt was a bead on my rosary.

Hail Mary, full of grace.

Semitrailers and SUVs blew past, whipping my curls across my eyes and spinning old newspapers and Coke cans into trashy tumbleweeds that we chased down the median. While everyone swapped stories of last night's conquest or crime tales in code, I kept my head down, trying to fill my bag first. I wasn't like the rest of the group. I'd had a momentary lapse of judgment. Lost control of my car on a notoriously dangerous San Francisco street.

Could have happened to anyone.

* * *

The growth in the Silicon Valley was stratospheric. Companies went to bed as start-ups and woke up publicly traded global behemoths. My international experience integrating Campari and SKYY had accrued new value, and recruiters were calling me weekly. Everyone who left SKYY was shunned. And God save them if they left for a lesser position; they became the butt of our bitchy happy-hour jokes. We were so high on our own supply that we couldn't imagine why anyone would leave our prestigious vodka-drenched familia. I'd pledged allegiance to SKYY, and leaving after everything they'd done to secure my place in the United States felt like a betrayal.

But the sheen was starting to wear off. Every filing I did with our regulatory agency—the Bureau of Alcohol, Tobacco, Firearms and Explosives— made the stark and dangerous reality of the product I was peddling clear. I may not have rammed my car into a pedestrian, but I was inadvertently killing people, and myself, for a living. During my time at SKYY, I'd become a magical trifecta: alcoholic, workaholic, sexaholic.

Protecting the family has its costs.

Instead of looking inward to take responsibility for my actions and behavior, or ask myself *why* I'd done these things, it was easier to make a move. I started taking recruiter calls, wooed by the siren song of benefit packages and company perks. Imagining myself as a *real* dot-com executive. Wrapping myself in the fantasy of who I could be, instead of dealing with who I was.

* * *

My friend Shereen was throwing a small Halloween soiree. I'd completed my three months of community service and had my driving privileges reinstated, but it was shame that was keeping my sobriety intact. I was, as they say, *white-knuckling* it. And without booze, I needed something to bring a little edge to my holiday. Maybe in character, I could knock out the yearning for a drink.

"Mademoiselle Sylvie at your service," I chirped in my worst French accent as Shereen opened the door. "Here to sweep zee skeletons from your closet."

"Oh honey, look at those stems!" Shereen whistled. Outside of soccer games, I kept my scrawny legs to myself. But Mademoiselle Sylvie was a naughty housekeeper, and she kicked her leg out and ran the feather duster up it seductively.

Behind Sheeren, I heard a catcall. When I pushed into the sweaty, crowded living room to see who it was, I locked eyes with an angel.

Complete with a feathery halo and sparkling star wand, the angel had intense round hazel-green eyes. With a golden tan and dirty-blond hair that fell into an easy wave at her shoulders, even in whimsical costume, she was an all-American beauty. No frills. Very vintage Ralph Lauren. As if she could charm the cowboy and rope his horse at the same time. Her smile was broad and clear, revealing white teeth that shined like she'd never had anything to hide.

I was so drawn in that I didn't notice her eyes running up and down my legs until they stopped. With a slight peak of her pierced brow, she shot me a look I'd recognize anywhere. That was *my* look. The one that said you're trouble.

"Silvia," she said, tapping her wand to my feather duster. "It's a small gay world, after all."

Fear must have shown on my face because she folded over laughing.

"Don't worry," she said. "Red Devil? Ozomatli?"

"Ohhhh, right! My God. Please forgive me," I said. "I meet so many people at work. Sometimes it's hard to put a face to a name."

It wasn't a lie, exactly.

She winked, and the tiny silver hoop gleamed above her right brow. "I'm Lori."

My God. She was the woman in the leather jacket. My heart thumped. About a month ago, we'd met briefly at an Ozomatli concert. She'd been wearing a black motorcycle jacket. Exuding the sort of rugged nonchalance I'd been trying to emulate in my Peruvian cowgirl days. A real rebel without a cause. I always needed a few shots to talk to women like that. Without booze, my bravado was deflated. When the drinking halted, so had my one-night stands.

I'd tried to get her to dance that night, but she'd refused sweetly, which led to my stumbling over conversation, trying to get a read on her. She seemed straight, mostly, but maybe gay, or maybe I just wanted her to be. Anyway, I hadn't been able to get a clear answer that night.

But now here she was, an angel at a very gay party.

Turned out that the naughty French maid wasn't just a telenovela carica-ture but a universal fantasy, and my outfit, the duster in particular, was kinky party fodder.

Around midnight, a chant rose from the drunken chatter of the apart-ment. "Endup! Endup! Endup!" The Endup was just that—where you *ended up.* A smoky windowless after-hours club fueled by late-night grinding and pulsing neon.

"I'll drive!" I piped up, proud to play sober and responsible for once.

Six of us packed into my black Jetta: two couples, Lori, and me.

On the dance floor, the couples disappeared, and Lori and I made a game out of dodging the torrent of straight men who swooped in. Lori hung close to me, pressing in to shout over the music. She'd grown up in Denver and lived on the East Coast before settling in San Francisco. A journalist for a food and beverage trade magazine, she told me she was focused on growing industry awareness of organics. "But my true passion is writing fiction." She said all this with such earnestness and conviction that I was turned on in a whole new way. A wholesome way.

I shared things too, snippets of my life, I'm sure. But all I remember is the seashell of her ear. My hot breath. The peach fuzz on my cheek humming with electricity as her face hovered next to mine, her lips grazing the outer rim of my ear as she laughed at my bad jokes.

Drunk, my libido had been a crude throbbing force with one mission. But sober, my body teemed with new sensations. As Lori talked, the electricity between my legs traveled up my spine, tingling and knocking along my vertebrae.

* * *

Just then, the sexy and contagious rhythms of Beyoncé singing "Naughty Girl" blasted all over the club. This time I didn't press Lori to dance; she just naturally grabbed my hand and took me onto the dance floor.

Our bodies slowly merged into the dance, a tender, caring sexiness bonding us together. I choked down my nerves, sober, and blurted out, "Can I kiss you?" With a sexy shrug of the eyebrow, her silvery ring glinting in the flashing violet light, Lori gave me all the permission I needed.

* * *

On our first official date, I took her to a Peruvian restaurant and ordered the staples, the dishes we Peruvians judge all Peruvian restaurants by: a mixed seafood ceviche, rotisserie chicken, and, of course, the pièce de résistance, lomo saltado.

Conversation flowed naturally.

"You seem so passionate about your work." I said.

"It's not the sexiest job," said Lori. "But I really think we can make a difference. These industries waste so much. No one even challenges it. They just need someone to shake things up."

I nodded and stabbed my fork into a juicy piece of lomo. She never broke eye contact as she spoke. It wasn't an attempt at seduction. More like she was looking past what I showed her to see who was really there.

"For example," she said, taking a swig of Inca Kola. "I was doing a story on Tyson, the chicken, you know? And for some reason they got it into their heads that I needed a hundred pounds of chicken to review. Now that I think of it, maybe they were trying to buy me off!" She laughed. "Anyhow, I had to rush and load this huge pallet of chicken into my car by myself and find a local shelter to drop it off before it went bad."

"Amazing," I said, charmed again by the purity of her desire to do the right thing. "You know when we first met I was trying to read you. The jacket said maybe gay."

"Leave leather jackets out of it. They are androgynous and shall remain so."

"Pardon me, my mistake."

"But no," she said. "I'm bi. I've had two live-in girlfriends and just split with a boyfriend."

I had been left for a man before, and it stung differently. With women, at least they'd stay in the gay fishbowl. Maybe I'd see them out again, and if fate and timing collided, there was always a chance we could get back together. But when women were lost to men, they were gone forever— swallowed up by the straight world. Going back to any man was going back to every man. But Lori seemed freer than that, and I wanted to trust her. Something was propelling me toward her. It was more than familiarity or comfort. She wasn't just someone to fill a void in my life. In Hawaiian culture, they say that seven generations of your ancestors live in your spine, and if that was true, it felt like they'd all woken up and were dancing on mine, telling me I was exactly where I was supposed to be. Not to screw this up. And if it really was *my* ancestors, I knew better than to question their guidance.

I was ready to take whatever Lori was willing to offer.

"I'm planning to stay single for a while," she said, scooping a spoonful of rice into her mouth. "Or . . . ," she glanced up at me, her hazel eyes softening to a sea green. "I *was*."

I never knew I believed in destiny until I felt it.

After dinner, we walked along carrying hefty containers of leftover chicken and rice. I was determined to send her home with all the goods. As we walked down Market Street, we passed a man crouched in a dark door- way. In the glow of the streetlight, I could see he was wrapped in a blanket, his face darkened with grime. He called out to us, and I picked up speed, but Lori stopped. "Hold on," she said, grabbing the bag and running into the shadows to leave the leftovers with him.

What did I have to offer a woman like that? Someone who stopped to share a meal with a person on the street. Who ferried a pallet of chicken across town in the middle of the workday. Everything she did was oriented outward. Toward the planet, her community, those in need. She was working to better the world, and I was working myself to the bone for money and loyalty. The sort of twisted loyalty that says even if it's killing us, we show up with a smile. We do not disappoint the family. The thing about trauma, about addiction, is that it locks you into a Groundhog Day of your own interior. I wanted to burst out of my own skin. To see what it was like to do something for others—no strings attached.

The next six months were bliss.

My youngest brother, Eduardo, had recently immigrated to the United States, and we found a loft together on Eleventh and Harrison in the SoMa district. Eduardo worked mornings as a security guard in a jewelry store, and Lori and I fell into an easy rotation between my place and hers. Through the fall and long, gray San Francisco winter, Sunday brunch was the highlight of my week.

Lori had a recipe that transformed a strange combination of milk and bread and baked potatoes into a killer French toast. While she cooked, we sipped mimosas and listened to her favorite, Al Green. She wasn't a big drinker, so I was letting her steer me toward responsible drinking. I imagined myself reborn as a casual take-it-or-leave-it drinker. A one-glass-and-I'm-done drinker. Lori didn't know about the DUI. About how bad my drinking really was. She didn't know any of my secrets. I'd given myself a clean slate, so our relationship deserved that too.

My days of sloppy hookups and amnesiac mornings in the ER were over.

While we ate, the buttery richness of Al's voice gave the loft a sultry mood. Determined to get my dance, I'd spin Lori from her chair into the living room, where the afternoon light of the Bay filtered through her sparkling floor-to-ceiling windows. While we danced, my head fell on her shoulder, and sometimes I let it lie there, feeling for once like I didn't have to take charge.

Sometimes I even let her lead.

"Let's Stay Together" was her favorite song, and she played it on repeat deep into the afternoon. I sang along, thinking that Al had taken the words right out of my mouth.

* * *

The deeper I fell, the more afraid I was of losing her. Some mornings I woke with a knot in my stomach, certain she'd call to tell me she'd fallen for someone else. A man. Lori hadn't done anything to confirm my inner thoughts. She always made a point to introduce me as her girlfriend and held my hand in public. But as I learned to love and be loved again, to partner, to see and allow myself to be seen, the fear of intimacy was always there—nebulous, looping, lingering. It was a low-grade undercurrent in all our interactions, especially when it came to the thing she was most passionate about in the world, the thing she said would put our relationship to the fire, would bring us closer than ever: Burning Man.

Burning Man is a ten-day festival held every August in a remote Nevada desert. Started in 1986 on Baker Beach in San Francisco when an artist burned an eight-foot-tall wooden effigy of a man that symbolized "the Man," it was a countercultural movement. Twenty years later, it had become an annual drug-fueled art party that drew thousands around the world who braved vicious daily dust storms to experience a world free of commerce. The dot-commers, artist types ate it up, saving and planning all year to let their freaky alter egos out in the middle of the desert.

They called themselves Burners. And they were Lori's chosen family.

She helped run one of the festival's biggest camps. It was a year-round job to plan, build, and fundraise for next year's camp. Most of the fundraisers were sexually charged re-creations of the Burning Man vibe, with sculptures and local art, topless women in feathers and body paint, and feminine men in heavy eyeliner. Men who were soft and dreamy, maybe just feminine enough, I thought, that they might be perfect for a bi girl like Lori. Lots of the Burners were wealthy tech executives the rest of the year, and the combination of communal, freethinking values plus the sheer wealth and capitalistic excess of the Bay Area tech boom made it a monied hippie fest set to a backdrop of deep house. One I both wanted into and wanted nothing to do with.

That spring, as the foggy mornings grew into longer days, Lori started begging me to go with her. Burning Man changes you, she said. And while I was looking for deeper meaning, a human experiment with polyamorous vibes was not it. To Lori, Burning Man was a model utopia, an alternative to our fast-paced capitalistic way of living. A place to learn what love really is, she said, which made it sound even more like a massive drug-fueled orgy.

Who even needed to be that free, honestly?

Instead, I threw myself into landing the dot-com job of my dreams. If I could only get a job in the tech sector, like Lori's Burning Man camp, I could turn my reckless life around. The fast-paced environment would feed my need for speed, and the cutting-edge thinking would keep me on my toes. Plus, for me, it would be the ultimate sign of success.

As spring broke into summer, I strung her along, letting her think I would be going to Burning Man, secretly hoping she'd let it go. I was terrified to just say no. The community there seemed so important, part of her identity in a way I was unwilling or unable to witness. I knew if I didn't go, I'd lose that part.

* * *

San Francisco's 2005 Gay Pride parade was the last weekend in June. We were invited to a party by a wealthy gay underwear designer who lived in a gorgeous penthouse overlooking the Golden Gate Bridge. With all the furs and feathers and glitter and go-go boots she'd collected from years at Burning Man, Lori's closet was Pride primed. As we got ready, I lounged on her bed and watched her fly through piles of outfits.

"No, no, no," she said, flinging out tutus and body chains. I flashed on my first Pride parade eight years earlier. Twenty-two, fresh-faced, and wondering what it would be like to kiss a woman. To celebrate with abandon. To feel joyful enough in my own body that I could find a freedom and ease I'd never known. It was the promise of freedom that had drawn me to San Francisco. Now about to turn thirty-one, I tried to remember the feelings of joy and freedom, but there was something in the way.

Dripping in leopard-print décor and gold finishes, the penthouse was a *Boogie Nights* island of scantily clad go-go dancers with free-flowing rivers of Ecstasy and coke running in both directions. The Veuve Clicquot was a bottomless lagoon.

All the biggest and best gay-boy parties took place Saturday before Sunday's big parade. I'd partied plenty, but the SKYY world was nothing like this. There were only a handful of women there, Lori and I with my friend Anne, a few other lesbians, some fag hags and their tag-along boyfriends. The rest of the straight men were gay for a night.

As I was taking it all in, Lori pulled me into the hall bathroom and handed me a circular baby-blue pill with the outline of a peace dove pressed into it. It was a godly little pill. She held another for herself, its chalky blue already coming off and staining her sweaty palm.

"Ready?" she said, her eyes sparkling.

"Ready or not." I shrugged and laughed nervously as we popped the Ecstasy into our mouths and chased it down with champagne. Bass rattled the crystal chandelier swinging above our heads.

Lori had dressed me in a sexy negligee, and herself in a sheer white top and hot pink fedora. We left the bathroom and flowed into the living room, a disco ball of a dance floor, sparkly shirtless bodies writhing. Anne yanked Lori onto the dance floor, and I beelined for the bar, determined to keep myself hydrated with champagne. Its cool, crisp bubbles sizzled down my throat as I drank one glass after another and waited for euphoria to kick in.

Maybe five minutes had passed, maybe an hour, but when I looked back, Anne and Lori were in their bras, dancing on a speaker. Men were surrounding them, their faces pulling and warping as they became slippery effeminate creatures. One pulled a rose from a vase on the mantle and handed it to Lori. She plucked off the petals, and as I watched them flutter down over his face in a slow pink rain, my legs went stiff. A surge of rage, of jealousy, of loss. Lori was right there, but I couldn't touch her. I was losing her. To them. But not if I left first.

* * *

At six a.m., we dragged ourselves into the elevator. My head was a clattering bell. My whole body felt like a wet rag.

"Something's off," I grumbled.

"What do you mean, baby?" Lori's face was glittering with sweat, her fair cheeks looked perfectly rouged. She *was* perfect. Too perfect. And free.

"Didn't you have fun?" she said breathlessly, pushing open the door to the building and throwing her hands into the dusky morning.

I hailed a cab, and as we rode, Lori oohed and aahed watching the sun rise over the Bay while I sat in silence, falling deeper and deeper into the darkness of my mind, and getting more and more agitated. By the time the cab dropped us off, I knew what I had to do.

"I can see it," I muttered, more to myself than to her. The words were a heavy sludge spilling from my mouth. "You'll leave eventually."

She whipped around, and I watched her face fall from the buzzy joy of dawn into the dark pit of my words. "What did you say?"

Instead of softening me, her sweet face stoked my anger.

"I'm sorry, Lori, we had a good run." I could hardly believe the words coming out of my mouth. They were cold, robotic almost. "But I can't do this anymore."

"A good *run*?" she practically spat. Her eyes pooled with tears, and her dilated pupils locked on mine.

"Give me my keys, Silvia." She was strangely calm. I obeyed, unwinding them from my key chain and handing them over.

Shocked, she stared at them in her palm. Then, without a word, she flung the door open and walked through the gate to her building. I watched her figure recede as she stepped into the elevator with her back to me. As the silver doors closed, she got smaller and smaller, until all I could see was a sliver, and then nothing.

She was gone.

I don't think I realized yet what I'd done, because instead of devastation, I felt only vindication. I'd done what I needed to do to stave off worse heartbreak down the road. For once, I was taking the high road.

By the next weekend, I was drinking in full force.

* * *

There are only so many ways to tell the story of oblivion. There was nothing new about my drinking. Nothing new about Saturday night. About bar after bar after bar. Blacking out in a stranger's apartment? Nothing new.

What was new was that Sunday morning, on the way to his shift at the jewelry store, Eduardo found me facedown in our loft entryway.

He crouched over me, shaking my arms. "Silvia! Hermana! What the hell is going on? Are you okay? Can you breathe?"

"Urrrggg." I propped myself on my elbows and wiped leftover puke from my face. My breath was a raunchy cloud, old tequila mixed with vinegar. Salad dressing long unrefrigerated. It made me want to vomit more, but it was also familiar. I'd been here before. At least I knew this person.

I knew what came next.

"I'm not feeling so well, need to lie down." My words were a slurry mess as Eduardo helped me to my room. Puke splattered the walls and floor of the first-floor accessible bathroom. It takes a lot of puke to fill a bathroom that big.

Belly flopping onto my bed, I stared out the window and tried to piece together the night as Eduardo called out vague words of concern, followed by the thwap of his boots and the click of the door lock. I tried to retrace my steps. To play a morning-after game of whodunnit. But I was tired. Not from lack of sleep or too much booze, but tired on the inside. Tired of running, of obliterating everything good, of breaking down walls only to build them even higher. I was tired of carrying so many secrets that I could no longer tell what was secret and what wasn't, so I just kept it all in—just in case.

All these drunken treasure hunts led to the same place. Me on a bed, sour tequila breath, alone and ashamed. There were no more mysteries. Only the long, sad days that followed. Except that this particular morning something actually was different. There was a witness. My baby brother, who I had promised to always love and protect, found me facedown in chunky puddles of my own shame. No one in my family had ever seen me that way. Eduardo looked up to me, but not anymore. How could he?

Then I did something I'd never done. I dialed home.

"Mama?" I said, close to tears when I heard her warm, rolling "Aló?"

"Mom, I need help. I drank too much and I'm struggling. I can't take it anymore."

There was a long sigh on the other end.

"I know, Silvita," she said. "Your brother told me. It is enough. Come home. Francis is going to help you."

My cousin Francis was the only doctor in the family. He'd done his medical residency in the Amazon, in the small city of Tarapoto. There he had befriended a French doctor, Jacques Mabit, one of the premier researchers on the psychological benefits of drinking ayahuasca. Ayahuasca is an ancient indigenous medicine made from steeping a jungle vine in chacruna leaves, which contain a powerful hallucinogen called DMT—also called the spirit molecule. DMT is found in the human body, but researchers and mystics debate its role. Some say the chemical releases only right before you die and is responsible for that moment in the movies when your life flashes before your eyes. They say that DMT takes you through death and spits you out on the other side, so that if you're lucky, you can see what you'd do differently.

In San Francisco, the use of native medicine had been reincarnated in hippie rituals, many practiced by the same Burning Man crew Lori hung with. But ayahuasca wasn't a recreational drug or something to be taken lightly, Francis told us. Because it involved ancestral knowledge, it was a spiritual undertaking to be done only under the guidance of a practiced shaman. Curanderos and shamans used ayahuasca to heal emotional pain and unlock higher states of consciousness. The vine sings its messages through them.

Francis had hosted an ayahuasca ceremony for my very Catholic mother, and during the trip, her father, Francisco, who'd been murdered when she was twelve, appeared to her. They had a conversation that let her seal a wound that had never properly healed. If she could find closure in a psychedelic vine, then maybe I could too. Heal from the things my family had never been able to talk about. Things none of us were equipped to handle.

I'd run in every way a person could. New country, new jobs, relationships, identities. I'd drunk myself into oblivion and narrowly escaped jail and killing myself, or someone else. There was nothing left to do but surrender. To go back to where the problems had all begun.

"Okay, Mama," I said. "Let me think about it."

* * *

The next week, eBay called and offered me a job in their corporate finance department. This was my Hail Mary. My chance to turn things around. Lori was gone, but she'd drawn out the part of me that wanted more, that wanted meaning.

My start date at eBay was set for September 6—my thirty-first birthday. I felt so guilty leaving SKYY that I gave four weeks' notice, which left me one free week. I bought a ticket to Peru.

It was now or never.

In addiction recovery, they say that the first step to healing is to admit that you are powerless over the substance and surrender to a higher power. Honestly, that sounded like a relief, but for me, God was still nebulous, and therapy was a place for people with real problems. Agreeing to take ayahuasca was my form of surrender.

In order to spiritually cleanse for the ceremony, Francis put me on a strict three-week diet of no booze, meat, sex, or sweets.

Francis managed to arrange the ayahuasca ceremony with María, a well-known Shipiba priestess, for a Saturday night in Carabayllo, a working-class district on the outskirts of Lima next to Puente Piedra, where my aunt Emerita and my cousin Felipe lived. The ceremony would last at least two to three hours.

My parents and I picked up Francis around midnight and started the long drive. He warned that the setup would be remote, rustic. He was very serious. If you weren't careful with the plant, he said, you could have a psychotic break. A somber quiet settled over the car. We drove in silence through the dark for what felt like a long time, and I imagined bumping down a dank ghostly road toward a decrepit cloaked mansion. My mood was resigned, as if I were marching to meet myself for the first time. Driving with both of my parents in the front seat because I needed help. Something I'd never said to them before.

In my family, we didn't name things aloud. Alcoholic. Pedophile. Rapist. Abuser. The things that haunted us were cloaked in euphemism and innuendo. With naming came shame.

Suddenly, a wild splash of salsa wafted into the car as we passed a string of blaring discotecas, people waiting in line, dancing in the street to flaring trumpets and timbales echoing from truck-sized speakers. The city was free and alive. From behind the glass I watched, remembering all the times I had danced, how free I seemed, but how heavy with grief my limbs were.

We turned onto a potholed dirt road. "Here!" Francis said, in front of a large white warehouse. "Stop."

"Here?" I said, second-guessing the whole thing. This was starting to get weird. Maybe my life hadn't gotten so bad after all.

My father parked, and we followed Francis through a side door that opened up into a large backyard. We climbed a set of rickety wooden stairs and walked into an open airy room lit by a hundred candles. In the middle, María, the priestess, sat on a royal purple cushion next to an altar, her face bottom-lit with flickering candlelight, casting a mystical aura through the room. On either side sat two young men—her helpers. In a semicircle in front of her, eight places were set up, each with a small mat, a white plastic chair, a blanket, and a bucket. Francis warned me that the worst part was throwing up. It was all a part of the purging.

I'd thrown up plenty. At least this time it would be productive.

The four others were strangers, I realized with a start—how was I supposed to do this in front of strangers who were already sitting cross-legged on their mats in silence? It seemed like everyone but me knew what to expect. Francis directed me to the seat across from María, while he took the mat to my left, and my mother and father to my right.

Who does ayahuasca with their parents?

My father had been at the first ceremony with my mother but had felt nothing. I couldn't imagine what my mother had said to get him to come again. She must have guilt-tripped him. Any conversations we had about the abuse ended in an argument. We had never tried family therapy to confront the issue, and he'd never apologized.

One of the helpers hit a gong, and its silvery vibration shimmered through the room. The other helper shook a rain stick, and little beads of sound dribbled down on us as María started an invocation in the native Shipibo tongue. She started mixing muddy liquids from various plastic bottles into a teapot, then added hot water. She pursed her lips, leaned over the pot, and began to whistle into the liquid and chant again in Shipibo. According to the tradition, whistling wakes up the powers of ayahuasca.

Francis signaled for me to step to the front of the altar and receive the tea. As I drank from a small cup, the thick, bitter liquid slowly chugged down my throat, and María kept chanting as one of her helpers shook a leaf rattle.

My mother followed me, then my father and the rest of the group. I walked back to the mat and lay down for the meditation phase as Francis directed.

After everyone drank the tea, María lit a huge cigar and began to puff on it rapidly, shooting out the smoke in little rockets. She then began to pray. From somewhere deep in her tiny body came a thrumming melody that vibrated the space, an endless hymn that shuttled me in and out of consciousness. I closed my eyes and pulled the blanket over my legs. The beautiful melody blew through the room. Singing fused with the sounds of the rain stick. I let myself get lost in María's voice.

The music snaked through my body like the vine of the ayahuasca unfurling inside me. The vine was the teacher, and the priestess, María, just a channel. The songs, called icaros, were the songs of the plant, channeled through the shaman. Even if you didn't understand the words, it was said that your spirit understood the message.

My cheeks began to flush and tingle. There was no need to open my eyes. Everything I saw I could see without them.

There was a rainbow drowning, a messy watercolor puddle of purples and reds and greens and oranges, and as I looked into it, it began to spiral, transforming into a vortex. Wrapped in María's song, I fell down into it, spinning, spiraling, dropping down to what felt like the center of the earth. Then silence. I could no longer hear the music, but there was a light. I walked toward it. It was the light of a house. My parents' house. I opened the front door, careful to be quiet, remembering how squeaky the glossy wooden floors always were, but they didn't make a sound. In the corner of the room there was a small figure. I had to see who it was.

I didn't feel scared.

As I got closer, I hunched down, and she noticed me. She looked up. She'd been crying and was still shaking a bit. I'd seen her before in a photograph. She had two ponytails. It was a little girl in a turquoise tracksuit. It was me at age six. I lifted her up and she clung to me, hugging me tightly, all her little muscles contracted. My heart started to flutter. I squeezed her tight and started to cry. Then a bolt of fire tore through my gut. Rage. Incandescent rage. Someone had hurt her. I held her tighter. Anger became bile, rising hot and fast in my throat. I jolted out of the vision, then lay back down, washed with a strange sense of peace. The little girl appeared again, and my adult self was standing next to her. As long as I was there, as long as I didn't let go, no one was going to hurt her again. There was an identical light glowing in our chests, and I leaned down to cradle her, sending waves of compassion from my body to hers.

Her face grew warmer, brighter.

In the distance, there was a great rumbling. We hovered at the entrance to something. Ourselves, maybe? All around, underneath us, the ground shivered and shook. I couldn't see anything, but she took my hand, and we began to walk. The air was crisp. We were in a thick patch of trees and grass, and something was forming on the horizon. Running toward us. Thundering.

But no, it wasn't a herd of animals. It was rocks. Huge rocks, no, mountains, pushing up through the ground, cracking the earth as if it were an egg. An endless valley unrolled in front of us as a ring of craggy peaks shot into the air, so high that they pierced the clouds and disappeared on the other side.

We watched in awe. When the rumbling stopped, I looked around cautiously to make sure it was safe. But the little girl was fearless. She clutched my hand in hers and pulled me deeper into the valley. As we walked, she noticed everything, blinking happily as she looked around at the birds and pointed out every little insect in the grass.

Her hand was warm still. She was at ease. At peace. Simply walking.

Music played again.

Then came voices forming incoherent words.

My eyes shot open, and I was back in Peru. My mother's face was soft and distant as she rocked on the mat next to me. Next to her, my father snored loudly, his mouth hanging open and his arms folded over his chest, the way he slept during afternoon naps. I closed my eyes again and listened more closely. My father's snoring had become a rumbling that had become a mountain. His snores had been the soundtrack to my vision. As I wiped away tears of laughter and release from my cheek, I let out a great bellowing sigh and collapsed into my mat. I chuckled as smoke from the shaman's incense drifted past my nose in a milky stream. The woodsy spice of palo santo flooded my senses.

Curanderos say the vine will give you what you need.

Apparently what my father needed was a nap.

They call ayahuasca "the Mother" because she reveals yourself to you. Like Everest, she is not always tender or nurturing, but like my own mother, who'd dragged my depleted, destructive self to this abandoned house in the middle of Peruvian nowhere, she tries to tell you the truth.

It's up to you to listen.

The little girl in the tracksuit. She was the one from the picture. The one I couldn't stand to see. The girl I had called weak, and whose image I had hidden away in the back of the closet. But in the mountains we'd been at peace. Were the mountains symbolic? Did it mean I needed to weather the peaks and valleys of life better?

Most of us have false bottoms. The lows we think are absolute. But often there is something even lower, and it's not always the most obvious or dramatic. For me, true rock bottom wasn't the DUI or heartbreak or the nameless one-night stands, or even being raped by my boss. Rock bottom was being seen by my brother. Having the depth of my pain witnessed by my own flesh and blood.

Reconnect to your inner child, Silvia. That's what the vine was telling me. Tend to her pain. She had something to show me, something inside that pain. Something I didn't understand until two weeks later, when, back in San Francisco, sitting at my new desk at eBay, it came to me.

The mountains weren't a symbol at all.

She wanted me to take her somewhere she could roam. Where her body could expand and move and feel all the things she'd been too scared to pay attention to. To feel free. Ayahuasca had helped my mother heal her biggest pain, and what had happened to that little girl was mine. Not only was I to carry her to the mountains, I was to take her—and my biggest pain—to the biggest mountain.

Mount Everest. Chomolungma. The Mother of the World.

Chapter 13

❦

TESTOSTERONE

I'm the only girl in the boys' club and I'm late.

The Adventure Consultants dining tent is hookah-lounge chic, a level of kitsch that at 18,000 feet looks like luxury if you squint. Bright bouquets of plastic flowers hang from the structural poles holding up the tent, a trio of egg chairs are clustered around a cozy electric stove, and two rectangular dining tables are set with bright oilcloth coverings, all the chairs draped in a psychedelic purple fabric.

The first table is already filled with very manly, very white, mostly balding men, cracking jokes and hollering over each other. Given that I've spent most of my life being afraid of men, I've picked an odd sport. Elite mountaineering draws out the most primal machismo characters I've ever seen.

Everyone seems to have their spots picked out already. Suddenly, I'm back in high school. At the back of the class. I take a deep breath and approach the other table.

"Hi, I'm Silvia," I say, waving. "Very nice to meet you all."

* * *

"Bloody day, you finally made it!" says a brown-haired tank of a man with an Australian accent. "We were about to give Danny the rest of your food supply."

The table breaks into laughter. I smile politely, trying not to be sensitive, but after leaving the girls, I'm a walking heart.

"Brian," he says, extending a hand, which I make sure to shake firmly. "Nice to see you. New Zealand by the way. The accent? In case you were wondering." Brian is also climbing the Seven Summits. Everest and Denali are the last on his list.

"I'm Rob," says a man with a short white beard and what I guess is another Australian accent, but I'm wrong again. Rob is an engineer originally from New Zealand but based in Adelaide. He's on his third Everest attempt. "Sit here. I have something for you," he says, dragging an empty chair over from the other table. He pulls a stuffed koala bear from a plastic bag.

"For me? Thank you," I say, a nervous smile plastered to my face. "That's so thoughtful." I'm unsure what to make of it, but Rob seems sensitive to the fact that I'm the only woman. Maybe he thinks a stuffed animal will help.

Who knows, maybe it will.

As we wait for dinner to arrive, the men barrel through the rest of the introductions. I try to keep up.

Tom, a balding white-haired man with a stringy, muscular neck, stands to introduce himself.

"If any of these hooligans give you trouble," he barks, "I'll set them back straight!"

"Keep an eye on old Tommy boy, you never know when he might be interrogating you," cracks Brian.

Turns out that Tom isn't just any military guy. He's a former member of the Navy's SEAL Team Six. He's also an ultramarathon runner who once completed two Ironman Triathlons in one day. As Tom lists his accomplishments, I feel myself shrinking. This is his first Everest attempt, but he seems *very* confident.

Next to Tom is Gabe, an Australian police chief, who jumps up in the middle of his introduction to bounce a soccer ball on his knee. "I'm planning to kick this guy around at summit. That's how you'll know it's me. Bouncing at 30,000 feet!"

"Oh, come off it, sit your ass down!" says Brian. *Brian.*

Seven summits, I think, trying to remember who is who.

My mouth falls open as the next man at the table stands to introduce himself. He must be close to seven feet. "Danny," he says. "Kiwi. Second summit attempt. First one was last year. During the avalanche. Devastating. Rob, there—koala man—was here as well."

The 2015 avalanche was Everest's most deadly. It killed twenty-four people and decimated the small citadel that is Base Camp. Not a single climber made it to summit that spring. It was the first time in forty-one years that that had happened.

"Were you in the avalanche?" I ask.

"Not buried under it," says Rob.

Koala bear Rob. Koala bear Rob.

"But we were caught at Camp 1 when the earthquake hit. We prepared ourselves to die that day."

I let out a low whistle. "I can only imagine," I say.

At the second table is John, a British financier who lives between Hong Kong and Tokyo—two of my favorite cities. His posh accent and square horn-rimmed glasses say professor, not mountaineer. He's on a private expedition housed within Adventure Consultants, and has hired Lydia Bradey, the first woman to successfully climb Everest without oxygen, as his main guide.

And finally, next to John, is Mark, a college professor who lives in Connecticut. Mark has a kind face and is more reserved than the others. He exudes a sort of gentleness that I'm grateful for after all the bravado. This is his first Everest attempt too.

Mike walks into the dining tent. I've met Mike only once, briefly, at the puja.

"Welcome, welcome, Silvia," he says. "Our team is now officially complete." He grins, his smile lines more like fault lines, deep creases extending from the corner of his eyes all the way down his cheeks.

"Thank you," I say quietly.

"Tell us a bit about where you've come from."

"Of course," I say, beaming with pride. I clear my throat and stand. "For the last ten days, I've been guiding a group of courageous young women to Base Camp. Women who, like me, have been victims of sexual violence. The hike was about getting in touch with their inner strength. I wanted Everest to show them how powerful they are. They're heading back down the mountain now. And I will continue here. With you." I finish with a flourish of the hand.

"Inspirational," says posh John, lifting his eyebrows. I can't tell if it's sarcasm or his dry British tone.

"Whew," whistles Navy SEAL Tom. "You must be exhausted."

"No kidding. Certainly not how *I'd* prep for Everest," says Gabe, the summit soccer jock. "You need to be on your A-game here. Guess we'll see how long you last."

His eyes are jovial, and everyone laughs, but something tells me he means it.

"Yes," I say with a smirk. "Yes, we will."

But he's right. I am exhausted. Not just physically depleted but emotionally.

Two young Sherpa men rush into the tent carrying steaming trays of food and a big pot of soup. Tendi, the expedition chef, runs down the night's menu: French fries, rice, dal, fried chicken.

"Okay, show-and-tell is over," booms Danny. "I'm starving. Let's eat!"

The first table stands, and we line up to serve ourselves buffet-style. Rob is in front of me and tries to put a piece of chicken on my plate.

"No thank you," I say, loud enough for everyone to hear. "I'm a vegetarian."

"Aww, a veggie, eh?"

"Well, on the mountain at least. And you?"

"Never."

"Anyone else?" I look up and down the line.

"Nope."

"Hell no."

"Carnivore reporting for duty!"

"Bloodier the better in my book."

Not only am I late and the only woman, but I'm the only vegetarian. A lesbian vegetarian allergic to gluten—the ultimate cliché pain in the ass. I almost can't stand myself, but I'm too hungry to dwell on it. Head down, I dig into a bowl of oily fries, rice, and more dal bhat. As the Sherpas say, "Dal bhat powers, twenty-four hours." What's good enough for the Sherpas is just fine for me.

The table thrums with testosterone—the live-wire energy of *Survivor* meets barroom arm wrestling. Trying to keep up with the dinner banter is like joining a story already in progress. While I've been focused on the girls, they've been acclimatizing, talking routes and gear, and trading war stories—literally.

It's clear that the next six weeks is going to come with a healthy dose of competition.

I finish eating quickly and pull on my coat. "I'm pretty beat, all. Going to get some rest." As I duck out of the stuffy tent and rush through the dark, frigid air of camp, panic sets in.

They're cast straight from a James Bond movie. A British millionaire? A rugby player? A seven-foot-tall Kiwi? *SEAL Team Six?* My God. My God. What the hell have I done?

I can't believe I'd ever been afraid of leading the courageous girls. I yearn for the tenderness we shared just hours before. For a decade, I've been working toward the big dream. "One day I'll climb Everest," I told myself and anyone who would listen. Well, "one day" has arrived, and even after all the climbing and training, all the delays and heartbreaks, I'm not prepared because I didn't just focus on that *one day.*

I unzip my tent and dive in, crawling into my sleeping bag. Once I'm cocooned in down, my eyelids are lead. I hope the girls made it safely back to Gorak Shep. I should call and check on them, but my phone doesn't have reception, and I can't go back to the dining tent.

Too tender. Too scared. Too tired. Too . . . too. Tired.

The blissful nothing of sleep washes over me.

* * *

"Silvia, Silvita! Wake up, levántate!"

My eyes open a slit. My mother is over me, shaking me, in bed. "There's been a bomb," she says, pulling me out from the covers. She runs down the stairs ahead of me. I'm watching my steps, trying not to slip, eyes barely open. In the courtyard, my family is standing in their pajamas.

"Silvia!" bellows my father. "The girl sleeps through anything. Even a goddamn bomb."

"They're getting closer," says my mother, caressing my hair.

I bolt upright. I'm zipped up to the throat in a mummy bag. My breath is an icy cloud. Somewhere in the distance there's a machine gun rat-a-tat. Avalanches. There are avalanches out there. I'm on Everest, not in Peru.

But Peru, it seems, is always with me.

I shake off the dream and wonder about the girls again. I hear a small ping and fumble around in the dark tent for my satellite device. Texts from Shailee light up the screen.

We are all good.

Everyone in great spirits.
Go and sleep, you must be tired.
We will talk tomorrow.

As I collapse into my pillow, a weight is lifted from my chest. All the space the girls have occupied for the last two weeks, two months really, as I got sober in San Francisco and funneled my energy into training and logistics, is empty now. In the space I held for them, old fears flood back in.

Everyone—me, most of all—likes to say that struggle makes you strong. I've lived, and practically died, by the ethos that to survive is to overcome. But again and again, mountains have shown me that strong is not the opposite of soft. That they are symbiotic. Strength alone is not enough. It may get me to the summit, but back at sea level, I'll still be adrift.

And now the courageous girls have shown me that I can bow at the feet of lamas and nuns, speak the language of the New Age, wear all the shawls and rosaries and prayer beads, and adopt the vernacular of healing, but as long as I neglect the muscle of softening, I will still be conquering where I wish to surrender.

I sob myself quietly back to sleep. Behind the thin skin of my eyelids, in dreams fraught with danger, massive hunks of ice tumble toward me, gaining momentum, exploding into waves of snowy powder. The cracking of the avalanche morphs into wailing alarms and explosions. I'm back in Peru. Men and bombs. The twin explosions of my youth. Where anything could crumble at a moment's notice.

Chapter 14

❧❧❧❧

THE GREAT WALL

A geographical cure—a geographic, in recovery shorthand—is the belief that a change in circumstances will change us. Will free us from discomfort, from the gnawing of loneliness or insecurity or depression or addiction.

It's the idea that we can outrun what chases us.

That we can outrun ourselves.

I'd done my community service. Picked up my trash without looking to see what it was. Gone through the motions of repentance while making no confessions. Instead of stopping to ask how I wound up there in the first place, I counted down the hours until I was done. Even after my first trip to Everest, my attention was not on how I ended up here, but what I was going to do next.

"So you're going to climb Everest?" Lori said, staring at me, her pierced brow raised in surprise. Her hazel eyes danced on the side of green that day. A cloudy sea green. A place to get lost.

"Yes ma'am," I drawled.

"Isn't that dangerous?"

"Of course! But that's part of my promise," I said, dumping raw sugar into my tea. It was a busy Saturday afternoon at Farley's, a homey coffee shop perched at the top of sun-kissed Potrero Hill. Farley's was Lori's favorite. Convincing her to meet me had been easier than I had thought. Just back from my hike to Base Camp, I was supercharged with purpose and dying to share it with Lori. After my ayahuasca trip, I'd come back to San Francicso and started my new job at eBay. But I couldn't get Everest and the little girl walking in the mountains out of my mind. My boss gave me one week off and I took my first trip to the base of Everest, where I promised I'd be back.

"I just have to become a mountaineer first," I choked out the words.

A mountaineer? God. It was the first time I'd said it out loud, and it sounded absurd, but Lori just smiled.

"I see it," she said, sipping her latte. A dab of foam clung to her top lip. I had to hold myself back from reaching across the table to wipe it away. "You can do anything."

The tips of my ears burned. Just thinking about Lori got me a little high. We hadn't seen each other one-on-one since the idiotic Ecstasy-induced breakup six months earlier, and I missed her badly. I was hoping my new lease on life could turn this whole thing around. Between slurps of syrupy green tea, I told her all about the ayahuasca and Base Camp. How my vision had unrolled like a carpet and led me to Kathmandu, how insignificant I felt when I first saw the Himalayas. And what a welcome sensation that was. How, for the first time in my life, I felt safe *and* free. How my lungs and legs had been surprisingly sturdy—so sturdy that I started to wonder if this was more than just a one-off vision, and something more like destiny. Like what I felt about Lori too.

I left that last part out.

Lori had been such a positive influence on my life. Hers was the kind of love that makes you want to do better. I guess sharing Everest was my offering. Maybe she'd see this purposeful glow in my eyes and be willing to give us another shot.

"I made a promise to Everest to return. I'm ready to make peace in my life," I said, meeting her gaze. "I'd love to give us another chance too."

Her lips curled into a shy smile, and I could see that she felt the same.

* * *

We came back stronger than ever. Fortified with a fresh outlook and a new job, I could finally love Lori without clinging to her. Without worrying that she was going to break my heart and trying to beat her to it. We were magnetic. Wherever we went, straight couples commented on how sexy we were. Bartenders sent us free drinks. It was a love for the ages. Or at least a good San Francisco lesbian rom-com, with all the essential highs and lows. Met while sober, broke up on Ecstasy, and rekindled after a spontaneous aya-huasca vision and a trip to Mount Everest, it was a psychedelic *L Word*.

Someone once said, *If it's not a hell yes, it's a no.*

It felt like the universe was screaming: *Hell yes.*

Even if I never summited Everest, my vision had brought me back to Lori, and that was enough.

eBay was one of the fastest-growing companies in Silicon Valley. At SKYY, the focus had always been on sales, but eBay was one of the first tech start-ups to talk about corporate responsibility. Early on, they established a foundation to give millions to nonprofits worldwide and created a platform for marginalized vendors in remote communities to sell their products. Lori was always volunteering at soup kitchens and looking for ways to help her community, and it was good for me to feel purposeful too, like my scope of work reached beyond getting models drunk in style. I'd spent years exuding a top-shelf image and dressing the part so that bartenders and VIPs would rec-ognize my importance. But at eBay, appearance was secondary. I was being challenged to think not just locally, but globally. In the same way that being surrounded by the Himalayas made me feel small in a good way, in my new role at eBay, for once, I was part of something bigger than myself.

Also, I couldn't drink while working there. Work was rigorous, and their San Jose campus was a professional, well-oiled machine. Crawling into work hungover in dark glasses was cause for concern, not an act of twisted cama-raderie. It was time to prove myself without the friendly haze of vodka to numb my desires, dreams, and disappointments.

Life was stabilizing, and the things I'd always envisioned for myself—what I knew I was capable of—seemed within reach for the first time, since, well, maybe ever.

I spent three to four nights a week at Lori's. During nights apart, our love-drenched, racy text exchanges put me to bed with a smile on my face. But there was no rush to move in together. Everything I'd rushed had crashed and burned. I wanted to do things differently. To slow down and allow things to evolve naturally instead of letting fear whip me into a frenzy, demanding *more more more* all the time. I'd given all of myself to SKYY. All of myself to hooking up. Instead of trying to control love, I tried to trust that no matter the details, the center would hold. I was trying trust. Trying moderation. Not just in our relationship, but in my drinking. If I could juggle a new career and a thriving relationship without pouring myself back into the bottle, then anything was possible.

Some mornings, I'd slip out without waking Lori to make the early train to San Jose. On the kitchen counter, I'd find a paper bag lunch with a note. "Just so you can be focused on your day. I love you." Or "Thank you, baby, for coming over. Looking forward to our weekend together."

We worked hard all week and kept our weekend Al Green and waffles brunch dates.

But one Sunday, Lori shot up in bed, panicked. Her face was bloodless and her flimsy white sleep shirt soaked under the armpits.

"What?" I mumbled, my eyes still crusted over. "What is it, baby?"

"I'm scared," she said. "Something doesn't feel right."

"About us?"

"No, no, about me. You know I get those headaches?"

I nodded. She'd started to develop horrible migraines, and her doctor had prescribed medication, but smoking a joint was the thing that usually helped most.

"Well, last Friday, I didn't work," she said, her voice like a slow scratchy record. "Actually I spent most of the day in bed, the whole time wondering if this was real."

"What was real, us?"

"No, this world. This place. If it was real or some sort of simulation."

Was she losing it? What did that mean, simulation?

"Do you have depression?" I asked, saying the thing I'd heard most discussed in the LGBTQ+ community or on the late-night commercials for prescription drugs with side effects that sounded worse than the actual disease they treated.

Lori nodded. "Sort of." She gathered the sheets up under her arms. Her sandy hair was matted in the back, her eyes flashing from brown to green as if trying to camouflage themselves. Hiding from some threat that only she could see.

"When I was living in Chicago," she said, "I had episodes of something called bipolar disorder. I would suddenly feel like everyone else was living in a reality different from mine. Other times, I became convinced we were all aliens living on an alternative world awaiting a liberation to see the truth."

"Umm." I stroked her hair, unsure what to say.

"I talked to a psychiatrist about some of my symptoms. They told me what it was called. But I've never told anyone else. Last Friday I started to feel it again."

"Have you talked to your parents about it?"

"I don't think they would understand. They might take me someplace and lock me up. Inject me with medication. You saw *Girl, Interrupted.*"

The more she explained, the more confused I was. I knew little to nothing about mental health. My family spoke of such things only in vague terms. "She's having a time," or "He's difficult." Things like that. It was hard for me to imagine a kind woman like Lori living with such torture. From the outside, she seemed so sturdy and bright.

The sort of person I aspired to be.

I wanted to show up for her.

"Let's drive to the beach," I said, pulling her close and kissing her forehead. Her skin was cold and slick against my lips.

That afternoon, I wrapped her in a warm blanket and walked her to the passenger seat of my Jetta. We held hands as I drove, and she looked out the window, her hair flapping in the wind. As I sped along the snaking curves of Highway 1, she gripped my hand, and for a moment, I felt a glimmer of her fear. Not just of my speed-demon driving, but about what was happening to her. We found a scenic spot on Poplar Beach in Half Moon Bay, where wind blew in and out like the tide. Without words, I wrapped myself around her and we sat there for hours until the sun set over the Pacific. The tighter I held her, the softer her cries became.

She was so fragile.

I'd never seen her like that, and every part of me yearned to protect her; to do whatever it took to make her feel safe. I stayed at her place for four days straight after that.

"Thank you for being here," she whispered the next morning. "I feel so much better."

That was what I'd been waiting to hear. That the pain had passed. That she was safe. That it was all over. That's how I saw it. I knew nothing about the inconsistencies of bipolar disorder, about its ebb and flow. After all, I'd never been to a therapist myself.

* * *

"So you've got the twenty-seventh through the fifth off, right?" Lori said.

Weeks later, we were back into our routine. "Mm-hmm," I said, nodding and grunting through a mouth full of toothpaste foam.

"You're gonna want a day on each end for travel," she said, pulling her tawny hair into a half bun.

"'Scuse me," I bumped her hip with mine when she swayed toward the door as I ducked under her arm to spit and swish into the sink.

"More if you can, babe. For time to recover. Trust me, you'll need it. This is going to blow your mind. Burning Man is indescribable. The art and the music, you've never seen anything like it. *I can't wait.*" She tapped an excited riff across the tile floor.

"That's all I can get," I said, splashing a handful of icy water on my face. "I'm sure." Patting myself dry with a hand towel, I ran a hand through my curls. Lori's fancy skin creams were doing some magic for me. Either that or love, but damn, I'd shed five years. Lori was beaming too as she pulled a mascara brush through her lashes.

"You know they say Burning Man can make or break a couple," she said.

"Mmm, do they now?" I raised an evil villain eyebrow. Lori just laughed. But her tone made my skin twitch. I wasn't a fan of tests. Especially ones I didn't know how to prepare for. At least I had until August to figure it out.

* * *

That March, I had a work trip scheduled to Shanghai. Part of my role at eBay was to support the expansion of international markets. Under the helm of Meg Whitman, we were focused heavily on the Chinese market, and this was going to be my third trip to China since I'd started. I was falling in love with the country. Lori had never traveled out of the States, and I wanted her to experience it, so I arranged for her to travel with me. She was just as captivated by China as I knew she would be.

She wandered the streets of Shanghai in awe. Her curiosity was a magnet. Her blonde hair and tall frame stood out among the locals, and though she didn't speak the language, she communicated somehow. She was one of those people who could talk to anyone, anywhere. The sort of person who is so earnest, so authentic, that you couldn't help but be charmed. What in others came off false or corny, in Lori felt generous and true. Strolling down Shanghai's Bund Promenade, she was giddy. She fell in love with the East's answer to the Space Needle, the Oriental Pearl Tower, a massive silver and pink structure that dominates the skyline. I snapped a photo of her that day in front of the tower, pure joy radiating from her.

When my work was done, we flew to Beijing, and after some Peruvian haggling on my part, I found a guide to take us to a remote part of the Great Wall. I wanted to treat Lori to a magical experience of one of the New Seven Wonders of the World. Something off the beaten path, something other than the typical Badaling tour that every tourist took—something no one else could give her.

We crossed through the gate and followed a dirt path that zigzagged up a steep incline. Just ahead, the Great Wall was a long, rocky spine cutting through lush mountains. We were the only foreigners around, and as we stepped up onto the wall, a woolly cluster of clouds rolled past, darkening the foothills to a moody blue green. The mountains of Beijing didn't have the height and grandeur of the Himalayas, but looking out onto the emerald folds of earth, I felt the same sense of freedom. Of possibility. I clutched Lori's hand, and we walked single file, stepping around piles of crumbled stone, until we came to a well-restored section. I tried to imagine the work it had taken to build the wall. Not just one generation, but many generations of Chinese who poured their lives into building it, this barrier, once necessary for protection, but now a relic.

"What's going to happen to the wall?" asked Lori.

"Seems they'll either restore it all or just let it crumble. Maybe let the earth take it back."

Every fortress has its natural end.

"You know," I said, "I've been waiting for a time to talk to you about this."

Lori turned to me, her face flushed. "Yes?"

"eBay wants me to consider moving abroad. It's just we're so focused on China, and there's lots of work in Europe. Being in California doesn't make sense for my role right now."

"That's great, baby. That's so great for you."

"Maybe you could join me?"

She kissed me but said nothing.

"Will you think about it?" I asked, my heart in my stomach.

"Let's get through Burning Man first."

* * *

That night in Beijing was oozy and dreamy, like a honeymoon. Giddy with laughter, we wove through the night market, high on each other as we ate BBQ crickets on a stick and sampled grilled scorpions and caterpillars. Lori settled for a starfish on a stick, which she thought looked appetizing "in an artistic way." It was terrible, but she ate two of the legs to prove her spirit of optimism and adventure. I let myself dream of a life abroad with her. We'd both be expats then, exploring a new world together. We could live among the European bohemians. I was the furthest thing from a bohemian— thriving in a set, strict corporate mentality—but being surrounded by artists and free spirits sounded romantic. Maybe Lori could become a writer for *National Geographic* or write the books she'd always wanted to, while I developed myself as a mountaineer.

Before we left China, we made a pact.

After Burning Man, we'd start a travel bucket list and check places off together. I bought Lori an expensive jade necklace as a token of our intention. A promise to travel the world together and embrace adventure wherever and whenever we could. "From Beijing to Burning Man!" I said. She pressed her lips to mine, and just like that very first night at the Endup, I felt electricity. By the time we got back to San Francisco, we were more in love than ever.

* * *

The week of Burning Man, I was not in the desert of northern Nevada with Lori. I was in Paris, wrapping up a three-course meal for one at a romantic brasserie and savoring the last of a delicious full-bodied Syrah. Shortly after our Beijing trip, eBay had temporarily relocated me to Europe. I'd begged Lori to come.

"They want to move me as soon as possible," I'd told her over dinner at my loft, buzzing with excitement. "And they're giving me two months to try out the different offices. There's London, Berlin, Paris, and Bern. Come on! We'll be international women of leisure. Well, working women—but international."

"Will you be able to come back for Burning Man?"

"I don't know; they haven't given me a timeline," I said, bristling. One of the biggest opportunities of my life and all she could talk about was Burning Man. "I might be in Berlin."

"Could you *ask* to come back? A special exception?"

"I doubt it," I replied sternly.

I'd finally joined the upper echelon, surrounded by Type-A minds with Ivy League pedigrees and supportive, prestigious families. Securing a spot in the aughts tech world had not been easy, and I wasn't brave enough to ruffle feathers yet. It was time to show them, and myself, what I was really capable of.

"What about our adventures?" I slid my finger along her clavicle and under the smooth jade stone she'd worn every day since we'd been back.

"Burning Man is more than just a party, baby," she said. "Don't you see? It's a way for us to see if we can manage a challenging environment like that as a couple. It puts you through things. Not just physical, but mental. Spiritual."

Hadn't we just been to China together? Was that not a challenge? What was her fixation on raging in the desert for a week?

"This is a big opportunity for me," I said, threading my arms across my chest. "I leave in two months."

As the weeks passed, I kept pressuring her, but she seemed to have an excuse for everything.

"It's a U.S.-based magazine," she said about her job at *Dairy Foods*, the publication she edited. "They want to have a U.S.-based editor."

"Alright. Well, what if you just quit your job and become a writer?" I shot back, proud of my quick problem-solving. "The kind you've always wanted to be."

Lori liked the idea of being a full-time writer, but during one of our Sunday Al Green brunches, she'd shared that she was too afraid to expose her writing to a public audience. But I figured there was no better time than the present. We could make a leap together.

"I wish I could," she said. "It's not that easy."

"Why not? Seems pretty straightforward to me."

I knew nothing about the life of a novelist. About what it took or how complicated it was. But my temper was flaring. Lori wasn't ready to become a writer or leave San Francisco or be without her Burning Man community. Excuses, all. Bullshit excuses.

"So if you don't come, what are we going to do?" I said, my anger softening to desperation.

"I want you to follow your dreams."

"But you're part of my dreams. I love you. I don't see why we can't give it a try."

"I'm sorry, baby." Her voice trembled. "But I don't think I can go . . ."

As deeply as I loved Lori, love had betrayed me. It had betrayed all the women in my life. My mother, who gave up everything for love, or for her version of it, which might have been nothing more than security in a life that guaranteed little to a woman like her. Meanwhile, my father yanked away any dream she dared to dream—but had never turned down a chance to advance his own career. Work had always been Segundo's number one. My brothers a close second; my mother and I, distant thirds.

Perhaps I was more like my father than I cared to admit because I didn't want to give up this chance to advance my career. I wouldn't give it up, not even for love.

This time Lori left me.

I was destroyed. Absolutely devastated. Positive it was the worst mistake she'd ever made, praying that it wouldn't be mine. Certain we'd fix it somehow, someday, some way. My love for Lori didn't fade, but her choice confirmed my suspicions that love was fleeting.

But ambition was a plant that thrived as long as I watered, fed, and tended it. If I could make executive, make it to the top of Everest, I could hoist the broken-hearted little girl on my shoulders where nothing could touch her ever again.

Work was my redemption.

If I could achieve greatness with eBay, a real company, the sort of company everyone who was someone wanted to work for, my brokenness would evaporate. Gone would be the woman who had blacked out in the bed of strangers. Gone would be the shameful gay daughter. The broken one. To me, success had a sheen to it so powerful I thought it could hide all the dark corners.

Of course, I failed to hear what Lori was actually telling me. That she'd found a safe community and sturdy ground. That she wasn't ready to uproot her bipolar disorder and depression and take them to a foreign country, with no one but me to rely on.

So as Lori raved in latex and flight goggles in the desert, I was nearing the end of my whirlwind two months in Europe and had discovered a new form of empowerment: the table for one. Sitting at a luxurious corner table alone felt bold. I imagined myself as the queer Hemingway, a real woman's man, dining on bloody steaks and fine wine. All I needed was a cigar.

As I savored the last of my Syrah, I remembered my promise to Mount Everest. Swilling wine and galivanting around Western Europe wasn't exactly conditioning me to climb. But I was learning about the Seven Summits— the challenge to climb the tallest mountain on each continent. Less than two hundred people in the world had done it, and very few of them were women. Maybe, I thought, my Virgo brain already assessing the order of things, if I just climb the mountains in ascending order, it'll be a natural preparation for Everest.

The easiest mountain was supposed to be Tanzania's Kilimanjaro, which the Masai called the "House of God." I wasn't completely prepared to go—I wasn't sure I had the right gear or enough training—but I wanted to see the glaciers at the top. They were supposed to be mystical relics from the ice ages.

I was closer to Tanzania now than I'd ever been.

If not now, then when?

* * *

When I came down from Kilimanjaro, eBay promoted me to head of financial systems for Europe and Asia and gave me my choice of cities. I chose Bern, Switzerland. Bern was a beautiful village built on the banks of the horseshoe-shaped Aare River, whose blue-green water glowed like a mystical lagoon. At first, living in Switzerland was thrilling. Even though I had my green card, declaring me a permanent resident, I'd never felt American. Europe just clicked. My new colleagues were bright, sparkly people from all over the world. Work was engaging, and we laughed the nights away during long wine-soaked dinner parties. It reminded me of SKYY at the beginning, when there were only a dozen employees. At the eBay offices in San Jose, there was so much competition to catch the attention of the top executives. But in Europe, maybe I could build a small community of like minds. Here I could be a big fish in a small pond.

But there was something missing.

In early December, I had one final trip planned to San Francisco to pack my loft into a twenty-foot shipping container.

There was nothing left for me in the city anymore. Nothing but Lori.

She'd been distant since Burning Man, but I called her after Kilimanjaro, and she laughed at my ignorant hijinks as only she could, making me feel more seen than stupid. Even over the phone, the space between us was thick with longing. Finally, she caved and told me about Burning Man. She was already planning the next year's camp. "I still have my jade," she said. "I wore it every day in the desert."

"Can I see you when I'm back?" I asked.

"You've got my number," she teased. We left it at that.

I was proud that I hadn't turned down a life-changing opportunity for her, but as I came to terms with leaving the United States for good, I saw it was more than just ambition. I no longer drank myself unconscious on weekdays, but I had taken on the mantle of workaholism with ease. In my family, alcoholism, any label really, was shameful. Naming it gave it limbs. Made it something we'd have to deal with, a gossipy label for the neighbors to cling to. Ambition, however, was a point of familial pride. As my mother used to say, "Por mi mejoría, mi casa dejaría." *For my betterment, I would even put my home up for sale.*

We don't set out to become our parents.

It seems they chase us even as we're running in the opposite direction.

Later, Lori left a comment on the blog I'd started to document my adventures abroad: "The city feels empty and ungenerous without you. Why is it that we only know what was good once it is gone?"

* * *

I had one month to settle my affairs in San Francisco and a one-way ticket back to Bern. Lori and I agreed to meet with each other Saturday afternoon at Barney's for tea. This was my final shot. I had to put everything on the line. Spill my guts. Tell her that short of leaving Europe, I'd do anything to be with her. All I could do was hope love was enough. The morning of our date, I woke to the sound of sirens. Eyes half-open, I glanced at the clock next to me. Seven-thirty a.m.

I was in a hotel in Sausalito.

I rolled out of bed and yanked open the curtains. Sun glimmered against the window, and for a split second everything went white. In that flash, the night before unrolled. *Sushi Ran. Celebratory drinks with friends. Too many celebratory drinks with friends. Sushi. Sake. Wine. Cheering. Toasts. Strangers joining the table. Congratulations! You're a European. An expat. One of us now. Oh God, I'm moving! I'm becoming an expat. I'm really, really in love with Lori. I'm too drunk to be driving back right now. I have to talk to Lori. So drunk. Sausalito.*

Sausalito. I'm still in Sausalito.

I found my car parked across from Sushi Ran and jumped in. My headache was dulled by the excitement of seeing Lori. The afternoon couldn't arrive fast enough. As I crossed the Golden Gate Bridge back into San Francisco, traffic was sluggish and aggravating, a rarity so early on a weekend. My legendary road rage was soothed by nostalgia. The bridge, the Bay, this drive, everything about the morning was tinted with good-bye. With the special sheen of knowing something is over. I noticed things I'd never seen before. Like how the sun backlit the grand archways of the bridge, deepening them from a flat red into terra-cotta, like something earthy and natural instead of a hulking piece of steel. In that light, the bridge seemed almost alive. Rolling down my window, I sucked in all the salty sea air I could catch in one gulp, then sighed it out, my limbs loosening and my heart full. Tony Bennett's "I Left My Heart in San Francisco" was playing on repeat in my head.

At eleven, I texted Lori to confirm our date.

Looking forward to seeing you at 2. Let me know if I should pick you up.

God, I thought as soon as I pressed send. *It sounds like I'm going to a business meeting. Be more alive. Expressive! This is a writer you're talking to.*

No reply. Not unusual for Lori. Christmas season was in full swing, and Lori was an avid decorator. She must have been caught up in her holiday cheer.

By one, she still hadn't replied. I called her and left a voicemail.

"Hey Lori, it's me. Let me know if we're still on for that tea!"

Arggg. Pathetic. You're trying too hard.

At two, still no word. I went to Barney's and waited on the sunny benches outside, where I bumped into a few of Lori's friends. They congratulated me on moving to Europe.

"Thanks," I said, and then, trying to be coy, "Hey, have you seen Lori around?"

"No, but I know she'll be at the party tonight," one said.

Perfect. She never missed the Ho Ho Ho Christmas party that our friend

Elena had started several years earlier as a fundraiser for local charities. It had become the mecca of lesbian Christmas parties.

"Awesome," I said. "See you there!"

By three-thirty, Lori was officially a no-show.

I was clutching a bag of treats I'd brought back from Switzerland for her. Maybe I'd just pop by and drop them off at her place. Just the thought of her face when she found the bag at her door made me giddy.

When I got there, her car wasn't parked in its usual spot, but I left the goodies in front of her door and shifted my attention to that night's party. I'd hoped to talk with her one-on-one, but I'd blown so many chances already that now wasn't the time for precision. It was time to spill my guts. To hold nothing back. To be brave and vulnerable.

That night, the party was packed, and looking for Lori was like playing a game of drunken telephone. Someone swore they'd seen her earlier that night; another person said she was *just on the patio. Or in another room, maybe, somewhere.* Everyone was deep into the spiked eggnog and swaying with Christmas spirit. I hung around 'til two in the morning, then drove back to my loft, leaving one last message on Lori's machine.

"Lori, I need to speak with you," I said, trying not to sound too desperate, but I was unraveling. Had I lost my chance? "I have something important to tell you, *really.* Please call me."

The next morning, I slept in. When I turned my phone on, there were twenty-five missed calls. As I started to scroll through them, the phone rang.

It was my friend Tara.

"Silvia, where are you?" she said as I croaked out a groggy hello.

"Home."

"Are you alone?"

"Yes."

"We're coming. Wait for us."

"Wait, why? What's going on?"

"Didn't you hear?"

"Hear what?"

"Lori."

"What happened? Is she okay? I've been looking for her. She was supposed to meet me."

"Silvia." There was a long pause.

"Tara?! What? WHAT."

"She jumped. Yesterday, she jumped. The bridge."

The Golden Gate.

"Silvia!" Tara called out. "Silvia?"

Yesterday I was driving over the bridge, looking down at the lapping bay, its calming navy blue waters. The sun glimmering on its foamy peaks. Tony Bennett serenading me. Tony Bennett reminding me that I was *not* going to leave my heart in San Francisco. That I'd come back to get her. Then something else. That stop and go on the bridge. Such strange traffic. Such strange Saturday traffic. Sirens first thing that morning. Had those been real or my alarm at the hotel? All those wailing sirens.

Water. *It was just water. Thank God. Lori had jumped into water.*

"Tara," I finally exhaled. "What hospital? Where is she? Where did they take her?! How many broken bones?"

Silence.

"Silvia, stay right there. We'll be there in ten minutes. Less maybe. Probably less."

"Tara, I need you to answer the question. Where did they take Lori?"

Silence.

Silence.

Silence.

"TARA!!!" I screamed.

"I'm so sorry . . . I know. I'm just . . ." The voice on the other end was no longer a friend of mine; it was no longer a woman or a person or any alive thing. It was a vacuum, sucking all the air from my lungs. My bedroom went gray. "She's dead, Silvia" were the last words I heard. "Lori's gone. We'll be there soon."

Gulping in the sea air as I crossed that very bridge, had I also been breathing in Lori's last breaths? Had I swallowed her screams, or did she jump in silence?

Chapter 15

∽∽∽∽∽

KIND IF YOU LET HER

"Sirdar," says Da Jangbu Sherpa.

"Cigar," I say.

Da Jangbu shakes his head. "Sir-*DAR*."

"Ci-*GAR*," I repeat, more slowly, but the syllables still roll off my tongue stubbornly wrong. Off to a great start, I see. When I slipped out before dawn this morning to pray at the camp altar, I was surprised to find Da Jangbu standing nearby. He wasn't praying, though, just quietly scanning the Khumbu Glacier.

Da Jangbu is our sirdar. At Base Camp, sirdars are like air traffic controllers. Essential. Invaluable. In charge of a lot. Each expedition's sirdar manages climbing logistics and routes, loads up the mountain, and communication between the guides, climbers, and Sherpa staff.

"Everest is a goddess," he says, nodding toward the glacier. I'm not sure if he's talking to me or himself. "Most important is to always be respectful."

"Of course, yes." I nod.

"Not like what's happened here."

His eyes darken as he scans the horizon, conjuring the wreckage of the last two years. Adventure Consultants alone lost six of its staff in the earthquake avalanche, mostly from the kitchen, and a dozen more were injured. I'd watched videos of the low rumbling, the sudden airborne tsunami of snow and icy scree flying down the mountain, all the tents flattened in its wake. When the powdery cloud settled, even the huge dining tents were upturned under reams of snow. Shiny tin pots scattered across camp like breadcrumbs.

And the year before that, in 2014, sixteen Sherpas had died when a ten-story-high tower of ice cracked off the Khumbu Glacier and crushed them.

In the sixty years since Tenzing Norgay Sherpa and Edmund Hillary first summited Everest, over three hundred people have died, some whose bodies have never been recovered. But in all its climbing history, there have never been back-to-back disasters with body counts like those in 2014 and 2015. Some Sherpas say that those years were cursed, and that the loss of life on the mountain was a result of something that came before. Not a natural disaster, but a human catastrophe.

The catastrophe of the Western ego.

When you're at 22,000 feet, energy is precious and oxygen low. But in 2013, no one was thinking about conservation when a brawl broke out between a hundred Sherpas and three famed European climbers after the climbers ascended from Camp 2 to Camp 3 against Sherpa orders. Rocks were wielded as weapons; punches and slurs were thrown. Both sides recall the story in their favor, but from what I can tell, it comes down to a matter of respect. The expertise of the Sherpas was challenged, and long-simmering tensions between the climbers and the Sherpas, to whom that mountain is not only a peak but a god, finally hit a boiling point. Elizabeth Hawley, the famed official Everest recordkeeper, later explained to the confused Europeans that their actions had shamed the lead Sherpa. "In Asian culture," she told them, "that is the worst thing that can happen."

Others say that fight was a long time coming.

"The resentment was always there," Tashi Sherpa said in an interview with *Outside* magazine. "Earlier, most Sherpas were uneducated, and they would grin and bear it. Earlier, we had suppressed our feelings." Tashi Sherpa is part of a new wave of young Sherpas, like the founders of Seven Summits Treks—a pair of Nepali brothers who've climbed all fourteen of the 8,000-meter peaks—who are no longer content singing backup for the legacy out-fitters, mostly European, Kiwi, and American.

Many older Sherpas are settled into comfortable roles with companies like Adventure Consultants and make up to $6,000 for an Everest season of work—a major amount when you consider that Nepal's average annual income is $1,100. Still, climbers like me pay around $45,000 at the midrange.

Those who are looking for more climbing support—they need private guides or want higher-end perks at Base Camp—pay upward of $100,000. Although Everest isn't a commodity that can be harvested and traded on an index, many locals feel the mountain is being sold to the highest bidder, and they are not the ones reaping the lion's share.

And this year, the year I chose to climb, is the twentieth anniversary of the 1996 disaster. Now, after three years in a row of chaos, whispers of a curse float around Base Camp. The air is unsettled, uncertain. So many are still grieving the dead. The spiritual homeostasis of Everest has been rocked, and I am treading lightly. If Sherpas consider her their goddess and church, I'll honor her just like my own.

"Pardon me," I say to Da Jangbu Sherpa with a little bow. I want to get my prayers in before breakfast.

"Hmmph," he grunts and goes back to staring.

The outdoor altar is a rustic stone tower draped with tattered prayer flags. Day-old fruits in a chilled still life. Perfectly round Asian pears and bite-sized lychee nuts with red skin so cracked it looks like it's been climbing too long without gloves. The ground being too rocky for me to kneel, I bow instead at the altar, trying to recall the four directions of a Taoist practice I had learned. Three times I bow to the north. *Be pleasant and charitable to your friends, relatives, and neighbors.* To the east, I bow three times. *To respect and honor my parents.* To the south, three times. *To respect and obey my teachers.*

And finally, to the west. *To be faithful and devoted to my life.*

Gripping my mother's rosary between stiff fingers, I slip into a Buddhist chant that Marta, my shaman friend in San Francisco, gave me to bring to Everest. I never asked what it meant, but her instructions were to repeat it 108 times. I'd memorized it on the plane.

"Om, Tare, tare tuttare, ture soha," I chant to the percussion of prayer flags snapping in the wind.

Om, Tare, tare tuttare, ture soha.

Om, Tare, tare tuttare, ture soha.

Omtaretaretuttareture소ha.

Somewhere around number 45, the words start to melt into one long sound.

Behind me, camp is coming to life. Pans clatter, and I imagine Tendi scrambling eggs and simmering morning porridge. When I peel open my eyes, I'm shocked to remember where I am. It's hard to take it all in at once. Everest is almost imperceptible. A little nub on the horizon. *That* is where I'm going? With my own two feet and hands I'm going to lug my body to the top of the world. Not happening. It's beyond what I can imagine, and I have a great imagination. Look at how I got here in the first place. But when I close my eyes, I just can't see it. I can't place myself at the summit. It's beyond my field of visualization. Everest is great as an idea. People love to talk about it at dinner parties. "Oh, you're going to climb Everest? Bold! Daring. I would *never. Tell me more.*" They lean in, with bated breath, body language suddenly more open. It's a real hero's adventure when it's all in your mind. But as I bow in the frigid air, an amphitheater of mountains rocketing into the sky around me, my knees start to twitch, and my palms go warm with slick sweat. I'm seeing the mountains with my body for the first time. And they are outrageous.

The idea of finding healing here suddenly strikes me as so absurd that I burst into laughter. Da Jangbu Sherpa flashes me a suspicious side-eye and with a polite nod rushes off to begin the morning's work.

Today, we begin ladder training.

A soft down of snow dusts my face as I weave through the sprawling maze of Base Camp. It's the beginning of the season, and there's a whir of activity as everyone sets up to live at 17,000 feet for the next six weeks. It's like the opening scene in *M*A*S*H*, but with yaks instead of jeeps. Everything is brought in by choppers that hover like hummingbirds over the helipad, dropping off supplies and people, or by yaks, driven in by Nepali porters in acid-wash jeans and ratty fleece. The yaks' gonglike bells jangle as they lumber into camp with plastic toilets, North Face expedition bags, and titanic sacks of food piled high on their backs. Base Camp is a mini citadel. Twenty expeditions. Forty to eighty people in each, including the guides, climbers, sirdars, and Sherpas. Sagging strands of prayer flags flutter above, creating loose lanes that section off each expedition, dividing the camp into haves and have-mores.

At the working-class end of town, where climbers pay the bare minimum, $30,000, all campsites look alike. There's a dining tent for meals and lounging, and smaller individual dome tents for sleeping, but the climbers lack the amenities of the high-end camps.

Two men walk toward me, and as they brush past without saying hello, I see that it's Russell Brice and Conrad Anker. Everest icons, whom few outside the mountaineering world would recognize. In 1999, Anker, one of the most respected mountaineers in the world, discovered the still-frozen body of British mountaineer George Mallory, who was part of the first Everest attempt and who died on the mountain in 1924. And Brice is one of Everest's best-known guides for high-end expeditions. His climbers pay for hot showers in private stalls and yoga-retreat perks like his famed geodesic-dome lounge with faux tiger rugs, a big-screen TV, and a clear panoramic viewing wall with a stunning vista of the Himalayas.

With five of the Seven Summits under my belt, I should be used to the collision of class and culture in mountaineering by now. But everything is amplified here. The hunger palpable. Everyone in this temporary village has one goal. To reach the top or get someone else there.

This is it: Everest.

The ultimate coup.

The crown jewel.

Parting the canvas doorway, I duck into our dining tent and exchange greetings with the crew before filing into the buffet line. "Good morning," says Tendi, as he ladles out mugs of oatmeal. Tendi lost his brother and his cousin in last year's avalanche. But like so many in the Sherpa community who make Base Camp tick, he came back. The Adventure Consultants camp sits solidly in the middle class, where climbers in performance fleece and nylon trekking pants shell out their life savings for one chance to chase the dream. Most of their local team has worked with the firm for over a decade. There's a loyalty, a pride, in knowing that every single member of the expedition is integral to a successful expedition no matter how many people summit. When he sees me, Tendi stops and fills a cup with hot quinoa instead.

"Namaste." I take the mug. "Thank you for remembering."

He has laced the grains with butter and cinnamon, and the rich, woodsy steam prickles the inside of my nose as I slide quietly into a seat next to Mark, the soft-spoken professor from Connecticut.

While we eat, Mike stands.

"As you know, rotations are staggered between expeditions to avoid congestion," he bellows like a general addressing his troops. "Training starts tomorrow."

Climbing Everest is not a bottom-to-top journey, but a series of ascents and descents done in three rounds called rotations. To inoculate our bodies to thin air, we have to climb incrementally. From Base Camp, there are five stops along the way: Camp 1, Camp 2, Camp 3, Camp 4, and Summit. Each rotation pushes to a higher camp and ends with a descent back to Base Camp to rest and recover, until the final push. The trek covers six weeks, and by the time we summit, *if we summit*, we'll have climbed the entire mountain almost twice.

I missed the first orientation because I was with the girls, and besides following the packing list and completing the at-home training Adventure Consultants required, I haven't studied the route or even let my mind wander up Everest at all. It sounds silly now that I'm here, but to memorize it was to make it real. Underpreparing is my secret weapon. Helps cut the anxiety. The inevitable *what if* of failure. Visualizing myself at the summit and not making it is worse than never imagining it at all. As the morning's quinoa turns to sludge in my gut and we get ready to start training, I'm no longer sure about my tried-and-true technique.

The next day, Mike and Ang Dorjee lead us to an open snowy field with small ravines and icy cliffs. Aluminum extension ladders are laid horizontally over the ravines like bridges, and others are bolted vertically to the cliffs. Nylon ropes anchored into the ground with ice screws snake down the sides of the ladders. It's like a firefighter's boot camp. By the time we make it to summit, we will have climbed up or over two hundred of these ladders, most of them in the Khumbu Icefall. It's early in the season, and we're one of the first teams scheduled to cross.

The Khumbu Icefall is a treacherous section of the two-and-a-half-mile-long Khumbu Glacier, which separates Base Camp from Camp 1. Sliding down the mountain as fast as four feet a day, the Icefall is a living entity. With a deadly obstacle course of ice towers called seracs, which can collapse at any time, the Icefall is fracturing and migrating, sinking and melting and refreezing, all the time. To call the Khumbu unstable is like calling Everest a hill. The Khumbu is volatile, erratic, moody. Seismic.

Where the ice cracks and pulls apart, it leaves behind massive chasms. Giant crevasses, some over 150 feet deep. At the beginning of every climbing season, the icefall doctors, a team of specialized Sherpas employed by the Nepali government, are the first to step onto the Khumbu. They work long days to chart a route up the glacier, installing a series of ladders and ropes for climbers to navigate the Khumbu's labyrinthine maze of icy canyons and spires.

The ice doctors are very skilled, but the system isn't as high-tech as you'd expect. They bolt aluminum extension ladders to the ice, sometimes even lashing two or three together with thick rope to create rickety footbridges over a crevasse or up a massive wall. Some years, there's a passage that calls for five ladders in a row. *Five.* Imagine crossing a dangerous river but instead of a bridge, there's a bunch of ladders from your garage roped together. Instead of rushing water, the river is a yawning icy abyss, and if you fall, you pray you die on the way down, because if you don't, odds are you'll freeze to death alone while feeling all of your broken bones.

We're silent as we step into and tighten our climbing harnesses. Glancing around, I note who's strapping in quickest—where I stand in the lineup. Gabe and Tom are swift and fluid, the rest of the men move methodically, and I fumble with the fasteners, sudden nerves turning my fingers to spoons.

Once we're harnessed, we clomp to the edge of the training course and fasten on our crampons. As we break into a line, I imagine the *Rocky* theme playing faintly in the distance.

Cozying up to Danny, who did this last year, I gesture to the training course. "Sooo. Does this look like what we'll cross in the Khumbu?"

"Not at all," he replies, with a sly grin. "This is a joke. Think ten times harder. Twenty, easy."

I gulp.

Ignorance is bliss, I tell myself, not for the first time in my life. *Stay present. There will be plenty of time to worry later.*

First up—horizontal ladders.

Up close they look even dinkier.

Two long ropes run like handrails alongside the outside of the ladders, and each rope is anchored into the ice at either end with specialized screws, like tent stakes. Only one person crosses at a time, and two others stand at each end, pulling the ropes taut to create firm railings for the person crossing.

Tom, the former SEAL, and Gabe, the Aussie police chief, sail across.

I'm up. From the other side, Gabe locks eyes with me and pulls on one end of the rope. Behind me, Bryan holds the other side.

"Most important thing is tension," says Ang Dorjee. "Feel the rope. Even through your gloves, you must perceive the subtlety. Balance between tense and slack is essential."

I clip the carabiner dangling from my harness onto the rope on my right, grab a rope in each hand, and begin to walk. The men leave me just enough slack to pull the ropes waist high, but not so much that the handrail effect collapses. The *Rocky* theme warps into circus music. I'm a performer walking a tightrope—the ropes in each hand my balancing poles. I smell the popcorn. Hear the scattered roars of the audience below. The heat of the swirling lights, the rumble of wild animal hooves, the glittering costumes. My limbs pulse with adrenaline. My skin is a heartbeat.

But there's a problem I have that the men don't. Their boots match the space between the rungs of the ladder, so that the teeth of their crampons latch onto a rung on either end of their boots and hold them in place. But my feet, a full six inches shorter than Tom's or Gabe's, are going to slip through the hole between the rungs. I have to balance both of my feet, crampons and all, on each rung and move extra slow, leveraging the tension of the fixed ropes even more delicately to keep myself upright. For the first time, I wish my fast soccer feet were giant man boats.

"Get comfortable with that flex and bend," calls Mike, as I edge myself from rung to rung. I flash him a death stare. "Bounce your knees!"

Back in San Francisco, my neighbor, a retired army specialist from Wisconsin, helped me run a twenty-foot extension ladder from my deck into his yard, angling it to re-create the wobbliness I needed to *become one* with. He spent Sunday mornings supervising as I crossed back and forth in crampons, trying to re-create the feel of Everest. *Become one with the wobble*, I'd chanted. But this. This feels different.

"Mmmm." I hesitate, shaking my head.

"Go ahead!" Mike pushes.

I bend my knees and press my weight down slightly. The ladder springs up, buoyant. More buoyant than I knew metal could be. My breath catches in my throat, my heart rapping against my chest as the twang of vibrating aluminum echoes through the icy canyon. I'm only five feet off the ground, but to me the gap below is infinite. A chasm. In all of history, there has never been a deeper, darker void.

"Follow the line of the rope," Ang Dorjee says. "Just keep your eye on the anchors ahead."

Locking my eyes into the line, I find a steady rhythm—right foot on rung, left foot joins, pause, breathe, rebalance, repeat. Each hollow chink of crampon against the ladder is a precious sound. Metal on metal means that I'm connected. When my crampon finally pierces snow on the other side, I let out a horsey sigh of relief. Hours, days, a lifetime has passed. I have aged a hundred years.

"Nice!" John shoots me a thumbs-up from across the crevasse. I wave.

After we all make it across, Mike and Ang Dorjee march us like ducklings toward a twenty-foot-high ridge of glacier ice with a vertical ladder screwed into its face. We nod as Mike runs down the basics of vertical climbing and rappeling.

"Number one!" he says, showcasing the ladder. "You see the ladder. TWO. Lock your carabiner into the safety rope. You are *always* clipped in. Two safety points at all times. Repeat after me, you are always clipped in."

"You are always clipped in!" hollers Brian.

"Not him, *you*," says Ang Dorjee. Brian's whole body rocks with laughter.

"WE are always clipped in," I chant, annoyed. I need these words drilled into my memory.

"Check with the teammate holding your rope," Mike goes on. "They're your lifeline. Make sure they look alive! All clear? Begin to climb and make sure the rope doesn't get tangled in your harness. Once you get to the top, unlock from the fixed rope, lock into the extension rope, and quickly move away from the edge to a safe position. Simple. Let's try it."

Mike scrambles up to the top of the ladder and hovers over us like a stern father, glints of sun bouncing off his polar mountain sunglasses. Ang Dorjee plants himself at the bottom of the ladder, arms folded over his chest, unsmiling in matching glasses.

"Most important," he says. "Look up. Only up! When crossing any ladder, do not look down."

The vertical ladder has only one rope. I clip onto it with my carabiner, which is pretty flimsy security. But for some reason we accept the wild danger of this. I suppose that's why we're all here and the people we love are comfortable at home not doing this.

Getting up goes quickly. It's the most natural thing we've done.

And now for the fun—rappeling. I've rappeled plenty, on Vinson Massif last winter, at Mount Rainier, and down most of the Carstensz Pyramid in

Indonesia, a jagged limestone peak near the coast of New Guinea. Carstensz is a highly technical one-day climb. More rock climbing than mountaineering. Getting down involves twenty long rappeling sections and a Tyrolean traverse—where you hang from your harness and pull yourself across the rope upside down.

I love free-falling safely down the side of a mountain and that hypnotic zip of rope sliding through aluminum.

I'm last and feeling confident as the group's eyes settle on me. But my first attempt starts out clunky. *You've got this.* I sweet-talk myself. *Just think smooth.* After the ladders, I need to show Ang Dorjee that I've got one skill down. That I've earned my place here. The air is a deep freeze, and my nose starts to run, trickling toward my lip. I bend forward to wipe it on the sleeve of my jacket. "Focus!" bellows Mike, throwing off my focus. I careen to the side, smashing my thighs into solid ice, bruising both my legs and my ego.

"You must master rappeling for the descent," calls Ang Dorjee. "This is imperative," he says.

I've got this, I want to cry.

Finally, I zip to the bottom and land with an exhausted thud in the snow.

For the next hour, we take turns climbing and rappeling, using the spiky tines of our crampons to inch slowly down. Ang Dorjee's eyes flit back and forth as he calls out adjustments. By the end, I'm back in the groove and flying down, high on the feeling of a controlled free fall. While others keep working the wall, I run back to the horizontal ladder. Bryan and John follow me and stand on either side, holding the slack for me as I cross again and again and again. I have to master any weak points now. We have a trial run on the Khumbu tomorrow.

"So the girls from San Francisco, that you hiked with? How do you know them?" asks John as I step methodically from rung to rung. John has a pied-à-terre in San Francisco and perked up when I mentioned the city. He's the only one who's taken interest in my trip with the girls. John, a former academic turned financier with houses all over the world, retains his refined flair, even when sweating and grunting up the mountain. A sort of decorum and manners that remind me of traveling in Europe.

"Through a nonprofit," I say. "I talked to a roomful of girls, and they were the only ones who didn't think I was full of shit."

"Aha!" John declares. "Smart girls, then. Classroom learning has nothing on this."

Tom saunters over to watch, hands on his hips. Advice on the tip of his tongue. I can feel it.

"I haven't done much ladder work," I say nonchalantly. "I'll get the hang of it."

"Listen," he says, with a little smile. "If you end up leaving early, I'll be more than happy to bring one of your dedications to the summit."

"Thank you," I say sweetly, biting my tongue. "That's very thoughtful of you."

But when I stumble during the next pass, I wonder if he's right.

What are my chances of making it, really?

"About forty percent," says John.

"Huh?"

"Your chances."

Oh, God. I'd said that aloud.

"And chance of death: do you want to hear that?" says Tom.

"Hey," says John, his tone suddenly crisp. "Men and women have equal odds of both death and success."

That may be true, but nothing about the stat is soothing. After training is complete for the day, I stop at the dining tent to try to reach the girls. Shailee's been texting me updates on the return hike. They should be at lunch in Phakding now, fueling up for the grueling final push to Lukla. I dial Shailee's number.

"Hey, Silvia," Shailee answers

Then a voice—two, three, five, maybe, I can't keep track. Everyone talks excitedly over each other.

"Silvia! We miss you!"

"Shreya! Is that you? I . . ."

"Mom!" cries Lucy. "You'll never guess what they're teaching me."

"What? What is it?"

"The Nepali Macarena."

They burst into frantic bubbling laughter, a happy swarm of voices. There's a new ease in their banter. I can see them huddled around the phone, arms draped over each other. A little family now, a sisterhood. Underneath the noise, I can make out Rubina's voice. "We love you," she says softly. "And we miss you."

"I love you too," I say. "I love you all." And I do. It's never been so easy to say and mean it.

"Please be careful!" says Lucy.

"Thank you for everything, Silvia." It's Jimena. Their voice starts to crack. "I will never forget this. I love you."

"Bye for now!" Ehani says abruptly in English.

More laughter.

They're so close. I know they'll make it back. They did it. They did this. Each of them is going to ride or fly back home carrying souvenirs known only to them. Private wisdom that no one can take away. Not now. Not ever.

I keep telling myself to let them go and focus on Everest. But maybe that's not how this works. Maybe they're with me now. For good. For all the training, for falling off ladders and getting back up again, for everything that comes next.

"Take it one step at a time, Silvia," says Shailee, just before she hangs up. "And remember, you have the Mother with you. She will be kind if you let her."

* * *

Tom doesn't even make it to first rotation.

"It's HAPE," Mike says as they escort Tom to the ER tent.

The death knell.

With High Altitude Pulmonary Edema, the lungs fill with fluid. The only way to reverse it is to descend immediately to a lower elevation. We watch from camp as a chopper floats down to the helipad. Tom becomes a tiny body on the tarmac. He's loaded in, and the helicopter glides off toward Kathmandu. Just like that, Tom and his dream are gone.

It's day five.

I'm in shock. We all are. Tom was a real-life action hero. American patriotism embodied. At sixty, he was the oldest, but arguably the most fit of the group. One of the world's best triathletes. A survivalist. Cut from the same cloth as the team that hunted down Osama bin Laden. Logically, I know altitude sickness has nothing to do with fitness or attitude. That it cares little about age. That it strikes at random and at will, and there's no way to predict what altitude will do to your body.

But if Tom, the true American hero, was leveled by our two trial hours on the Khumbu, what the hell chance do I have to make it to the summit? Tom had it all. The focus, the muscle, the grit. And it still didn't protect him.

At dinner, I gobble down my food in ravenous silence. My nerves are raw. Our first rotation starts tomorrow, and the Khumbu is haunting me.

"Breakfast at one," says Ang Dorjee. I groan. It's already eight o'clock. So much for beauty sleep.

"Sleep hard!" Mike says as we shuffle out of the dining tent. "You're going to need it."

I wave goodnight and collapse into the little cave of my tent. Its nylon walls quiver in the wind as I crawl into my mummy bag and zip it up to frame my face. I will sleep to come. *Please, please.* At home, no matter how exhausted I am, as soon my head hits the pillow, a fresh surge of energy pushes me up. I have to read until two or three a.m. or distract myself online or do anything I can to work myself to an exhaustion so deep that my mind can no longer fight my body. Sleep has never come easy. It took me a long time to make the connection. To realize that for some people, bed was a relaxing place, not a door to memories they had tried to forget. In my dreams, anything can happen. As long as I'm awake, on the move, I'm in control.

But here in the mountains, I have to surrender. Here, obeying bedtime is a tiny mercy.

It's one of the things I love most about climbing. The militaristic order of camp. At first, it's a struggle, but eventually it's a relief to let go and do as I'm told. To quell my inner Tasmanian devil. Being on the mountain, climbing with a team, demands the type of structure that evades me in everyday life. Here I have to take care of myself.

Here, rest is not a luxury. And drinking is not an option.

By nine o'clock, I drop into a dreamless sleep. I'm so tired I don't even hear the avalanches cracking in the distance.

* * *

Ang Dorjee begins to chant as soon as he sets foot on the Icefall. We file onto the glassy terrain behind him, one by one, scattering dried rice that the kitchen staff tucked into our palms this morning. The rice is our offering to the mountain. *Breathe and trust*, I tell myself as the beadlike grains spill through my fingers. My cheeks are chilled porcelain. My breath, a crystalline cloud. We're asking for safe passage. *Breathe and trust.* For protection. *Breathe and trust.* For kindness. *She will be kind if you let her.*

I really want to believe that.

It's just after two a.m.

It's best to cross the Khumbu in the middle of the night, when the glacier is the most frozen and its network of icy lattices holds tight. As the day goes on, the searing Himalayan sun starts to soften the ice, creating soggy pockets more prone to collapse. We climb in total silence and darkness, the path lit only by warped yellow circles of light from our headlamps.

Mark, Bryan, and Danny are ahead of me; John, Rob, and Gabe, behind.

The sound of our crampons chopping into snow is meditative—like splitting firewood or chopping vegetables, it's a mantra marking every step.

As we move deeper into the icy chambers, the crunch of our steps echoes, and the slick walls glow from the inside, producing an eerie white glare that competes with our headlamps. Sherpas say the spirit of a dead body stays close by for weeks. I wonder how many ghosts haunt these icy tombs. Shadows play hide-and-seek. At one angle, craggy columns of ice resemble sinister faces; at another, they disappear. The Khumbu is a Rorschach test—every frosty formation an inkblot.

At the two-hour mark, we hit the first series of ladders. Every crossing is ceremonious. As we cross one at a time, the rest of us wait quietly, as if any sudden sound or movement might tempt the mountain to swallow us whole. And it might. In the Khumbu, sudden loud sounds can set off an avalanche. If an avalanche hit now, it would pick us up like jacks and fling us down the mountain.

As I cross, I count the chinks of my crampons on the metal rungs. 1–2, 1–2, 1–2, 1–2. Beneath me, the crevasse is a wide, hungry mouth. *Whatever you do, don't look down.* Ang Dorjee's warning echoes in my mind. But the total absence of light below is hypnotic. There's a pull to the darkness—one that feels familiar. I can almost smell the nothingness calling me.

Trust, Silvia. Trust that my team will hold the ropes taut. *Trust* that they'll give me the exact tension I need to balance. *Trust. Trust. Trust.* If I keep repeating it, maybe I will feel it. I can't remember the last time I put this much trust in men.

We're at the fourth ladder now, a horizontal one that leads to a vertical ahead, and I'm surprised to feel more at ease as I step onto the first rung. Steadying myself, I glance quickly down into the crevasse. My foot almost slips.

"Always ahead, Silvia!" Ang Dorjee's voice is a whisper scream.

At four a.m., the night starts to break, and the sky becomes a sea. Deep marine blue. Majestic blue. Not soothing baby blue or hospital blue, but a pigment so lush and pure it's almost fake. Blue like the origins of the color blue itself. And the stars? A million crystals tossed against velvet. The moon? Lighting our pathway with pools of silvery light.

This is how I would describe the beauty of the landscape if I were sitting at home, watching us climb. It would demand that sort of poetry.

But all I see is the oblong sphere of light in front of me. The blue-black bruise of the ice as night's curtain rises. All I can see is a massive chunk of ice crashing down any minute to pulverize me. All I can think about is the irony of being killed by a place so beautiful.

That's the funny thing about Everest. For all its lore and beauty, when you finally get here, most of your energy is spent eating, sleeping, and trying not to die.

Around five a.m., dawn shoots arrows of light through the ice. Frozen stalactites drip like long sharp teeth over house-sized banks of snow. In aerial photos of the Khumbu, it looks approachable, like a series of decent sledding hills. But as the sun starts to rise, the stark drama of the landscape reveals itself. It's a frozen Sahara of undulating blue-ice dunes and craggy archways of snow carved out by time and the melt of ancient water.

What little I can take in is astounding.

"I wish my wife could see this."

"Huh?" A voice snaps me out of my trance. I crane my neck to look back. John's behind me.

"She would be blown away," he whispers.

John's wife is sick. That's how he said it at first. But over the next few days around the dinner table, I learned it was clinical depression. He's been worried about leaving her, but this is his big dream, his one shot.

I nod, focused on putting one foot in front of the other.

"I'm sorry she can't see this."

The rest of the ladder crossings are swift. A human relay, we make it through two ladders, then five, then ten. There are no flat areas. No easy parts. There is only up and over. Up and over, over and up. Falling into a seamless choreography, even our breath is starting to sync, frosty clouds coming out in labored huffs.

It's dangerous to stop for too long. The ground is a shifting island. We take few breaks.

When the ladders end, which they do on some vertical banks, we spiderman ourselves the rest of the way up icy ridges, hanging on by the teeth of our crampons and activating our shoulders and back muscles to pull our weight up with the rope. My calves are scorched as I stop for water at the top of what feels like the hundredth ladder. We've been going for four hours.

As I'm gulping down half a Nalgene, Mike suddenly shouts, "Silvia, move faster!" *Shit, shit, this is it. An avalanche! I knew it. Padre Nuestro . . .* I start to pray, making the sign of the cross as I scan the horizon for the telltale plume of snow.

"That's not Silvia!" Brian calls from below. I can hear him laughing. "She's already ahead of us. This isn't Silvia's butt. It's mine."

Just then, Brian pulls himself over the top of the ledge. "Hey, I got your ass according to Mike. What an insult."

"I . . ." I'm not sure if it's a joke or a dig. With Brian, it's hard to tell.

"An insult to you!" he cries. "But an honor to me. I didn't know my behind was so diminutive."

"Guess you're my butt double now." I shrug. "Never know when I might need one."

He roars, slapping me on the shoulder. I wince. My arms are throbbing.

We keep moving. The temperature is rising. From –10 degrees Fahrenheit to hovering around zero, it seems to be leveling out.

By six a.m. we're on the Football Field, a massive amphitheater of stepped ice that looks like bleachers. To the left, the western shoulder of Everest flanks us, rising at an imposing fifty-degree angle. Suddenly the pace quickens. Peeking around Danny, I see Ang Dorjee in the lead, striking toward the Golden Gate, the site of the 2014 disaster.

They say it was more like a rocket than a typical avalanche because there was so little snow. A sixty-ton serac, a spaceship's worth of ice, cracked away from the glacier and shot down the mountainside, crushing sixteen Sherpas to death. They dug up one body, and nine more were stacked underneath.

A sadness settles over the group as we catch up to Ang Dorjee. He's standing where they found the men, pointing out exactly where the glacier fractured. As he retells the story, his voice is a deep rumble. The Icefall is about fifteen hundred feet long, he says, and this, where we're standing—the middle five hundred feet—is the most dangerous part because the ice shifts so rapidly, sometimes by as much as three feet a day.

I keep thinking about what Tashi Sherpa said in his *Outside* interview about the Sherpa view on Everest.

"Everest is a goddess. We worship it before embarking on an expedition," he said. I knew that the Sherpas thought climbers from the West only saw Everest as a physical challenge, as a way to see how close they can get to death. To the sherpas it was a sacred place—one that should inspire humility more than bravado.

For two decades, the official South Col route has run under this same serac because it's faster than the original, safer route established in the 1970s.

Now, it's a ghost town. Broken ladders are crystallized in the rock-hard ice. Torn ropes swing over the crevasse.

The still-life leftovers of tragedy.

Frozen bodies arrested in ascent.

Like what remains of trauma.

Sometimes we have to return to the site to begin to heal.

* * *

The final push for the day looks like another death-defying circus act. Five aluminum ladders are lashed end to end with nylon rope and bolted to a hundred-foot-tall wall of sheer ice. It's a fully vertical staircase above what looks like a snowy nowhere below. And it's pretty much all that stands between us and Camp 1.

Mark is already halfway up, and as he climbs, the aftershock of his steps vibrates the ladders all the way down to the bottom, where I stand nervously awaiting my turn. When he finally disappears over the top ledge, I approach the ladder. My crampons pierce the ice. My skin screeches. Every sensation is amplified. The volume turned all the way up.

I take a deep breath and brace myself against vertigo.

Breathe.

I clip my carabiner to the safety rope on the right.

Left boot, right hand.

Right boot, left hand.

My crampons grate against the aluminum as I climb.

Breathe.

Do not look down.

There *is* no down.

Down does not exist.

There is only up.

Only this ladder.

This one rung.

This moment.

There is no past. No future.

Only this moment.

This ladder.

This ice.

This shimmery wall of ice. This tiny square of beautiful blue ice. Ice really isn't white when you see it this close. It's translucent. A milky blueish white. The sort of white that exists only in the paint department on a swatch with a silly name: Soft Cloud, Alabaster, Whale's Mouth.

Deadly Blue Ice.

Left boot, right hand.

Right boot, left hand.

Breathe.

Maybe I'll paint my living room deadly ice blue when I get home. If I make it home.

No future. No past.

This moment.

This ladder.

This rung.

This ice.

Look how the ice is melting there. Oh, cool. The way it drips down the wall, very poetic, like a trail of tears falling down, down, down to—do *not* look down. Hell is down. Heaven is up. Look up. Ohhhh, look, I'm almost halfway.

Yes.

I'm ascending.

Right boot, left hand.

I'm climbing. I'm pushing. I'm changing.

The ladder starts to wobble. I must be in the middle now. The jiggly belly of the beast. Hot fear floods my body as metal bucks against metal, a distorted cacophony of grating and bending and warping. It's the fear orchestra, and it is loud, symphonic. Cymbals clash in my mind, banging out *fear, fear, fear.*

Ángelito de la Guarda . . .

This is it. This is the end.

If heaven is up and hell is down, this must be purgatory.

This stupid ladder is the last thing I'm going to see before I die. How anticlimactic. *Death by Ladder* is not what I imagined would be etched on my gravestone. *Here lies Silvia. It wasn't the vodka or the avalanche that got her, but the Feld Fire ladder.*

Wait, I'm past the fourth ladder. One more to go. My God, I can do this.

There's a face. A Sherpa. He's looming over me, pointing to something. The safety rope at the top. Clip into the safety rope before clipping out of the ladder. Do not forget, Silvia.

In before out.

There's a moment between releasing the ladder and stepping onto the ridge above when I am hovering. I hesitate. I'm not ready to let go.

"It's okay, it's okay," the Sherpa is saying, waving me up aggressively. Everyone says being present is the ticket to happiness. To freedom. Is this what they mean? No escape. No way to go faster or slower. To turn around or jump ahead. Marching through the long, slow pain of every moment. If so, if this is what the saying meant, have I ever been truly present in my life?

Half my team is on the ground, waiting to climb. Getting back down will be harder. There's nowhere to go but up.

The Sherpa reaches out his hand. *In before out.* Clip in. Clip out. Pull rope. Grab his hand—warm and steady wrapping around mine. Final step off the ladder. A metallic twang as it reverberates behind me. Land crampon on ice. Push down harder to ground it into the ice. Step down into the snow and let out a gasp. I'm on solid ground.

Ang Dorjee, John, Mark, and Rob are all patting my back, my arms.

Even inside the down gloves, my hands are frozen. Adreneline shuttles through my veins, my heart palpitating as a cold sweat prickles my skin. Under my arms, my base layer is soggy with sweat, but on the surface, I'm freezing. Ang Dorjee bends his knees and swings his arms front to back, reminding me of a circulation technique to warm up the body.

"Of course," I say, sheepish. "How could I forget?"

There's so much information to take in. All of it feels essential, so much of it life or death. It's like my whole body, my entire sense of self, is adapting to this environment. Soon, I hope, it will all be second nature.

I bend my legs and swing my arms, drawing blood back into my fingers.

"Okay, Silvia," says Lydia, sidling up behind me. "You're really making it. You're strong. I'm impressed."

"Thank you," I squeak, my throat parched. I should be flattered. Lydia is an Everest legend. And some small faraway part of me is squealing. *I did it. I'm doing it. Lydia sees.*

But mostly I'm shell-shocked. Nothing we just did makes logical sense.

"How long was that?" I ask Mark. That climb was the longest hour of my life.

"About three minutes," he says.

"*What?*"

"Time is relative on the ladder," he says.

"Damn."

I don't look down to get perspective. I'm done looking back. Only forward from here on.

After everyone scales the wall, we make it to Camp 1, which is ringed by massive crevasses deeper and wider than anything we have just crossed. Our tents are perched at the edge of a vast, windless, snow-covered bowl.

The Valley of Silence.

Two days later, Gabe is gone.

The mood is somber as we watch a cherry-red chopper circle low in the distance, looking for a place to land. The wind torques the tail up, and the pilot keeps flying up and dipping down again, trying to angle into a successful landing. Gabe strained a rib muscle, and the side of his torso was sickly blue black, making it hard to breathe. In a place where oxygen is already limited, a simple injury like that can set you back too far. By the time we made it to Camp 2, it was getting worse, and Mike and Ang Dorjee made the call.

We watch Gabe disappear into the body of the helicopter. Mike flashes a thumbs-up as it flies away, tracing the ridge down and down, until it disappears from sight.

"And then there were six!" booms Brian.

My whole body contracts. First Tom, now Gabe. I'm panicking and unsure why. When Gabe bounced that soccer ball on his knee, I had no doubt he'd make it to the summit. He saw himself there so clearly. *He* had no doubt. But it's becoming clear that the rules do not apply here. That ego and brute force—everything I've watched men build their lives, careers, identities on, and what I've tried to emulate in my most go-getter macho times—guarantees little. Miyolangsangma may be the goddess of inexhaustible giving, but her patience for those who climb Everest with hubris appears to be exhaustible.

The ones who barrel into the world; whose intent is to conquer, no matter the cost; who want to reign over nature, over the land—they have been at it for decades, centuries, millennia. I'm just one more climber in a performance down jacket, but before my father chased a better life into Lima, he, and his people before him, were of the mountains. My bloodline is Andean. It carries the stories of conquistadores, the ones who tried to destroy the indigenous way of life. Sendero Luminoso brought so much terror to Lima for so long, but for some rural peasants, a revolution was the only way to return the land to its rightful stewards.

For people like them, for the Sherpas here, the land is everything. Losing two of our most brute, bold men within the first week reminds me that Everest is a spirit to be honored, not a peak to conquer.

I've been asking myself if I'm strong enough to keep up, to make it to the top, but maybe that's the wrong question. Maybe I should be asking if I'm soft enough to listen. To yield. To trust something deep inside, something in my bloodline, my heritage, that undercuts logic and strength.

I still can't visualize myself at the summit. But maybe that's not a bad thing.

Chapter 16

⁂

LOS DIVORCIADOS

"Gruetzi Miteinander. I'll have the latte macchiato and a grüner Tee, please," I said, flexing my very basic Swiss-German to greet the barista.

"Of course. I'll bring them over to you," he replied calmly. The small Siddhartha café below my office in Bern was my daily tea spot.

"Thank you, darling," Margaret drawled as the barista set our drinks down. As soon as he disappeared behind the counter, she turned to me. "So as I was saying, you know that I'm a witch, my love." She winked. "A good witch, that is."

I sucked my hot grüner Tee down like it was icy lemonade, the spiced liquid scalding my throat as I thought of something to say. The platinum wedding band on my ring finger felt cold and heavy. The truth is that I knew next to nothing about the strawberry blonde woman sitting across from me except that in just the right lighting, she had a mythological glow.

"Oh, wow." My eyebrows peaked in what I hoped was curiosity and not a dead giveaway of the panic rising in my throat. "No, I didn't. I didn't know you were a witch. Please, tell me more," I said politely. This was the sort of vital information a second date would have provided. Instead we'd skipped right to the wedding

We had said "I do" two years after Lori died. We met at a mutual friend's party when I was back in San Francisco on a work trip, and I was captivated by Margaret's English accent, svelte five feet eleven frame, and pouty, seductive lips. Margaret was the life of the party—bombastic and bold and incredibly sensual. A free spirit who loved belly dancing, wore lots of clinky gold jewels and feathers in her hair. She was funny and warm and had a Boston terrier named Bo. We went home together that night and never looked back.

When I returned to Bern, within a week, Margaret confessed she was deeply in love but couldn't do long distance. Most of her family still lived in the UK, and she was willing to move to Switzerland. Just like that. Last time I'd second-guessed love, I had lost Lori. Lori knew I loved her. I told her all the time. But there's a difference between saying, "I love you," and showing it. When I had left for Europe, I was cavalier. I figured we'd have time. I didn't ask Lori for a trial period. I didn't tell her that she was pivotal in my life and that taking this job would help me grow into a better person not just for me, but for us. I was still too guarded to make it clear that even though I was taking the job, I wanted to make us work. Maybe that would have made a difference. If she had known how much I cared, maybe she would still be here. Her death showed me how fragile love is.

For better or worse, in sickness and in health had actually started to sound pretty good.

I still hadn't gone to a therapist, but after six weeks of long-distance dating, I married one. In addition to being a good witch, Margaret was also a Certified Marriage and Family Therapist.

When my mother found out that I'd gotten married, she was hurt that I hadn't invited her. Part of me bristled. *Why would I invite her to my wedding?* She'd never acknowledged my relationship with Lori, or how devastating it was to lose her. If love is love, then loss is loss.

"I'm sorry you lost your friend" was all she could manage.

We'd never gone more than a week without speaking, but I couldn't forgive my mother for stripping away the romantic aspect of my relationship.

We didn't talk for a year.

Back in Europe, I was traveling a lot for work, which meant lots of high-end business-dinner drinking. Margaret didn't seem to mind, or more likely she didn't care. She was on a sabbatical from work, trying to transition her therapy practice into creating what she called a global "priestess-ordained ministry." She was into *awakening the priestess inside every woman*. Something along those lines. My life was still measured in corporate meter, but I kept ending up with women who were into the mystical, the *woo*, as I called it. With Margaret, at first I didn't think much about it. It all sounded vaguely nurturing and altruistic enough to pass muster without my needing to press for details. My critical thinking was not at its peak.

* * *

Silvita. Llamame.

The subject line of my mother's email was stark, but the body of the message was empty. My spine prickled as I dialed the number by heart.

She picked up after a single ring and sat silent on the other end.

"Qué pasó, Mama?"

A long, deep sigh.

"Mom!"

"Silvita, I don't want to lie to you. I'm *not* going to lie to you."

"Okay? What the hell. What is it, Mom?"

"I've been diagnosed with cancer—lung cancer."

The blood drained from my limbs.

"But haven't you been doing your checkups?" I said. "Even after the hysterectomy and polyps? You promised you were going to do your checkups."

"I know, I know. But I got busy with so many other things to do over here."

I wondered how long she'd been keeping this from me.

"I'm starting chemo next week. Miguel will be here. And you'll be here for Christmas, yes? We can talk more."

I traveled solo to Peru for Christmas, but my mom and I talked little about cancer. Instead, I found myself on a whirlwind mission to bring joy and toys to all the little children of Santa Cruz de Chuca, my father's hometown in the Andean foothills.

"Stone sober, sí?" My mother badgered the driver as we climbed onto an overnight bus at the station in Trujillo. Roads into La Sierra were chaotic ribbons of rutted asphalt. Every few months, a night bus crashed, usually piloted by a driver who'd had one too many glasses of chicha de jora, the potent fermented corn drink popular in the mountains.

If only my mother had seen me, lit beyond a prayer, swerving down San Francisco's snaky roads. In the Andes, one drunken nod-off or slip of the wheel would send us sailing to the bottom of a canyon, where we'd become vulture food.

Mom shuffled down the aisle, scanning each seat. She seemed at ease on the crowded, uncomfortable bus, nodding to everyone as babies cried and families shouldered big loads of rice and supplies back from the city. She was dressed in a zip-front purple tracksuit and white Reeboks, with a fanny pack slung casually at her hip, and her laissez-faire confidence was a joy, and a surprise, to watch.

"Here!" she declared, pointing out two seats still near the front. "Scoot in," she whispered. "I'm keeping my eye on him."

I plopped down next to the window while she perched on the aisle, her eyes locked straight ahead.

The door shut with a big hydraulic whoosh, and the gravelly rumble of the engine came alive. I leaned onto her shoulder, my eyes fluttering shut as I breathed in a cloud of Trésor and Lancôme face cream. White lilies, musk, and milk. She'd smelled like that for as long as I could remember. Cloying and fresh at once, the smell cut through the troubled tunnels of my mind and straight to the heart. It was a balm. A rich floral lullaby.

The smell of my mother.

I had never imagined a life without her.

* * *

Santa Cruz de Chuca was a typical Andean village. Rows of boxy two-story buildings surrounded a palm-lined central plaza with a stone fountain and giant bushes carved into bubbly abstract shapes and cartoon animals. Peruvians groom their parks with a flourish. The central plaza is the town living room, and each place adorns theirs with pride.

Twin streetlamps with curlicue iron flourishes lit the park at night, and a soft haze of fog often rolled down from the surrounding hills in the morning, snaking its way through the cobblestone streets as if to wake everyone up.

My father always wanted more than this place. When he and his brother, Walter, got the chance to live with a wealthy uncle in Trujillo, a big city in comparison, he jumped. Maybe he hoped his uncle would be a surrogate father—his own had abandoned the family to marry someone else. When my father tried reaching out to his father after years, he was turned away.

After all of us kids left Peru, and my mother became a grandmother, she started taking trips to Santa Cruz de Chuca. She'd gather money from my siblings and me to help modernize my father's hometown. Over several years, she worked to gain the trust of the townspeople, and together they established a craft workshop for the children, revamped the region's medical post—a rural bare-bones urgent care station—and built a better infrastructure for the 150-student elementary school my father had once attended. During the Christmas season, she'd started a holiday gift and chocolatada event. It had grown to almost three hundred people.

At first, I found it strange. After all those years and everything he had put her through, why would she dedicate her free time to yet another thing centered on my father? Was it a gesture toward healing an unhealable man? Providing for the children of the village in a way she couldn't for all of her kids? Was she tending to the little boy my father had been? But during our Christmas trip, I saw that it wasn't about him at all. Or at least, not how I'd imagined.

As we approached the central plaza from the hostel where we were staying, a procession of children and their mothers, dozens of them, came marching down a dirt side street led by two young girls proudly holding a hand-painted banner that read: BIENVENIDA SRA. TERESA LAVADO. The road sloped down into town, and they marched past rows of tile-roofed stone houses painted in earthy browns and robin's-egg blue. As the dirt turned to cement, more people came pouring down the side streets, and soon there were hundreds gathered at the central plaza. We walked through the crowd, dipping our arms into huge bags to pass out gifts to children with ruddy cheeks and matching bowl cuts in little tracksuits and jean jackets. Others in polo shirts one size too big. There were the mountain grandmas in flowered dresses and cardigans wearing long socks under slippers, and mothers in traditional Andean bowlers or the tall white thatch hats that signaled mixed Incan and Spanish heritage.

Five women on a side street stirred huge metal vats of chocolatada, the special Peruvian hot chocolate. We ladled it into tin teapots and walked the sidewalks, filling the colorful plastic mugs of excited children, and placing in their outstretched hands mini panettones, a once-a-year treat.

My mother was like the Santa Claus of Santa Cruz de Chuca.

She seemed at home there. Back in Lima, in the monied social circles my father aspired to, people were classist and ruthless. Around them, especially the women, my mother's natural exuberance was inhibited. She seemed shy, deferential almost, as if speaking too much might expose her as an imposter.

Being a divorced mother from La Victoria who'd never finished high school was a story she was happy to leave untold. But around the working class, the poor, those who lived closer to the ground, hand to mouth the way she'd grown up, her confidence and generosity, her sense of humor, was electric. She even carried herself differently. Her chest open, her shoulders back. It didn't strike me until I watched her bustle through the cobblestone streets laughing as she filled the children's cups, that her mother had been from the Andes too. From Cochabamba specifically, a remote district in the foothills of the Cordillera Blanca, the highest tropical mountain range in the world.

Her roots were undeniable. *Our* roots were undeniable. And they started to show the higher into the mountains we went.

* * *

Two years later, my mother's cancer had progressed to Stage IV. Margaret and I were living back in San Francisco, and things were rocky at best. eBay allowed me to work remotely part of the time, and I spent my free time flying back and forth to Peru. Margaret rarely traveled with me.

Wheeling my mother to oncology appointments became a sacred duty, like taking her to Mass—somewhere a miracle might occur. I needed to believe in miracles then. Whatever it took to keep my mother alive. My drinking was in check, but only circumstantially. I was afraid to lose control in front of my family, and though my mother never confronted the issue, she constantly reminded me not to drink too much. Marianela had told her what had happened with Beto, and the memory of Eduardo finding me facedown in my own vomit was still fresh. Growing up Catholic, I had inherited a sense of shame. We were never asked to examine our actions, to understand *why*, but to simply repent and stop, or in my case repent and repeat. Shame was the only thing stronger than my thirst.

In Peru, even the doctors ran on Latin time. Especially the most in-demand ones. We waited for hours in long hallways with glaring white walls. We waited alongside others like us—patients and families of patients. Some who looked sicker than my mother, some who looked better. And as we waited, we settled into each other. For once, my mother had stopped moving, and I had the chance to *be* with her. There were no errands to run off to, no juggling of secret lives. There was only this. Me and her. Together. Fighting for her one life. It was the most time we'd ever spent alone, and while we waited in hospital lobbies, in doctor's offices, for surgeries, for drugs, for news, for a cure, slowly we started to become friends. This unknowable woman, a woman I'd idolized, began to fill out before my eyes.

With nowhere else to go, she caught me up on all the family gossip. As she explained the ins and outs, I grew to understand more about her role as a matriarch among her sisters. She'd become the sounding board when tiffs arose between extended family members. The wise one who took care of everyone, the one with the empathy and compassion.

Doctors cut out two-thirds of her left lung to stunt the cancer. After her surgery, I pulled an empty bed next to hers and squeezed her left hand between mine, kissing it softly, while her other hand drooped at her side, weighed down by the IV drip.

"Mamita, I got it!" I said, snapping my fingers. She was bald by then, her head a shiny dome. Her already fair complexion now appeared pale and bloated, but her cheekbones were still sharp, and a blissful aura emanated from her.

"You look just like Casper, the friendly ghost!"

"Jijijijiji," she laughed her funny little laugh. Her cherubic face glowed. The sicker she got, the saintlier she appeared. Wrapped in fringed shawls and blankets, waving to everyone from her wheelchair, she tossed out kind words like candy. She'd become a regular Mother Teresa.

My mother, Teresa.

Santa Claus, a saint, the family diplomat.

I wondered if this was who she'd always been.

Back home after the surgery, we transformed the living room into my mother's bedroom to accommodate the massive oxygen tanks that nebulized medication for her lungs. "Mom, when you get better," I told her on one of my last trips, "for your birthday we'll go to La Bistecca." A buffet-style restaurant, La Bistecca was the closest thing Peru had to a Sizzler, her favorite restaurant in the U.S.

There were two phone lines at the house—one for my father's dying business and another for everything else. Eventually, calls from her relatives and friends flooded both lines. A steady stream of guests visited her in the "presidential suite," as she called it, and she received them proudly from her hospital-style bed.

"Let me tell you," she'd brag. "We're going to go to La Bistecca. It's almost as good as the Sizzler!" Her hands danced and flitted as she emphasized just *how good* the twice-baked potatoes were or how juicy the steak was, as if Sizzler was beyond anything they could imagine.

"Un cafecito?" she'd chirp. Someone—me, my brothers, Meche—would make coffee, and she'd sip hers from bed, nodding along as her visitors unraveled their daily dramas. A matriarchal Don Corleone. For once, she seemed in total control of her domain.

My father, in his late eighties by then, had a hard time walking and had already set up a small bed downstairs in his former office. I used to marvel at him spending his days there in his perfectly starched shirts and crisply pressed suits, dictating to his secretary or craning over tidy stacks of papers, one hand on the calculator, adding for hours, never stopping to check if his fingers were hitting the right keys. In that room, he'd been a concert pianist. A maestro.

But outside his regimented world of numbers, I began to see how small my father was. As my mother got sicker, he holed up, ignoring the constant stream of visitors and calls and only shuffling in and out of the kitchen for meals. He didn't come to the bedside to hold her hand or check her vitals. When she tried to talk about her health, he spoke over her.

"What if I go first?" he'd snarl like it was a competition. "I'll be the one dying first!"

"Shut up!" she'd tease. "Yerba mala nunca muere."

That got me every time.

A bad weed never dies.

We tried to move her to the United States, where she'd be near her children and grandchildren. After years of working at it, Marianela had secured her a green card. But no matter how hard we pushed, she wouldn't leave my father. She'd accepted the duty of her loveless marriage. And my father? He had no desire to move. He couldn't speak English and was too old and stubborn to learn. He'd never been able to claw back to his original wealth after losing all that money to the pyramid scheme when I was in college, and then he'd started to age out of the industry, undercut by accountants who were younger, hipper, and cheaper than he was. Despite his relentless preaching on about the permanence of the calculator, things had changed.

Everything but him.

In the United States, Segundo Vasquez would be just another immigrant starting from scratch; while in Lima, at least he still had memories of the glory days.

My marriage was barely hanging on. Right before our first anniversary, on a business trip to Singapore, I had cheated with a woman who reminded me of Lori. I confessed to Margaret, but she forgave me, and we had stayed together. After we had moved back to the United States and she started to pull away, spending weekends away at retreats with titles like "Harness the Divine Feminine," and "Tap into the Goddess Within," I cheated again. This time with a close friend.

To say that I was unfaithful because my father had been is too easy.

Nothing true is that simple.

But it would also be untrue to completely deny that it was in the blood. In the *name*. That I came from a long line of men with second families and secret children. Of women who turned the other cheek, and then the other, often because they had no choice. While I rejected the options Peruvian culture gave me for womanhood, in the process, I slipped into another stereotype. The unfaithful man of the house. The dog with a bone.

As my mother got sicker, she started leaving voicemails for each of her kids. Her final wishes. She implored each of my five siblings to build their families and stay close. To me, she said: You're so smart. Get a master's degree.

My mother had finally gotten her high school diploma while she was in the early stages of her chemotherapy treatment, and education represented freedom and the possibility of a different kind of life.

She'd also become the social center of her world and loved listening to the ins and outs of everyone's moral dilemmas, but whenever I'd tried to share my early marital gripes over the phone, I got a polite chorus of *mmm, mm-hmm, yes, okay,* punctuated by the electronic shuffle of cards in the background. She was playing online solitaire.

It was as if my being gay scrambled her whole system. Because she couldn't sanction my life with a woman, she wrote off *my* family—the thing she valued most—altogether.

After coming out, I'd never imagined myself getting married either. Maybe because of where I'd come from, marriage was something I could only envision with men. But once I said those words—"*I do*"—I was surprisingly determined to make them stick.

Margaret and I weren't happy, but as we said in Spanish, "Peor es nada."

Having nobody is worse.

I was too afraid to get divorced. It would be yet another failure.

I'd fallen into the same trap my mother had, using marriage as a shield. Clinging to its false security, its hollow promises. I was more invested in the identity of being married than in my actual marriage. As if marriage was a safeguard against chaos and dysfunction. Of course, I should have known better.

By mid-2012, the cancer had spread to my mother's spinal cord. She was now bedridden. A tumor left her paralyzed from the waist down. She was being treated with steroids, which ballooned her weight from 170 pounds to almost 230. By Thanksgiving, both Miguel and I had moved home. Every night I slept on the long, low couch beside my mother's bed in the presidential suite. Her breathing was slow and labored, and the night nurse who slept in the next room came in often to check on her. She'd turn up the oxygen, and I'd watch my mother's breathing stabilize. Tracing the oxygen's invisible path through the tube and into her bloodstream, seeing her eyes grow bigger, her breath stronger, I became fascinated by how a little extra air might help me climb higher than what was humanly possible. I started teasing her—putting the extra oxygen mask on myself.

"I'm going to climb Mount Everest one day," I told her.

"Silvita, no," she said. "It's too dangerous. You can die. Please don't do that."

"But Mom, it was very special to be there the first time, you know. And I'll train hard. I've already climbed Kilimanjaro and Mount Elbrus."

I didn't tell her how unprepared I had been on Kilimanjaro, because everything I didn't know on Kilimanjaro, I learned on Elbrus. It was Elbrus that turned me from a climber into a mountaineer. Plus, I learned how to self-arrest—how to stop myself from sliding down a mountain to my death if I fell. I didn't think that was the best point to make with her.

"I just don't think doing that will be very smart, hijita."

As she pulled the oxygen mask from my hand, I imagined it as a lifeline. What if it sprang a leak? What if the tank got dented? What if my whole life depended on it?

When I first met Margaret, I told her that I wanted to climb Carstensz Pyramid in Papua, but she discouraged me, too, saying just what my mother had said. That it was too dangerous. So for a long time, I stopped climbing, stopped talking about climbing, even, funneling my desire for *more*—giving more, being more—into work. Climbing remained a low buzz at the back of my brain, but real life marched on.

* * *

I took my mother's swollen left hand in mine, cradling her newly chunky fingers, absorbing the warmth that meant she was still alive.

Everest will always be there, I told myself. The mountains will always be there.

This was a special time. Time I'd never had.

Time for Mommy and me.

On a sunny Saturday morning in mid-April 2013, I woke to my mother gasping for air. The overnight nurse rushed into the room, and I grabbed my mother's hand while the nurse sedated her and called the doctor. Her lungs were failing. It wasn't the first time. It'd happened several times in the previous five months. It'd been terrifying to see her like that, but now that she was unresponsive, I longed to see her pant for air, to see her fight.

Her oxygen capacity was plummeting.

Her nurse began to cry.

I knew this was it.

Miguel stood next to the bed, holding her right hand, and I clasped both of my hands around her left. My father stumbled in and slumped down on the couch next to us.

"Mamita," I said, leaning closer. "I love you. I love you, Mamita. I know you hear me, Mamita. I love you so much, Teresita. Can you hear me? I know you can. I am here for you, Mamita. I am here with you."

I pressed her hand to my cheek. It was lukewarm, spongy—white lilies and cream.

I'd lost Lori before I could tell her how much I loved her. And all the love that I'd held in and twisted up poured out like an incantation. Like an anointing that I alone had to offer my mother. She would have no doubt about how I felt.

"I love you, I love you, I love you. Mom, I love you," I chanted, each word softer than the last.

At three p.m., the pulse oximeter hit zero.

Miguel released a guttural cry, and I collapsed onto her body, listening for one last exhale, a final sip of air. But there was nothing. No more breath, no more her.

My mother was gone.

* * *

At first, her death didn't affect me as much as I thought it would.

At first.

I took solace by throwing myself into work and fantasizing about how Margaret and I might start over. Spending the last few years with my mother had affirmed the importance of family and shown me that healing, or, at the very least, acceptance, was possible. Maybe Margaret and I could repair things too.

I was invited to give a talk in Tokyo about a pilot program eBay had unveiled with one of our technology partners. Tokyo was one of my favorite cities in the world, and they flew me over first-class, rolling out the red carpet. The organizers set me up in a room with floor-to-ceiling windows overlooking the skyline, at the luxurious Prince Gallery hotel, whose futuristic bar served dishes like gold-leaf shrimp tempura. The morning of my talk I walked into a small auditorium where 120 men in near-identical crisp dark suits were broken into two groups on either side of a low stage. Behind me on the stage stood two female Japanese translators.

This was my father's dream. To have the attention and honor of a room full of Japanese executives. He saw the Japanese as the pinnacle of elegance and professionalism. And here I was, his unlikely gay daughter, with two Japanese women ready to translate my every word to a room full of conservative men. I bowed in introduction and began to speak. After each pause, the women alternated translation. Then, in the middle of a slide, everything just stopped. As I stared at the slides—slides I'd spent days perfecting—my mind was blank. It was like holding one of those huge seashells to my ear, the ones where you hear the rush of ocean. The sea whooshed through my mind, washing out every thought, and I was left suspended somewhere, floating.

It was like someone had pushed pause on the moment, and I had stepped out of the scene. As if I'd been playing Superman and was suddenly exposed as Clark Kent. The mask fell off. The cape crumpled to the ground. All the men in matching suits stared at me. Politely waiting. I didn't want to say one more word about the new technology we were building. Not now. And not ever again. All the passion and excitement I'd become known for evaporated right there on the stage.

I was lost.

I was now a motherless daughter.

And I was done with it all.

I managed to pull myself together and fumble through the rest of the presentation, but the glitch was obvious. Not just to the audience, but for me. It was more than just work burnout. Whatever had been trying to push and pound its way through the compost of my psyche for the last decade was blooming and unfurling as I bowed and thanked the audience and rushed out of there as fast as I could.

I'd done more than my father ever would.

And just like that, his power over me evaporated.

Still, I returned home hopeful.

But when I got back to San Francisco, Margaret's half of the house was packed, and she was gone. She left a flowery notecard saying that she was sorry and that she cared for me. We were "on different paths," she said, which would have been shockingly clear by date three if we hadn't already gotten married. Even aside from the cheating, from the very beginning, we had a hard time finding each other, and my time with my mother in Peru had only widened the gap. I got involved in a dysfunctional marriage because I was dysfunctional. But that didn't make Margaret's leaving hurt any less.

I turned to my usual. Drinking. But this time, it was different. It no longer soothed me. Even the thickest bourbon stupor wouldn't stick. I'd pass out just fine, but every morning at five a.m., I shot up in bed, wide awake and in pain. Not from the echoing throb of a hangover or the anxiety cloud of tallying what I'd drunk the night before. But raw pain. Like my skin had been turned inside out. Like my heart was in a vice grip. Plastered to the bed, I felt the empty place beside me where Margaret had once been. And it seemed like an endless abyss. One that had swallowed Margaret, my mother, and Lori. That threatened to swallow me again.

For once, the pain was worse than the hangover.

Even on the days I didn't drink, I woke in the dark with tears in my eyes. I'd beg the sun to show itself.

"Please wake up with me. Please wake up now. I'm suffering. Please come out. I need light. This is too dark, too painful."

The sun never rose when I needed it to.

One evening I climbed into my car in the dark and drove at full speed toward the Golden Gate Bridge.

Cool, damp air clung to my face as I parked and walked toward the Bay. Under the bridge, the city lights were a distant halo. The water a midnight oil slick. I tried to picture them dredging up Lori's body from the bottom. Search and rescue teams diving for her at the exact moment that I drove across in the other direction, oblivious, humming to Tony Bennett. Thinking, once again, that my feelings were right on time. That I had a shot. That I could just keep bulldozing through life and wind up where I wanted to be when I was ready. I was on the bridge when Lori jumped, but I was never close enough to reach her.

I had been running for as long as I could remember. And I'd run all out. Of reasons. Of people to cheer me on. Of second chances. Of fresh starts. With no Lori, no mother, no marriage, and a career that I suddenly cared little about, I had nothing. There was nowhere else to run.

I was truly alone.

I was in pain.

And for the first time in my life, drinking wasn't numbing it.

I resigned myself to getting help. On a friend's suggestion, I signed up for the Hoffman Process, a one-week meditation retreat focused on understanding negative patterns we learn from ages five to twelve, which mold who we become. In a group circle on one of the last days, the facilitator said, "This work will allow us to climb our inner mountains." Suddenly, I was in Nepal, at the base of Everest, remembering how crisp and sacred the air was, how making it to Base Camp in half the time had felt like a special grace, an omen almost, that the mountain was going to guide me. Standing in the shadow of Everest, I'd felt propelled by something bigger than me. It clicked then.

Christmas was close, and I was dreading the first one without my mother. It was her favorite holiday. Laborious and full of love, her holiday feasts had been a master class. The juicy turkey, apple and cranberry purees, yellow mashed potatoes, her signature green beans and infamous Waldorf salad. I couldn't imagine not sitting around her table. Not spending New Year's with her nagging me to uphold the Peruvian tradition of wearing yellow underwear and eating twelve grapes at midnight—six purple and six green—for good luck each month of the coming year.

If I didn't do something drastic, I could end up drinking myself into a coma. When I was climbing, I wasn't drinking. I both feared and respected the mountains, and miraculously that kept me sober. I hadn't summited a mountain in six years, but I had the holiday off from work, and expeditions were cheap, so I booked a trip. The next peak on my Seven Summits list was Aconcagua. In school, we always took pride in Aconcagua, the tallest mountain in all of the Americas. My territorial mountain, the highest peak on my own continent, on the land that I came from.

After so many years away from climbing, I was unsure I would make the summit. Climbing one mountain didn't necessarily mean I'd be able to climb the next. Thirty-five percent of climbers don't make it up Aconcagua the first time; even some Nepali mountaineers who have summited Everest struggle. Proximity to the Pacific creates brutal weather conditions on the mountain. Cruel winds and driving snow make for whiteouts. At the summit, atmospheric pressure is 40 percent that at sea level, and the dry environment increases the chance of altitude sickness. But the biggest challenge is that there is minimal time for acclimatization. Summiting Aconcagua is a straight-shot climb. Every mountain has its own challenges, and Aconcagua just happens to have them all.

Just like my first trip to Nepal in 2005, I was following a vision, a sliver of conversation from my time at Hoffman to explore *the mountains within*.

I was grouped with two men—Mike, an American from Atlanta, and Rajat, an Indian man living in Dubai. Right away we had one thing in common. "Los Divorciados" became our team name.

After ten arduous days, we were on the verge of the summit. At 22,000 feet, the air was thin; the light, sheer. We'd departed from Base Camp and pushed to the three upper camps in back-to-back days, without rotations. Just one straight driving line. A few climbers had already turned back, and at times I wished I'd gone with them. The whole thing—climbing a mountain to change something—started to seem ridiculous. The truth is I was pissed at life. Fueled by grief, I'd come to take it out on the mountain. To kick the shit out of a giant rock. But it kicked back. And harder. The mountain would always be stronger than I was. Climbing wasn't going to heal me any more than having a fancy tech job or marrying the perfect blonde woman would.

The night before I attempted the summit the air was still with little wind. In my tent, I shivered, fighting off the crushing throb of an altitude headache. The only sounds were the occasional chatter of climbers passing by and the serrated snores of my tentmate. Curled into a ball on my side, I let a few lone tears fall. Then a few more. And as they started to accumulate, out trickled all the loss and grief and sadness and fear and anger. I cried for all the love and time and possibilities that I'd lost. For my mother and the women in my family before her who had suffered. For all the people I'd hurt because I couldn't find my way out of pain. I cried because I thought I wasn't going to summit. I pitied myself—that my dream, this whole mountain climbing thing, wasn't meant to be. My body jerked in silent spasms, and I sobbed as quietly as I could into my pillow so as not to wake my tentmate. I cried until I was empty. And into that emptiness stepped the outline of a little girl. A girl who'd been trying to climb out, who wanted to shed this suffering once and for all. A girl who was tired of being alone. The girl in the turquoise tracksuit hadn't given up on me.

She was waiting, patiently, her hand outstretched.

Right before Lori jumped, she'd isolated herself from everyone. Later, I found out from mutual friends that she'd stopped returning their calls. Skipped out on fundraisers and parties. Once upon a time, she had stabilized her bipolar by finding a community to care for, by building giant art cars and planning all year to build a glittering camp in the middle of the desert. I wondered what had come back to eat her. What had Lori not been able to outrun? She never wanted to burden others. Like my mother, Lori kept the darkest parts of herself hidden, then dug her way back to life by giving herself to community. After my mother's kids had left Peru, she crafted a whole new life through giving back. In Lima and in the Andes. Over a thousand people had come to her funeral to pay their respects. People I'd never even seen.

If someone had been looking down on that bitter cold night on Aconcagua, they must have seen the star-choked sky split open above the red speck of my tent and the universe pour compassion down on me, because once my tears were spent, I fell into a deep sleep. When I woke the next day, I was flooded with grace. I reached the summit with time to spare, almost as if my tears had cleared the way. Summiting, like healing, I was learning, demanded surrender. *Vulnerability.*

As I stood looking out at the view, the answer was so clear I couldn't believe I hadn't seen it before. Everest was not about me. I wasn't supposed to be doing it alone. I wasn't supposed to be scaling mountains and staking my flag at their peaks like some modern-day conquistadora. It was about what I had to offer, what I had to give to a community—to women, to girls, like me. I had to keep my promise to climb Everest, but I was supposed to bring others with me. Other women like me. Survivors. That had been the message all along.

When I went back to San Francisco, I could feel the vacuum of my mother's absence. But there was something else under the sadness. Freedom. Invited to speak at One Billion Rising, a rally against sexual violence, organized by Eve Ensler, I stood at the podium and told my story to a crowd of thousands. They roared in support. It was the first time I'd said it aloud since I had crumbled to the ground on the azotea twenty years earlier. The first time I could tell my story free of guilt. Without worrying that it would shame or hurt my mother. I'd found my voice.

Now it was time to find the others.

❦

Chapter 17

THE VALLEY OF SILENCE

Sometimes when it's cold enough and the air pressure and all the scientific components align just right, snow experiences a metamorphosis.

It's not just the slope of the mountain or a sudden boom that unlocks an avalanche. At the atomic level, it's about the structure of each snowflake. A snowpack made of layers and layers of powdery snow that has fallen over time and bonded together is mostly secure, but say one day, given the perfect temperature gradient, a layer deep down spontaneously metamorphizes and becomes faceted. Somewhere deep in the snowpack there's a weak point. Given just the right shake or rattle or boom, that layer may crumble, triggering an avalanche.

* * *

Descending to Base Camp in the early morning, the mountains seem so alive. The sun hovers high over the glacier, but massive spires of ice shadow us from its rays. It's said that getting down a mountain is just as hard as getting up, and this morning's sinking realization is that to get back to Base Camp, once again we have to descend the ladders we crossed on the way up. As we drop deeper into the Khumbu, I hear the sound of water, of ice melting, of snow breaking down.

Rob is the last to make it back to camp. He pushes aside the canvas flap of the dining tent and collapses into a coughing fit. He's been like this the whole way down from Camp 2, and without making eye contact with anyone, I know we're all thinking the same thing. The high altitude hack. The dreaded wheeze of failure.

The Khumbu cough.

A dry cough born from the perfect collision of cold weather, low humidity, and exertion at altitude: it's the Everest phantom. And once you catch it, it's hard to shake. Because we're basically sleeping inside a freezer every night, it's expected you may pick up a cold, but the Khumbu cough can kill a climb.

Bodies heal slowly at altitude, if at all. The higher we go, the less of a chance there is to recover. Unlike other sports where athletes condition and train, getting stronger and faster in preparation for a big race or playoff game, the higher we climb, the weaker we become. By the time we reach the summit, *if* we reach the summit, our bodies will be shutting down. Our appetites will be nonexistent; sleep, elusive; even our breath will be bottled. Even at Base Camp's elevation we're expending more energy than at sea level, sometimes twice as much, but food somehow seems less appealing, and by the time this is over, some of us will have lost the weight of a small child. We're conditioning our lungs and bodies by living at altitude, pushing our limits a little further with each rotation, but we're not getting stronger in the traditional athletic sense. By the time we reach the summit, we'll be actively dying.

Sometimes descending to a lower elevation is the only option.

* * *

Tendi rushes over with a mug of ginger tea, and Rob nods, mouthing a gentle *thank you* as Anthea points him toward the doctor. After lunch, it's confirmed. He's caught the Khumbu cough. This is Rob's third Everest attempt, and he isn't ready to give up yet, so Ang Dorjee and Mike agree that he should descend to Periche and rest for a few days. If his cough improves, he can join us for the second rotation. Maybe a few days in an adequate bed with proper meals and hydration will kick the Khumbu cough. That doesn't sound bad, actually. I'm tempted to go along.

Rob leaves with little hassle, promising to send updates. We walk him to the edge of camp, shouting lighthearted *Get well*s and *See you soon*s as he heads down the trail, but as he grows smaller, loss settles on us like fine dust. The unspoken question lingers—*Who's next?*

From our original eight, we are down to five: Brian, Danny, John, Mark, and me.

Two days later, John starts to waver.

It's one of those incredible Everest mornings where the sun is so hot, we're stripped down to T-shirts and SPF. Lots of SPF. The Khumbu Glacier is a sheet of tinfoil threatening to fry us. Everyone is hanging around Base Camp, recuperating and preparing for our second rotation. John and I are sitting on plastic patio chairs outside the dining tent, our feet kicked up onto a pile of rocks. He had a rough climb to Camp 2 and hasn't been the same since. He's quieter, withdrawn even.

"I'm worried about my wife," he says. "I just . . . she's there all alone."

Meeting his earnest blue eyes, I can almost see what he's thinking. How would his wife manage without him? What will she do if he dies up there? What will *he* do if she dies while he's gone? I know what he's thinking because I think it too. Every night, to the lullaby of rockslides and crumbling snowbanks, I wonder what it would be like to die here. Sometimes I think it would be alright. There's no one back home depending on me, though—not like John.

"Do what's right for your family." It's all I can think to say. "Everest will always be here. Our families . . . well."

He nods, examining a small patch of melting snow under his feet. The long dimples that form so easily every time he smiles are gone.

"Maybe try giving her a call?" I say. "See what she says."

* * *

Even while recuperating, we have to keep active. If you don't move at all, you're more likely to get sick. Continuous motion is the best way to manipulate our bodies into believing that we can fully operate with limited oxygen.

Every two days, I trek the two miles to Gorak Shep and back. On every loop, my return times are shaved down. My pace is pretty fast, I'm learning, almost as fast as the locals'. It feels good to find my rhythm, to see that I have a place here. That I'm not just the woman, the lesbian, the vegetarian, the underdog, the one no one expects to make it; but that my body is adapting to the harsh environment better than others' are. That maybe I'm made for this, after all.

Most nights, I linger after dinner and talk with John. His business acumen reminds me of my father. Talking with him is like a brief window into a life I could have had. One where my father was kind and our relationship was reciprocal. Instead of engaging in aggressive one-sided sermons, John is curious about my experiences in business. It has been hard to find trustworthy mentors. Even at Millersville, I had an accounting professor, a real intellectual from the Midwest. He was young and witty and preached strong conservative values. He reminded me of my father too, but it was his fervor, his overbearing conviction that I had recognized.

During a late-night tutoring session for a tax class, he tried to kiss me. Shocked, I pulled away. He was married with a young family but assured me that it was okay. He'd been watching me all semester, he said, and he saw my potential. I left his office and steered clear of him for the rest of the year. When I got back from summer break, I found out he'd been fired for sleeping with students.

He went back to Indiana, and I was left, again, without a mentor, without any man I could trust to guide me without belittling, assaulting, or trying to sleep with me. When sexual harassment laws were passed, thankfully, eBay was serious about enforcing them.

Maybe it's his mannered British demeanor or the ongoing fear that an avalanche could kill us at any minute, but it's easy to open up to John. A worldly businessman with an artist's eye, he's proper but warm. The only man in the expedition who is clean shaven every morning, and his cologne lingers after he leaves the tent. He's even been to Burning Man, and though he doesn't tell me with whom, it certainly wasn't his wife.

Chuckling to myself, I imagine him in neon latex and feathers instead of thick black glasses and performance down. John reminds me of the "Burners" I met through Lori, the men I'd been jealous of her dancing with even after she laughed it off. "Trust me," she'd said. "These aren't the kind of men you need to worry about." Did she mean they were good men or gay men? I'd never figured that out, but many of them were technologists and financiers who seemed very comfortable with their softer sides. Not at all like the men I was raised around.

"Burning Man wasn't how I expected," I tell John.

"How so?"

"Well, I figured it'd just be a lot of drugs."

"Naturally," he nods.

"But I was sober the entire time, for five days. Time didn't really matter there. There was always something going on. It was like a twenty-four-hour Cirque du Soleil. I think I realized that it was about art and community more than drugs or sex."

"Not that they're mutually exclusive," quips John. "But yes, it's certainly a colorful explosion of the subconscious. Not one to be missed."

"Indeed," I smile, fighting off a pang of regret that I hadn't just gone to the stupid festival with Lori. I'm not sure why, but I stop short of telling John about her. That she's the reason I went the year after she died. That after missing my chance, after she died, I went to the playa and painted my body in her honor, then built her an altar inside the Burning Man Temple.

It took me too long to see that all those times she begged me to come, it wasn't a test but an invitation. She wanted to show me what community meant to her. Everything took me too long to figure out. It's hard to see others when you're so cloaked in your own pain.

As Danny and Mark and Brian file out of the tent for bed, John leans in closer.

"Silvia," he says firmly. "I'm going home."

"No!" It slips out before I can catch it.

"I need to be home," he says. He's already there; I can see it in his eyes. There's no talking him out of this. And at this point in the climb, there shouldn't be. No matter how much I want John here, he has to want it more. More than anything, really. More even than what awaits him at home. He has to be willing to risk it all.

The mountains are both sanctuary and pressure cooker—purifying and bringing the deepest truth to the surface like a splinter. All the things we want, think we want, and what we are hiding, reveal themselves. Everest is a divining rod, dowsing for clarity of heart and purpose. And she's working fast.

Who she keeps and who she turns away is surprising.

After breakfast the next day, I walk John out to the helipad. As he climbs into the cockpit, he turns to me and tips his invisible cap.

"I wish you didn't have to go," I shout over the chuf-chuf-chuf of the helicopter.

"Me too," he calls. "But Silvia, my dear, love is complicated." And with that the door clicks shut, and the rotor blades start to churn faster, whipping air into little tornadoes around my head.

How could he have known? I'd never even told John about Lori.

* * *

Long rays of morning sun settle on the Western Cwm. It's almost seven a.m., and we've just made it to Camp 1 after five hours in the Khumbu. In the last week, a minor avalanche hit parts of the Icefall, and the icefall doctors had to shift the route. It was shocking to see ladders we'd crossed on our first rotation lying torn and twisted at the bottom of deep crevasses, massive chunks of ice sitting in their place. And even on the ones that remained, there was a wobbliness I hadn't noticed before.

We're two weeks into the climb, and our route, the South Col, has been traversed by about three hundred people now. Each group crosses and ascends the same ladders, pulls their weight up the same icy cliffs via the same fixed ropes. All that weight tugs at the ice anchors, widening the holes and weakening their holds with each pass, a nano-shift imperceptible to the eye. But it all adds up. Meanwhile, the glacier is alive, expanding and contracting, melting and freezing.

Each rotation up the mountain is less secure.

This time, we don't stop at Camp 1 but push straight through the Western Cwm toward Camp 2. The Cwm is a huge glacial valley carved out by the Khumbu Glacier and hugged by the base of three peaks: Nuptse to the right, Lhotse straight ahead, and Everest to the left. The Triple Crown. Three of the world's tallest mountains all in my line of sight.

It's another hot day, and the snow-caked walls of the valley are like a greenhouse, radiating so much heat that we start to cook inside our down jackets. Like being roasted inside of the world's biggest walk-in freezer. The temperature dances just under 90 degrees Fahrenheit. Because the high canyon walls trap heat and the snowpack is so dense, on days like this the Western Cwm is prime avalanche territory.

The air is windless and eerily quiet. We march in silence. Our crampons thudding softly on the snowy trail and labored huffs are the only sounds.

Ahead, in the center of the valley, a series of lateral crevasses are cut like slices of cake into the snowbank. There are dozens of them, all deeper and wider than anything we crossed in the Khumbu. Between each crevasse is a narrow plateau of snow, and as we get closer, I watch them fan out like waves. We veer to the right, hiking toward a snug passageway called Nuptse Corner. We have to avoid the worst crevasses in the center, which are too dangerous to cross.

We reach the edge of a large crevasse. Its edges are shaggy with ice. It feels like more of a slot than a gap. A ladder runs down, and another runs up the wall on the opposite side. This time, we're descending into the voids instead of over them. Sounds about right. Every new challenge is some sort of quixotic metaphor. When will it end?

Halfway up a crevasse, a sharp pain hits above my pelvis. "Aghh!" I cry, contracting my stomach. The ladder rattles as I claw my way up another two rungs. A twisting throb. *Not now. My God, not now.* Usually, my prayer works. The one where I pray that I'll skip my period while I'm on a mountain. I'm not sure if it's my daily devotionals or the fact that exertion and altitude can actually stunt a period, but so far it has worked.

I swallow the pain and push to the top of the ledge.

"Ang Dorjee!" I call out to the front of the line. "I have to stop."

"No stopping!" He shouts back without looking. The ice cliffs are prime avalanche territory. "It's too dangerous here. Keep going."

Warm liquid runs down the inside of my leg.

"I have to stop! *Ang Dorjee.*"

Finally, he glances over his shoulder. All the men turn and look with him as I make dramatic swirling motions near my pelvis. There were no directions for this during orientation.

"I need, erhm . . . a moment."

"Fine, fine," he calls brusquely. "Stay with Pasang."

Pasang, one of our Sherpas, hangs back, clearly unsure what to do.

I take another step, but the pain drops me to my knees. Clutching my belly, I bow toward the snow, praying for it to end. My uterus is being wrung out like a sponge. *Breathe in the mountain air. Breathe out the pain. Breathe one thousand, two thousand, three thousand, four thousand. Breathe.*

Ouch. Ow. Dammit.

Pasang is pacing, practically hovering over me, unsmiling.

"We move," he says. His English is bare-bones, and I'm in too much pain to pantomime. *I need a minute!* I want to scream.

Thankfully, I'm carrying extra pads, baby wipes, and hand sanitizer.

"I need some *privacy*," I say, waving Pasang to turn around while I crouch over a snowy nook.

"Hurry," he barks after a couple minutes. "I must hurry." He starts to walk away.

"It's my period," I holler. He turns back, looking confused as I pull my pants up and stumble out of the shadows. Jumar in hand, I point to my ovaries.

"Blood? I'm *BLEED-ING*," I enunciate, swirling my hands around my belly again. Pasang looks alarmed. Have these men never heard of a period? What do they call it here? My God, what's the magic word?

"Pasang, do you have a sister?"

He nods.

"Okay! She has this. Your mom. Your sister. They both have it."

He shrugs his shoulders.

"The moon, *the moon*!" I practically screech, pointing to the faint sliver of moon hanging over the peak of Nuptse, then back to my ovaries. I feel like a kindergarten teacher playing a weird game of reproductive charades. Without the Sherpa word, I can see Pasang won't get it. And it shouldn't matter, really, but the longer he stares blankly at me, the more I feel like a bleeding lunatic. Suddenly, I'm desperate for him to understand. Hasn't this happened to other women? Where *are* all the women on this goddamn mountain?

No matter how hard I push to keep up, I have to deal with something the men don't. Something they're oblivious to. Something that forces me to stop and be a body with needs and demands, a soft bloody thing, instead of a machine that I can force into motion with sheer will.

Even on this mountain, my body demands to be heard.

* * *

At 21,000 feet, Camp 2 is nestled in the shadow of the Lhotse Face. When we came through on our first rotation, there were thirty people here, but now there must be two hundred clustered into yellow-tent pods. Momentum is building on the mountain as rotations start to overlap.

We have one night to rest before pushing to Camp 3, which is the final test to determine who will go on to summit. During the summit rotation, we'll be using supplemental oxygen from Camp 3 on. But if we look sluggish at Camp 3 on this round, Ang Dorjee or Mike will cut our climb right there.

We have to be strong, vital, for them to trust that we can withstand what's ahead.

The next morning, the ropes up Lhotse Wall are caked in snow. A storm surged through overnight, and as I step out of my tent for morning tea, flurries of wind laced with icy bits of snow lash against my face. Climbing an exposed face in blizzardlike wind like this is way too dangerous. Ang Dorjee makes us wait it out at Camp 2 for another day.

Thank God, I think, smiling. Maybe it'll take a couple days to clear up. To be honest, I just want to sleep. I could sleep for a week, a year, a lifetime, right now. But the guys head off on an exploratory walk to the base of the wall, so I tag along. Keep moving. Always moving. Always acclimatizing. Tricking my body into thinking that this is normal, that this is totally fine. The mountain hasn't been climbed in two years, but trash from previous years is half-buried in the snowbanks skirting camp: plastic toilet casings, broken tent remains, food wrappers. The ethics of modern mountaineering is Leave No Trace. Everything should have been wiped of any human debris. But some of this trash is from before the environmental awakening. Ironically, the rising temperatures of climate change are melting the ice and exposing all the decades-old trash. We pick up small pieces whenever we can, but most of it will need to be hauled out eventually.

After lunch, I duck into my tent, ready to crawl in bed and nurse my cramps.

"Gonna be a rough one!" Mark says, already curled up on his side with a book. "Do you need privacy to change or anything?"

"No," I say, shivering. The tent walls thwap and shimmer against howling gusts of wind. "Too cold. I'm not moving out of this bag unless it's for food."

"I hear that."

Lying on the ground, a thin foam mat separating me from the snowy earth below, I watch my breath make frosty cloud shapes. "Hey, that one looks like a dog," says Mark, looking up from his book.

"Where?" I ask. "How?"

"See the snout right there." He traces it in midair with a finger. "And the eyes, one and two, and . . . ooohhh, it's gone, they're gone."

I hold my breath for a full minute, then shoot out a huge mouthful of air.

"Oh!" I cry. "A bird, look. Swan, maybe?" As we watch, the neck stretches and breaks apart, scattering into cloudy nothing bits.

When I was a girl, fear snatched my ability to admire and notice all the little things. I don't want to let it steal another moment away, not even a silly little game with Mark.

At dinner, Mike gets the all-clear weather report from Base Camp. "Camp 3 in the morning," he announces. Before bed, I pray that the weather will turn again so we can sleep another day. There's no set altar at Camp 2, so I cobble my own together with a few rocks. Every camp must have an altar. Every morning, I pay my respects at the altar. It's mostly just me honoring Miyolangsangma, praying to the Virgen del Carmen, and begging that I can last one more day, but I'm positive my prayers are the only reason that Mother Everest has let me get this far.

Last night's prayers must have gotten twisted in transit, because we wake to a clear, bitter cold morning, and by six-thirty we're hiking toward the Wall. Mike wants to be first on the ropes to avoid the human traffic jams that happen as more people accumulate and start to climb. It's like an airport—the later in the day it gets, the more chance for logjams and delays. Just ahead, a constellation of lights bobbles through the valley. Headlamps. Another group is up already.

I follow the scattershot of their beams and watch as the rising sun starts to meet their brightness, absorbing them completely by the time we reach the base of Lhotse, a 4,000-foot exposed face with a 50-degree incline. Running up the face like a lifeline is the beginning of hundreds of feet of rope that we'll follow to the summit. Ropes that are going to take me to the top of the Mother of the World. *The top of the world. Who could even imagine? When I was a kid looking out onto the hills beyond Lima . . . Focus! Silvia. Clip in. Stay clipped in at all times. Watch your step.*

For two hours, we slog straight up without a break. At least, it feels like straight up. Notching my crampons duck-style into the snow, I inch up the wall, barely moving, maneuvering over slippery icy bumps.

One step at a time.

Snow, then ice.

Like climbing stairs for hours with no reprieve.

Breathe.

Calves in searing pain.

Snow, then ice.

The higher we climb, the clearer the day gets and the sharper my breath becomes. I monitor it like a new mother hovering nervously over a newborn, paying close attention for signs of a headache, of altitude sickness.

Breathe.

Breaking to hydrate, I glance back over my shoulder. Thousands of feet below, the earth seems like it pulsates. I can see all the way to Camp 1, where the tents are doll toys, and the humans, tiny ant-like specs. The perspective on how high we've climbed is surreal.

Then *BOOM*.

My brain is a balloon. Disconnected from my body, floating. Dizziness, a flying sensation. Like if I just let go, I might lift off. *My vitals.* Am I breathing? Yes. My hands are still moving. Yes. Are these my hands? Wiggle your fingers. Okay, I'm in control. Still in control. It's nice actually, like a warm, fuzzy high. As we break to take in a balcony view, my breath is short and my mind is slack.

I've felt this before.

In Aconcagua. Right before the summit. The last three hundred feet maybe. All woozy and sweet. An escape from the body when everything feels so real and raw and dire.

Start climbing again.

One step at a time.

Snow, then ice.

Trust the crampons. Trust that they will hold. Trust the razor blades on your feet to pierce and grip the snow.

Breathe.

Tents.

Tents?

Yes. The tip-top of little yellow domes. Camp 3.

A final lunge over the top of the wall and I collapse onto flat ground, my hands gripping the packed snow. My head is still spinning as Brian pulls me in for a hug.

"We did it!" he bellows.

"We did." I nod, letting myself relax into the hug. Then, over his left shoulder, I see it. For the first time since leaving Base Camp, in full view, nestled behind the tents at the far end of camp. The iconic black pyramid of Everest's peak.

"Chomolungma," I whisper.

Brian turns toward where I'm pointing. "No, that's not," he says. "That's not Everest."

"Hey, I've got better eyesight than you!"

"You're bloody wrong." He snorts.

When I look more closely, he's right. It's another distant peak. I haven't studied the skyline of the mountains like Brian has.

"Well, it's the closest I've ever been, anyway," I say, shrugging.

"I'll give you that," he says, thumping me on the back. I don't cringe. He's actually starting to grow on me.

Camp 3 is a high-altitude bird's nest no bigger than a gas station parking lot. The clouds seem close enough to touch. As if the top of the world is really within reach. At 23,000 feet, we have only 6,000 to go. Mike is standing in a clearing a few feet from the ledge and calls us over. We sit in a line in front of him, securing our harnesses to a rope strung along a line of tents.

"Looking good," says Mike.

Before we descend, everyone scarfs down energy bars and nuts and chugs all the water we can hold. I finish quickly then take a walk through camp, trying to etch every detail into my brain. Anything I might need to recall during the summit push.

"Time to head out!" Mike hollers.

"Coming!"

Just as I turn to head back, I notice a cluster of yellow bands in a snowbank ahead. Tents. Long abandoned and buried under the snow. "Ang Dorjee," I call, jogging to catch up. "What are those tents?"

"Who knows?" He waves me off. "Other expeditions, possibly."

For a moment I wonder if they're left over from the 2015 earthquake. If they're the tents of people whose dream ended here.

On our way back to Camp 2, we slide past the high-altitude Sherpas untangling rope, hundreds of feet of rope that they're anchoring to the ice, one screw at a time, to build a road all the way to the summit.

Back at Base Camp, the days toggle between mundane and live wire as we wait on news from the Sherpas, who are still working their way to the summit. No one can climb until the ropes are set and the weather is pristine. Every night we huddle around Mike's walkie-talkie like an old-timey family and listen for updates. It's exhilarating to hear the deep voices of the Sherpas broadcast down from so high in the sky. Anthea and Mike receive fourteen-page weather reports via fax with in-depth analysis of wind trends and all possible cloud activity. Every hypothetical wind or storm pattern is analyzed at all angles from multiple altitudes, but nothing can predict avalanche or earthquake.

We have to have a perfect five-day weather window to depart for the summit. Until then, there's nothing to do but wait. It's anxiety inducing—sort of like being on call. We have to remain calm and healthy but be prepared to leave on a moment's notice, in the middle of the night, for the final climb.

Richard, the Peruvian mountaineer I ran into in Lukla with the girls, is camped nearby at the Seven Summits camp, the largest expedition at Base Camp. I stop by to visit. Seven Summits Trek is so big, they have multiple dining tents. Over mugs of green tea in one of them, Richard reveals that his expedition isn't going great. On his first solo attempt to Camp 1, he caught the Khumbu cough and had to descend to Periche for ten days, just like Rob.

When I saw him back in the teahouse, Richard was so assured, so prideful about what he planned to achieve for our country. He seemed superhuman. A national idol. But his spirit has dampened. There's this look in his eyes. Something jittery and hooded. I've felt it so often here that now I'm learning how to spot it in others: fear. *Insecurity.*

Attempting to climb without oxygen is a massive challenge. Something that only purists—old-school mountaineers or climbers looking for new boundaries to break—take on. With a compromised immune system, Richard is understandably wary.

"I'm pushing ahead anyway," he says. But I can see he's lost some of his enthusiasm. We talk about his family in Peru. Then we talk about the joy of climbing. And as we start to focus on the dream instead of the hardships, his light comes back on. Just like all those times I talked about climbing Everest. Even though I rarely believed it myself, whenever I spoke it aloud, the dream grew. No matter how absurd it sounded, how impossible it seemed, dreaming got me closer to executing.

I thank Richard for the tea, give him a Peruvian kiss on the cheek and a big hug. "Buena suerte, Richard," I say. "Whatever happens, you are a star. I truly admire what you're doing. Can't wait to celebrate once you reach the top." He nods and flashes a large warm smile, but there's something sad underneath it.

Something I won't be able to shake for days.

It's not just the mental aspect of waiting for the summit window, of doubt that starts to creep under the door like a persistent draft; I've also been battling cold symptoms. After willing it away doesn't work, Rob returns and shares a magic medicine that he brought back from Periche: Sancho.

It's Vick's VapoRub on steroids mixed with eucalyptus. The smell alone is enough to get you high. Everyone is clamoring for a dose.

"We'll need to get a pot of boiling water," says Rob, setting up a make-shift station for us in the dining tent. "Okay, now put several drops of San-cho into the water, cover your head with a towel. Right. Now bend down and inhale the steam."

"What is this, the Everest spa?" Ang Dorjee jokes, walking into the tent.

"Sancho!" I call.

"Ahh, yes," says Ang Dorjee. "The original Sherpa steam bath."

We start taking turns during the day, Rob and I, doing Sancho steams. And then, after all the playing, it's Tendi who gets sick.

When he doesn't show up to work, Mike and Ang Dorjee check on him and find him wheezing and hacking in his sleep. Right away, they order a helicopter and send him to a doctor in Kathmandu. Just like that, Tendi—strong, sweet Tendi—is gone too.

I'm stunned.

"Tendi must be heartbroken," says Ang Dorjee. "He didn't want to leave. He would never. We had to force him."

"Why?" asks Danny.

"Being at Base Camp is incredibly important to him. He's been with us for the last fifteen years. We are family. It'll be a huge letdown that the season got cut short."

During my very first dinner at this table, I was skittish. Just coming off my hike with the girls, I was suspicious and tender and really, *really*, not looking forward to going toe to toe with a group of macho army-ranger men for the next six weeks. But the table has opened up to me. Shown me what can live inside the hearts of men.

After dinner most nights, we lounge and bullshit or walk around camp to keep the blood flowing. We've all lost a ton of weight; the no-fail Everest Diet:

"Results one hundred percent guaranteed!" says Danny, as we assess our new bodies.

"You might have lung damage for life," I joke. "But hey, your clothes will fit great!"

"Hey, Mark, speaking of," says Danny. "Where'd your ass go?"

"Seriously, mate," says Brian. "I've been wanting to ask 'cause I swore you had one when we started. Not that I was checking it out."

"Damn!" I holler. "Now, Danny and Brian, you're the last people I expected to keep tabs on Mark's butt. Truly."

"I am sure my students will be happy once they see me," Mark snapped back.

"The return of the assless professor!"

We burst into laughter. It's hard to get a read on Mark, and I'm surprised to see how well he takes a joke. After weeks together, I still can't tell where the boundaries of his personality are.

Brian, on the other hand, continues to surprise me. We start walking together after dinner. He becomes my new John. He tells me about his family. How he married his high school sweetheart and had two sons.

"My youngest, Georgy, just came out," he says, as we stroll through camp. "As gay. He's gay."

I nod but say nothing. I can't tell if Brian is for or against what Georgy told him.

"Good for him!" Brian shouts. And then, softer: "Good for him."

"It can be tough at first," I say, setting a hand on his shoulder.

He nods. "Thanks. It's certainly an adjustment. But I'm a proud dad. And this changes nothing. How old were you when you came out?"

"In my twenties. It was hard because my parents disapproved."

"Why?"

"Mostly the Catholic Church, but also because of the negative perception of people in Lima. It is a critical society. Especially for women."

"That sucks," says Brian. "I don't want my son to feel like that. When he came to me, he was crying, you know, and it just tore me up to think he was so sad." He sniffles and dabs his eyes with his sleeve. "He thought he was going to disappoint me. But I just want him to be the happiest he can be. To find the perfect loving partner."

"Now *I'm* going to cry!" I glance tenderly at Brian.

For so long I'd dreamt of my own mother saying those exact words. Envisioned her walking next to me carrying a big white PFLAG sign—parents, families, and friends of LGBTQ+ kids. Imagined her making fast friends with the other mothers, the way she'd tried during my catechism, the way she had always tried to be part of so many things my father kept her from. Flashing that sweet, shy smile of hers, the little giggle she used to disarm people before speaking her very bad English. I could almost hear it now: *Jijijiji. Me speak little English. Please verrrry slow!* And the words I wanted to hear most of all. *I proud my Silvita is gay. I am proud mother.*

"I'm so proud of you, Brian," I say. "I wish I would have had a father like you. Georgy is really lucky."

When I first met Brian, his boisterousness put me on alert. I was a cat ready to pounce or run. Just hearing his voice—and it was hard *not* to hear it—made me jumpy. He embodied the alpha male, the big talker, all brash and loudmouthed. Where I come from, the loudest men take up all the air, leaving no space for softness.

Seeing Brian's eyes glisten as he talks about Georgy makes me trust him. Maybe it's his tenderness, or maybe I'm emotionally raw from being ripped to shreds this past month, but the details of my story tumble out.

I tell Brian about my relationships in San Francisco, my mother's denial, all the support I wished I'd had and things I wished I'd known. I tell him about Lori. How my mother couldn't acknowledge my grief because she'd never acknowledged my partner. How people in the gay community too often have to live with this split: people who love them but can't accept, or see, entire parts of who they are. Who we love is part of who we are, I tell him.

When I pause to take a breath, I realize we're standing still and that Brian is facing me, not posturing or shouting or sucking up all the air, but with tears in his eyes, quietly hanging on every word.

"Silvia, I'm so sorry about your loss. That must have been excruciating."

That is all I'd ever wanted my parents to say.

"And for her parents?" he says. "What a tragedy."

"I know," I say, the tears welling up. Every time I manage to speak calmly about Lori, my heart breaks a little. Losing her is a deep wound I'm not sure will ever heal. I've just learned how to cope.

* * *

We have less than three weeks before the monsoons start and rain starts to fall by the truckload, soaking the surrounding valleys and shrouding Everest in mist. If the weather doesn't cooperate, we might run out of time. The glacier keeps melting. We keep waiting. And once we get the okay to leave, we have one shot. We're no longer on our timeline but at the total mercy of the mountain and her weather.

On top of all the uncertainty, I'm anxious about how my body is going to react. Mike, Ang Dorjee, and Lydia green light me for the final rotation, but that doesn't mean my body is ready. I have several friends who attempted Everest and hit a wall somewhere between Camp 3 and the summit.

A few sites over, my friend Masae's expedition is waiting for their summit window. Masae is a young Japanese climber attempting Everest. We met last year in Antarctica climbing Vinson Massif. It's easy to make friends climbing because you're forced together, and there's a special bond between the women, because we are so few. But they're also hard friendships to maintain. Everyone is always on different expeditions and schedules or climbing a different rotation, attempting a longer hike, or staying warm after a cold streak; it is hard to keep in touch with fellow female climbers.

The sky is blue-jay bright. A perfect day for lunching *alfresco*, I think, as if Masae and I are meeting at a bistro in the city instead of crouching on fold-up chairs 18,000 feet above sea level. When I get to Masae's camp, she's distressed. Her crew has just returned from a very challenging second rotation, and Masae tells me it was marred by what she calls "male entitlement."

"It was Camp 3," she says, sipping her tea. "The guides decided to stay overnight to acclimatize. They assigned me a tent to share with a climbing Sherpa. In the middle of the night, he rolls over and starts touching me. Here, here, here!" Masae points to her chest, her belly, her crotch.

"What?" I stand up out of my chair.

"At first I thought I was confused, you know, like maybe I was dreaming or it was just the altitude getting me loopy. This can't be real, right? Happening right here? That would be a bad dream."

"A nightmare," I say under my breath.

"But I realized it was true. That it was happening. I shoved him away and threatened to report him. Of course, he backed off then, mumbling some *I'm Sorrys* or *No, No, No,* acting like I had it all wrong."

The next day, she told her guide, and the Sherpa was fired on the spot, but since the team got back to Base Camp, Masae says, the energy has been tense.

"They're all looking at me like I caused him to get fired," she says. Her forehead scrunches into a worried V. "Now I'm at the final leg of this trip, the summit, so important, the summit. But I'm scared of retaliation. I just don't know if I can trust my team."

As I am learning, on Everest, team trust isn't a luxury, or even really an emotion—it's a matter of life or death. It's an essential function. A practical necessity. We spend weeks building that trust, and the fact that it got snatched away from Masae by some horny guy, and that the incident could possibly threaten her chances of breaking a world record, makes me furious. I've always said that mountains don't discriminate. That being gay or a woman or Peruvian here doesn't matter when it comes down to it, because we are all at the mercy of the elements. I've always approached climbing as an equal playing field. If you have what it takes, your gender, race, or creed doesn't matter.

Mountains were my escape. My sacred places—places of healing—natural places that accept all without judgment. But even here, even in this sacred place, there's no escaping the hands of men. And just as I'd begun to trust the ones around me. I'm livid. I rush back to camp and find Lydia and Anthea relaxing in the sun. "This has to end!" I shout, after telling them about Masae. "This is ridiculous! In the middle of this intense climb?"

"Oh yeah," says Lydia. "That's the mountains for you. I've experienced my share of harassment. Just the way it is."

"The way it is?" I whimper. "The way it is? We have to change the way it is . . ."

"Listen to me," says Lydia, patting an empty chair next to her. For the next hour, I listen to Lydia and Anthea pinball stories back and forth about "sexism" in climbing. Their takeaway seems to be that battling the machismo environment is unpleasant and uncomfortable, but they don't call the behavior assault. All I can think about is Masae having her world-record climb compromised. That isn't unpleasant. It's an attack. On her body and on everything she and the women who came before and will come after her are trying to accomplish.

Where's the Gulabi Gang when you need them?

When Jimena told us about their vigilante college crew, the ones who beat up a rapist, it wasn't just about the assault, but the collective rage of not being believed. Like the Gulabi, a band of Indian women vigilantes, Jimena's crew were Brown and Black, indigenous, and Asian. Not believing women is the status quo, but for women of color, the violence of the disbelief is even more dangerous. Even after Ehani, Shreya, and Rubina stood up to one of the most horrific traffickers in their region, and even after the Nepali government found him guilty and gave him a record sentence, they still faced daily death threats. Sometimes even from their own neighbors.

All for telling the truth. The simple truth.

People go to incredible lengths to keep us quiet. Even convincing us that it's our fault so that we'll bundle up the shame and carry it like a close friend, for years, protecting ourselves from what they really don't want us to know.

That none of this is our fault. And that just because it's the way it is does not mean it's the way it has to be.

After an hour of getting nowhere with the women on my team, I'm boiling over with frustration and emotionally exhausted. "I have to go and lie down. I'm going for a nap," I snap. I never nap, but it's the only way to process this. Otherwise, I'll explode. I crawl into my tent to try and nap, but my heart is pounding. Stewing with rage, I think of all the dreams stolen from women around the world, women who've been told that this mountain— that any mountain—is too big for them to climb. That women aren't mountain climbers.

And then, when the few women do get here, they are always, always at risk. Sexual violence thrives on the assumption that no one will tell the truth. That's not the *why* of it, but it's what keeps it alive and thriving just under the surface. J was never brought to legal justice. I'd been too traumatized to take him to court like the Nepali girls had done. Instead I'd watched him marry and have kids of his own. Before I told my mother what J had done, he asked my parents to be the godparents to his twin sons. They said yes.

My mother later told me one of his twins died of pneumonia.

That I considered proof of a just God. Of karma. The universal courtroom. A tipping of the spiritual scales.

Tears water my resolve as I call on Everest, the Mother of the World, on Shakti, who is mother, lover, destroyer—whatever necessary. For once, maybe I can use destruction for good.

Suddenly, there's a rapping on my tent.

The sun is down. I must have been asleep for hours.

"Silvia." It's a woman's voice. Lydia. "Summit's on," she says. "We leave tonight after dinner."

"Tonight?" I squeak.

"Yes. Tonight."

Shit! Frazzled, I scramble to gather my things. *Where are those flashlight batteries?* I think while staring directly at them in the palm of my hand. This is like packing for the end. For a trip I might never return from. At dinner, I'm surprised to see Tendi cooking. He fought his altitude sickness to make it back in time to give us a proper good-bye and send along his blessings for our trip. As we eat, Anthea asks how we want to be announced by the Adventures Consultant news wires if we make it. I take a deep breath, pause for a moment, and say: "Silvia Vasquez-Lavado. The first Peruvian woman to have summited Everest." Hearing it aloud swells my heart with pride. I have a chance to rewrite this legacy of pain. To show girls and women everywhere what's possible. I want to tell them that the strongest men on my team are long gone. But here I am. And I'm going to make it to the top if it kills me.

Not for me, but for them. *This isn't about you anymore, Silvia,* I think, but standing there, speaking my existence into being at the top of the world—Silvia Vasquez-Lavado, first Peruvian woman to summit Everest—I realize *it never was.* It was always for Masae; for Lucy and Jimena and Shreya and Rubina and Ehani and all the other women and girls at Shakti; for whatever Lydia lived through that she couldn't make a fuss about. This is for Silvita and all the Peruvian girls who were hurt like her; all the girls around the world who've been abused and told they were trash or would end up trash, and who, like me, believed it for far too long. And maybe still do.

I try to get some sleep—we're leaving for the summit, *Oh my God, oh my Goddddd*—but it's useless. When Mike screams, "Time to wake up!" around midnight, I spring out of bed, ready.

I am a woman on fire.

Chapter 18

❧

THE DEATH ZONE

I'm on my knees, curled around my oxygen tank, and my hands tremble as I beat back terror. Outside, the wind thrashes against my tent, blowing the walls in as snotty tears roll down my cheeks. This is it. This is as far as I'm going to make it. I'm done. Waving the white flag. I give up. You win, Mother. You *win*. The mountain is going to swallow me, bury me alive like the yellow tents. Like the bodies that never decompose because the air isn't warm enough.

For weeks, death has buzzed at the back of my brain. But even when I flirted with the idea as I had during so many dark nights back home, it was still hypothetical. But now, here it is, gnashing at my tent while I cower stone sober and wide-eyed, looking death in the face for who she really is. I'm never getting down off this mountain. Away from this. This storm. This burden. This weight. Maybe it would be a relief to just give in. To join the other bodies in the frozen ice. The ones whose journey was cut short. If that's what it takes to end this sorrow, to make sure I never pass it on, that it never hurts another person, then maybe it's best.

Maybe Everest *is* my death wish.

I never called myself an alcoholic. I never said it out loud. Maybe it's textbook denial, or maybe in some twisted way I don't think of myself as an alcoholic because booze has just been a symptom of my insistence on survival. At one point, drinking was the only way for me to access the abyss buried under a lifetime of keeping quiet. It was the only thing that enabled me to shed the mask; the only thing that dragged me down deep enough to touch the white-hot center of my own pain. In some ways, booze was once a beacon, drawing me to where I needed to go.

Until it wasn't, and it became death itself.

When I called myself a survivor, it wasn't with pride, but with a corrosive mixture of arrogance and resentment. Survivorship was a suit I'd worn to hold all the loose, bloody pieces together. But I was starting to see how dangerous it was to assign merit to survival. To make it part of your identity. Because one day you wake up and realize that surviving is all you know how to do.

Survive.

And it's not nearly enough.

But it's too late now for me to choose life or death, in the shadow of this mountain; it's no longer my choice.

The girls are gone.

Lori is gone.

My mother is gone.

I am nothing but a lost child, alone on a mountain.

Wind snaps against my tent, and my teeth chatter. Another sound cuts in. A deep, melodious lullaby. A humming. The Deboche nuns. Their voices are a hundred hands stroking my hair. A blast of warm air. *You do not have to be good*, they're saying. *You do not have to be obedient or successful for love. You don't have to achieve anything at all. You don't have to cut off parts of yourself in order to become whole. Accept them. Like we accept you. Love them. Like we love you.*

Please, tell me it's okay, I beg. But the nuns are gone, and the sound of my own voice echoes back. *I don't want to die*, I cry. Something bursts from my chest. It's the sound of long-buried grief. A great wild howling of pain leaving my body. It's the sound of something that wants to live, wants to fight. I'm wracked with sobs and shaking as the zipper on the tent door starts to jingle and Lydia stumbles in. I glance up just as she's closing the flap.

"Silvia!" she says, touching her hand to my back. "Are you okay?"

I look into her eyes. They're the color of sage. Her face is ruddy and wind chapped, but her eyes have a softness I never noticed before.

"I don't think I can go on," I mutter, hanging my head. I don't want to see her disappointment.

"Look, I'm really sorry for shouting at you back there," she says. "This storm is horrible. One of the worst things I've experienced on a mountain. I was scared."

"You?" I perk up. Hearing this gives me a strange sense of comfort.

She nods.

"Sure. Mike and Dorjee considered bringing us back down. Most of the Sherpas have gone back to Camp 2."

Camp 3 is higher and more exposed than Camp 2, so staying overnight puts us in a more vulnerable position in the event of bad weather, but a better position to stay on schedule for our summit push. Sherpas can make up the difference in little time, but for us climbers, descending to Camp 2 and coming back up after the weather has cleared would put the entire summit bid at risk. All we have is this five-day window.

"So," I say, slowly, my lips frozen stiff. "This weather isn't normal?"

Lydia shakes her head. "Not at all. That was as bad as it gets."

As bad as it gets.

"It's okay to be scared, Silvia," she says. "You are a really solid climber. A strong climber. You are going to be okay. We're going to the top, yes?"

Mountaineers are rugged people who throw themselves into the elements because they want to feel more alive, because they like nature more than people, and, mostly, because they want to see what they're capable of in this one life. They aren't famous for their warm fuzzies or inspirational speeches. When challenged, their default is often stoicism. But Lydia's reassurance is an unexpected kindness. A warm bath when I need it most. A sense of calm settles over the tent, and I release my grip on the oxygen canister. My fingers unclaw and cramp as I stretch them out inside my gloves.

Then, another voice. A memory. A man's voice. Ed Viesturs. The most legendary American climber and the only one to climb all fourteen of the world's 8,000-meter peaks. The fifth person in the world to do all that without supplemental oxygen. Five weeks earlier, on one of our first nights at Base Camp, Ed joined us for dinner. I sat next to him, giddy to be in the company of a legend.

"Ed," I asked him. "What's your biggest advice for me during this journey?"

"You'll have an awful day, if not many, on this mountain," he said. "You'll want to quit; you'll question why you're here. But when that happens, know that it's just an awful day and that everything will be different when you wake up the next morning. Everything changes when you just keep going."

That night, I'd nodded at the platitude, grateful for his time, but not particularly moved. I couldn't have imagined what those simple words could mean in action.

Mountaineers have a way of under-exaggerating danger.

Ed hadn't said what an awful day might look like—me crying and spooning an oxygen tank, first praying to die, then praying to live. I've had more than my share of bad days. Days when I woke up not knowing where or who I was. Years really. I've had days when I wanted to die. But death wasn't actually banging at my door. Here I see clearly what a bad day can really mean.

This is just a bad day, Silvia. It's just a bad day.

I pull on my oxygen mask and open the valve. Thin lines of cold air snake up my nose, filling my lungs and the deflated tire of my Everest dream. Instantly, I feel clearer. Brighter.

Two hours of lying awake in my tent and the wind has finally died down.

"Are you alive?" Someone screams from the next tent over. *Brian!*

"Barely!" I shout, letting loose a big stuttering sigh.

"Look outside," he says.

Lydia steps out of the tent first. I step out next, and what I see is stunning. I stumble a few steps forward. Behind Lydia, rays of sun beam down on Brian's tent. The snow is a dusting now, not a squall. We're perched high above the Western Cwm, and the whole valley is soft with the peaceful hush of freshly fallen snow. The sky is a crisp marine blue, but the valley isn't sunny; instead, it's half-shaded by a massive shadow, the fused shadows of Everest and Lhotse. And the shadow seems alive like a shelter. A friendly refuge. A place to rest and hide.

All around, my team starts to climb out of their tents and look around, chattering and recapping the storm. I watch the edge of the shadow and see that, like snow, what seems gray or black at a distance has many gradients of color and light up close. When I first came to Everest, its shadow was dark enough to swallow mine. It was so ominous that I felt small, and my problems felt smaller too. Standing in the shadow of the mountain, I could see outside myself for the first time. But now it feels less like a place to hide and more like an invitation to settle in, to let go. It feels expansive. Less cloak than companion.

The shadow feels like home.

Being up this high feels sacred. Like swimming in the darkest parts of the ocean, where an entire ecosystem unknown to us and not meant for us reveals itself. It doesn't need us, but if we're lucky, we might be allowed to witness it.

At the other far end of the Cwm, the shadows of Nuptse and Lhotse meet in a perfect V. Looking through the V, I can see the cone of Pumori, a 23,000-foot peak that climbers call the daughter of Everest, but in the Sherpa language, it means "unmarried daughter." The unmarried daughter, the daughter of Everest, stands at the border of Nepal and Tibet. Beyond her, the Tibetan plateau unrolls itself into wide brown plains, broken up by more snow-capped peaks draped in wispy clouds.

By four p.m., the sky is clear and freezing. The air, invigorating. Even the little hairs inside my nose tingle.

By six p.m., we get news: we're moving up. Tomorrow is going to be a clear day, so the plan is to get a good night's sleep and get up by eight a.m. After a few iffy appetite days, my hunger is back, and eating feels amazing. At dinner, I gorge on my secret dish for secret strength—a rice and quinoa blend. I shovel it into my mouth, suddenly ravenous. I can't get enough.

By eight p.m., it's off to bed.

It feels like I've lived an entire week in the last twelve hours. As I drift off to sleep, I say a prayer of thanks for Lhotse and Everest and the solace of their shadows. I give thanks for Mother Nature, who continues to show me mercy. *Just a little longer, Mother, just a little more is all I need.*

I cuddle up to my oxygen tank like it's a metallic teddy bear, and I pass out.

* * *

When I sit up the next morning, my body pitches forward. We're on a steep incline. Which apparently didn't rattle my sleep at all. I slept so long and hard that yesterday seems like a distant nightmare. I'm feeling reborn. Basking in the peace that comes after a storm.

"Breakfast!" shouts a muffled voice from outside.

We're pushing to Camp 4 today. *My God.* Camp 4. And from there, depending on the weather, we might leave tonight for the summit. *Holyyyy shit.* I have a real shot. Scrambling, I pack my bag and get dressed. As I tighten my 8,000-meter pants, the ones I had to buy last-minute in Kathmandu, I laugh remembering Ang Dorjee's stern look of disappointment back at the Hotel Annapurna. For such a hot mess, I've made it pretty far. The guides seem to believe in me, so maybe it's time that I should too.

Breakfast eaten and bags packed, we place our oxygen masks on and open our tanks. A tiny valve turns on the flow of air. Cool air streams into my nose; inside the mask, my breathing is hollow and raspy, Darth Vaderesque.

* * *

The major steep, technical climbing is behind us now. The rest is a fight against gravity and oxygen. We start off at a gradual incline, climbing laterally across a broad, snowy face that runs toward Camp 4. There's one fixed line strung all the way from Camp 3 to the summit. Our lifeline, it'll catch us, God willing, if we fall. In our penguin-like summit suits, we clip into the fixed rope with our jumars. A second carabiner—which we'll use as security for passing other climbers—dangles from our harnesses. We're a single helix, flowing, grooving, all sync and no stress this morning. People going up the mountain stay to one side of the rope; those coming down use the other.

My thighs hum with dull pain. My shins burn from pulling my boots through dense, powdery snow. It's like climbing a steep sand dune. But my legs just keep going. No car. No train. No helicopters. I've walked all the way from Lukla to here, my two ordinary legs powering every step.

Just ahead, a line of climbers is backed up already. Ang Dorjee picks up the pace and rushes us around them. He is moving so fast, hardly looking, as he clips in and out, in and out, moving around three, five, ten people, with the fluid mechanics of someone who's learned to breathe underwater. It's almost embarrassing. Like we're pushing our way to the front of the line. But there's no time to second-guess him, and I wouldn't dare. Following his lead, we clip in and out, moving swiftly around each climber, and after a while, it becomes rote, mechanical, like slipping past someone in a crowded subway car.

This is what Dorjee means by practice, by committing life-or-death actions to muscle memory. If we screw up here, or worse, higher up, it's an easy slip to an icy death. Over the last month, danger has become so normalized that sometimes in moments that are less technical or terrifying I have to slap myself to remember the stakes. Maybe we climbers have a high danger tolerance to start, but there's also a tapering down of attention. You can't think about life or death every minute of the day. You have to live in the kinetics of the climb. Everything becomes nano. The plonk of a crampon into the snow. An arm reaching up the rope. I'm not curious about the summit or the obstacles ahead, but about what happens if I just keep walking. Maybe it's so hard for adults to experience awe because we're thinking too much about what happens next.

* * *

Two hours into our climb, I feel good. I mean, I feel *wow*. I feel *great*. My body is on autopilot, powering me up the mountain, while I soak in the incredible views. There's no wind this morning. Not a single cloud in the sky, and the glare is intense. Sweat rolls down the back of my legs. Dorjee warned us about taking pictures. "One tiny slip and your camera is gone!" But I have to try. Pulling my camera from an interior pocket, I snap a few photos, trying to frame the moment. But nothing can capture the meditative crunch of my gait, the immensity of the majestic, craggy landscape. It's surreal. It's like looking down on a 3-D topographical map. We're above the clouds now, sky walking in a frosty heaven. It's easy to see why after visiting the Himalayas James Hilton wrote about the mythical Shangri-la, a utopian city above the clouds where everyone lives forever.

What a contrast. Yesterday I was ready to quit, to die, and today the sweet chirp of cartoon birds loops through my mind. Then a rumble. At first, I brush it off, marching happily along, but there it is again—a low, deep growl. *Shit*. Not now. Yes. NOW. I couldn't poop before we left Camp 3, but now I need to go. *Bad*. There are no toilets. We each carry disposable bags. The camp rule is we pack out whatever we produce. Leave No Trace means leaving no waste behind, not even what comes out of our bodies. I glance around for somewhere to squat, regretting how enthusiastically I pounded my "power meal" last night. Because of my celiac, I eat mostly pots of rice and quinoa, which find their way out at the most inconvenient times.

How am I going to squat and keep myself upright? The incline is too steep. At our next break, I signal to Ang Dorjee.

"I need to find a place to poop," I try to say quietly.

"Absolutely not," he says, stoically. "You're not clipping out here." The

only thing holding us to the mountain's face is the razor's edge of our crampons and one long rope anchored to the ice with hundreds of little screws. I
know clipping out could be fatal, but I have to take a serious shit.

"We'll be at Camp 4 in ninety minutes. Hold it 'til then."

"Wait, what?" Ninety minutes? My God. What if I can't? I don't think I
can. But I nod and step back into line. Whatever Dorjee says goes. It's much
too dangerous. I need to focus on holding it in. The sun is blaring down and
getting stronger by the minute. It's close to midday. By our next break, my
stomach is a pot about to boil over. I can't take it any longer.

"Dorjee!" I shout. I'm beyond shame. "I don't think I can hold it. I seriously have to go."

"Silvia!" he roars. "It's too dangerous. You're likely to fall. See that final
push over there?" He points wayyyy down the path toward a big scramble
of rocks. "That's the Geneva Spur. After that, Camp 4 is around the corner.
People have fallen here. Just hold it!"

It seems unfathomably far, but if I squint, I can see people climbing
around the rocks where he's pointing. Maybe I can do it. Ooooh, I don't
know. My stomach churns. Screw it. Ang Dorjee might yell at me, but I have
got to go. I turn to step off the trail just as someone shouts: "Pack!"

Somewhere on the line ahead, a backpack gets unclipped, and all of a
sudden it shoots past my face like a bullet. It scares the shit right back into
me. I can make it. If I don't, Anthea will have to revise my summit announcement: "Silvia Vasquez-Lavado, the first Peruvian woman to fall off the face of
Lhotse while attempting to poop." I can't put her through that.

The Spur is in sight.

"Por favor, Virgencita del Carmen, ayúdame para que no me salga la caca.
Ayúdame a aguantarla."

Please, dearest Virgen of Carmen, help me not let my poop out; please
allow me to hold off.

Also please forgive me for praying to you about poop.

Most of the day has been a slow, steady walk, which made it easier to
hold, but the Geneva Spur is a massive anvil-shaped rock buttress, a mixed
face of ice and rock that's almost completely vertical. And it's more slippery
than it looks. Pulling ourselves up with the fixed line, we have to zig and zag
around big nubby boulders, looking for patches of stable snow to sink our
crampons into. Every step demands total focus. First, to avoid slipping, and

second, well, . . . *Come on! Come on, Silvia.* I'm sweating and panting. Not from the searing sun but from the sheer effort of not crapping my pants. Thirty feet from the top of the Spur, I'm pulling myself up and over a low boulder, my jumar sliding smoothly along the rope, when my foot slips on an icy rock. Panicking, I jerk my body to brace myself, and lose control.

Shit.

And it keeps coming. Oh my God. Please God, let me get over this stinking rock. I pull myself up and over the Spur as quickly as I can. At the top, I turn to the right and spy a small flat spot, and faster than you can say pit stop, I whip out my compost bag and squat right there, still clipped into the line and everything.

"Silvia!" Dorjee yells again. "Hold it."

But the time for a climber's decorum has expired. Lucky for me, I can't smell a thing inside my oxygen mask. Climbers pass me with my bare ass hanging out, and I'm surprised to feel no shame. Nature always wins. Luckily, my teammates are too tired to properly tease me. As I pull up my pants and take a sip of water, I see rising from the earth, like a primordial arrowhead, the triangular face of Everest. Big icy breaths wrap themselves around its peak. A chill runs down my spine, rattling my tailbone. I imagine the first people who attempted the climb. What hell they went through. The first woman. Junko Tabei, a tenacious Japanese climber. I'm sure she had bigger problems than crapping her pants.

I need a nap.

Once we make it into camp, I find an isolated nook away from the tents and try to scrub my pants clean with antibacterial gel and handfuls of snow. A mountaineer's bath. Maybe I could use one myself. I haven't showered in weeks. There's a moment, that's not now, when I'll laugh at this—I know it. When I'll see the metaphor in my hands. When I realize that we all have to deal with our crap eventually. And isn't that why I'm here? But today is not that day. Dammit. My summit pants of all things. They're the only thing warm enough to wear to summit. And mine are not in great shape.

We're in the South Col now, at 26,000 feet. I'm scrubbing my pants at the altitude at which planes fly. Once they're as clean as they're going to get, I stroll through camp on the way to my tent. The term *thin air* is starting to sink in. Even with oxygen on, every step I take is draining. At the lower camps, there was a social aspect, a climbing camaraderie and chatter among expedition teams. But here, Dorjee and Mike have discouraged socializing or wandering around—*waste of oxygen, waste of energy*—advising us to stay in our tents instead, and try to get some sleep, which is supposed to be next to impossible at this altitude. Still, there's a scene. A handful of climbers stroll, strut even, in their oxygen masks and summit suits—a cross between a snowsuit and an astronaut's getup. It's spectacular watching them parade around camp in a show of strength, the oxygen mask a status symbol. One man in a neon orange suit matching the orange tank slung casually over his back looks like he's ready for a rave in an arctic nightclub. I've really come full circle, from blacking out in the back of a gay bar to hobnobbing with the high-altitude elite. Entry is quite exclusive.

Walking back to my tent, I crane my neck up and gape at the towering pyramid of Everest. I can make out two potential routes. The one straight up from camp looks treacherous, if even possible; the other is a gentle, curved path that weaves around to the right of the peak's base. Tucking into my tent to rest, I drift off, dreaming that someone will wake me soon with good news: that we're climbing tonight and that our way up Everest is the sweet little path to the right.

By seven p.m., the guides call a meeting. After deliberating, Lydia comes back to deliver the options. We can push to summit tonight or wait it out until tomorrow, when the weather looks marginal.

"If we go halfway and if it's too windy, can we try again tomorrow?" I ask innocently.

"Silvia," Lydia speaks slowly through her oxygen mask. "There is only one chance. If we have to turn around halfway, that's it. That's your summit bid. There's not enough oxygen to go again."

I'm torn! Should I go or wait? Go or wait?

Brian and Danny are game for tonight. Mark decides to wait until tomorrow.

"Let's do it," I say.

"Wait, Silvia, before we take off." Lydia's face expression changes. "The guides discussed it and, well, you've got a problem."

My face flushes.

"We're going to have to clog you up. We can't take a chance with your bowels," says Lydia firmly. "Too dangerous." Lydia hands me a dose of Imodium. It's such a small thing, but at this stage of the climb, it can be the difference between life and death. As it travels down my esophagus and into my stomach, I imagine it releasing into my bloodstream, sending its chemical signals to my body to hold it in. One final time of being asked to hold it in, keep it down, to be smaller, to be ashamed, to keep quiet, so I can make it to the top. For this it's worth it. But I pledge to myself that this will be the last time.

By seven-thirty p.m., we're in our tents chasing sleep. For three hours, I flit in and out of stress dreams and whorls of nervous excitement. No one sleeps at this point. Who could?

At ten-thirty, it's –20 degrees Fahrenheit as we clip in and begin to walk. It's so dark that the light from my headlamp is swallowed up, and all I can see is the small circular beam tracking my feet. The reflection from the snow helps a little, but we're throwing shadows everywhere. For the summit, we've each been paired with two Sherpas, so the guides can focus on monitoring the route and technical issues. Chewang Dorji, one of the Sherpas assigned to me, climbs just ahead of me. I can hardly see his back. Each step is an exercise in trust. Kami Rita, my other Sherpa, is just behind me. Dorjee is leading us all.

I'm in my summit pants and an insulated summit parka. Under the down pants, I have two pairs of thermal pants, one thick, the other thin. On my hands, a hyper-thin lining called one-minute gloves, then a thicker pair of fleece gloves, then my summit mittens. My head is covered in a balaclava, a fleece buff, ski goggles, and a beanie. Accessories include a headlamp, harness, jumar, and ice axe. My crampons are well-sharpened, and my boots tied tight.

My oxygen mask is in place.

The triangular face or south slope is the steepest route to the summit. This is the route that I had hoped we were not going to climb. If I had studied the route, I wouldn't be so shocked. It's exhausting. My legs feel leaden and glued to the earth; catching my breath is a joke. We're taking in two liters of oxygen per minute, but weirdly it doesn't make it much easier to breathe or climb. The canister is a mix of compressed gas and ambient air that increases oxygen flow by only 2 percent. It's like a low-grade A/C feeding sips of air up into my nose: enough to keep the brain from swelling, but not enough to gulp down or fully expand the chest. Imagine breathing through a coffee straw.

Slowly, as we start to move up the path, my eyes adjust. Together, the headlamps create a bubble of light. Together we're safe. The air is still.

Crystalline. Shot through with a million stars. Stars that look close enough to reach out and pluck from the sky. Are they? It's May 18, and for a minute, I wonder what that means for the constellations here, where Tibet, Nepal, and China meet. Maybe there are entire formations I've never seen.

Just ahead, in the velvety darkness, it looks as if a strand of Christmas lights is strung up the mountain, stretching from the South Col to the Balcony, one of the last flat resting spots before the summit. Vertically, the Balcony is less than a mile away, but it'll take us three hours to reach because of the grueling incline, thin air, and the last thing you'd expect at the top of the world: traffic. We should add that to life's guarantees. Death, taxes, and traffic.

We have to get in and get out of here fast.

Brian and Danny are on fire. We're keeping good time, moving right up the line. Clipping in and out and shuffling around bodies has become automatic, though I'm still strangely ashamed when I pass someone. The stakes are higher up here. The ridge is more narrow and steeper than the climb to Camp 4, and I have to push my body against other bodies to slide by. One extra step to the left and I could be pitched right off the mountain. Pushing past in silence under the half-lit Himalayan sky feels intimate, like squeezing past a stranger in a narrow doorway at the sort of party where anything could happen.

Climbers who started before us, some as early as six p.m., are reaching the Balcony now, their lights clustering together like a constellation of fireflies. It's surreal to see the string of lights inch slowly up the mountain. To know that each one is attached to a person, riding the engine of their own two legs; and each person has a dream, a particular, singular dream, a dream that maybe only they know about. Each light represents a reason for climbing. A dream, like mine, that is so commanding they are willing to risk everything.

By midnight, I need a nap. I'm hoping Mike will call it. Just a little rest. Five minutes is all I need. Every rock looks like a La-Z-Boy, its snowy surroundings a pillowy down comforter. I dream of bed. An actual bed. Floating, woozy, flying.

My body. My body. What *is* my body?

By two a.m., we reach the Balcony. We try to eat something and hydrate. From the inner pocket of my coat I pull out a 500-milliliter thermos of hot water. The bottle that Ang Dorjee made me purchase back in Kathmandu.

Now I see why. One sip of the warm water and a tiny bite of my favorite raspberry energy chew is enough. It's hard to get anything down. Food is alien. Even candy, which I usually love, tastes like cardboard.

Someone jostles my arms, and I turn to see Danny. Danny Boy! He's pointing to his oxygen tank, mouthing something. Oh, right. I turn back to Chewang Dorji, who motions me to unclip my tank and swap it with the new one he's holding. Everything is in pantomime. There's no energy for real words. Real food. Real feelings.

We swap out our tanks and begin walking again. Dorjee pushes on toward the South Summit, which marks the final stretch before the infamous Hillary Step. It's another five or six hours to the top. Almost ten hours total to climb one mile. It's dark, steep, and incredibly cold. It's not just my limbs and face that are cold; my organs and cells and bones feel like they are made of ice. All sensation has been switched off. I'm a machine, an assembly line of a person—step, breathe, step, breathe.

Breaking 27,600 feet, we've officially entered the Death Zone, where atmospheric pressure drops to a third of sea level, temperatures never rise above 0 degrees Fahrenheit, and any exposed skin freezes instantly. Over the last six weeks, our bodies have slowly been acclimatizing. We have manufactured more red blood cells; our hearts have even started beating faster. As we climbed higher, nonessential bodily functions like digestion were suppressed in order to funnel all our body's energy to the cardiopulmonary system. But there's no acclimatizing to the Death Zone. Cell mitosis has stopped completely. Our bodies are deteriorating. But that's not even what kills most people on Everest; it's the brain fog and disorientation that lead to lethal decision making, like sitting down to rest and never getting up, or stepping sloppily and falling. Drunkenness and altitude sickness mirror each other. Slurred speech, confusion, the inability to walk straight.

Ahead, there's a cluster of little points of light that seem to merge and scatter, a painting in motion. Headlamps. It's hard to make out shapes in the dark, but there's a shadowy outline of people ahead. The sky is spectacular, a deep blue-black bruise. I feel like I'm walking on the moon. The closest I'll ever get to becoming an astronaut. Walking on totally exposed terrain, we tower over the surroundings. The landscape of the last six weeks—snow, ice, rock, mountains—suddenly feels surreal, hyperreal. Human minds weren't made to be this high up. I'm an arctic bird. We keep walking. Short, heavy steps. You can't drag your feet. With each step, you have to pick your crampon up and then press it down hard to reestablish contact with the ice. Everything takes so much energy. People are crouching at the side of the trail, panting, looking defeated. One shakes their head, pantomiming to the other.

And just like that, they turn around and head down the mountain.

That could be me. Any minute now, it could be any one of us. Not a single breath is guaranteed up here.

My limits have already been demolished. Every step is a new edge that I'm skating.

By three a.m., the darkness starts to lift, revealing a glittering pea-soup sky. A dainty sliver of moon.

Traffic starts to back up as we come to a standstill at a series of rock benches—a smaller version of the Geneva Spur. Thirty to forty people have to scale the slippery, rocky steps, pulling themselves up the rope one careful step at a time. There's no passing. We have to wait for each person to climb, which, at altitude, with diminishing energy and low oxygen, demands tremendous effort and risk.

At first, the break is great. I really look around for the first time. On the horizon, in the direction of India, I see a storm. Cloudy gray pillars of rain. And lightning, *wow*. Veiny bolts of blue-green lightning strike the earth— one, two, *four*. Across the valley, the headlamps of people attempting Lhotse are candles flickering low in their votives.

I jiggle my hands and feet, wobble my torso, circle my head around, hoping constant motion will scare off frostbite. My team is getting restless. It's been thirty minutes and we've barely moved. Up ahead, people are stuck on the ropes. Frozen in fear. Backing up the whole line. It's just too much. We are clipped to a rope without much room to move. Every additional step to warm our bodies will consume the little energy we have left. Too much for any one person.

People start to give up. One by one they peel away from the flock and turn back down the mountain. It's too dark to see their faces, but I imagine them shaking their heads in defeat as they inch their way back down the rope. As they pass, I feel a flicker of connection. They're not strangers. Every single one of them has endured the beauty and brutality of the past six weeks just like me. They've sacrificed so much time and money, for many their life savings; eschewed the security of their families and loved ones. They've

trained, mentally and physically, often for years. Climbed many other mountains. Crossed dozens of terrifying rickety ladders and stared into the chasms
of themselves. They've all had their own "awful days" and woken up the next
day and kept going. Against all logic and comfort and sense, they kept going.
They wanted to quit—we've all wanted to quit—but they didn't. They gave
everything they had to be here. For a chance to stand at the top of the world
for twenty minutes. And maybe to see, from there, just how big that world is
and how small we are; yet how capable is each small, imperfect life. Everyone
linked together on this one rope climbing up the side of the mountain has a
dream they are willing to die for. In that, we are all the same.

My heart goes out to those who pass. All my impatience, my cold jitters,
my body's demands, give way to compassion.

We wait for one more hour. My cheeks, fingers, feet are going numb.
I'm getting worried. This is a perfect recipe for frostbite. A light wind starts
to pick up, and at 28,000 feet, it's no longer breezy, but a frigid, pummeling
cold. The thick arctic cloud that wafts out when you open a deep freezer. I
feel my hands getting hard. My circulation has never been great. I have low
iron. Anemia.

Mike, who's at the tail of the group, calls up on the radio.

"Everyone, hey," his voice crackles. "How is everyone doing? The wind is
picking up. Can you take the cold? Anyone want to turn around?"

Should I turn around? My teeth chatter.

I am so cold. But we're so close. I picture blackened fingers and faces—all
the Everest amputations that come from frostbite.

But I'm not going to be the one to give up. Not now. If the group wants
to go down, I'll go along with it. Brian and Danny are ahead of me. They
shake their heads no.

"We will continue," says Dorjee into the radio.

It's close to four a.m. Dawn is crawling over the horizon, and we still
haven't made much progress in the traffic jam. The sky is pastel. In the distance the vast brown plains of the Tibetan Plateau unroll, the outlines of
Kanchenjunga, Lhotse, and Makalu emerge. I'm overwhelmed by the poetry
of it all, and the feeling lasts a good three minutes until the cold overtakes
all my senses again.

I'm starting to lose patience.

My cheeks are freezing. Frostbite could be hitting already. It's hard to tell.

I am starting to get scared. I pray faster.

"Hail Mary, full of grace."

Oh God, the line is not moving. Come on! I don't think I can do this.

I look toward the sky. Toward the horizon of where the summit must be. *Mama, Mamita!* I think. *Ayúdame. Mama! Mamita! Ayúdame. I don't know if I can do this. Please help me! Are you there? Mamita?*

Music comes flooding into my ears. Something familiar.

What the hell.

Chewang Dorji looks back at me.

"Did you hear that?" I ask.

He just stares at me and growls. I take that to be a *no*.

But there is it again! The unmistakable thumping rattle of the iconic Latin Christmas song "Mi Burrito Sabanero."

In front of me, smiling and laughing, just like the last time I saw her standing with ease, is my mother, fully alive and animated and dancing across the snow to the goofy song of my childhood about a donkey on his way to Bethlehem. Holding her fists in front of her face like a boxer, she shimmies her shoulders to the sound of the maracas and throws her head back, smiling and singing along to the chorus:

"Tuki tuki tuki tuki!"

Tears stream down my face. After her Christmas feast, we'd go to my aunt Irene's house to celebrate with all of her family—my aunts, uncles, and cousins. My cousins. Marianela. Rolando. Ramiro. Before I knew who they really were, they were my sweet, playful cousins. We would tear through the house while Mom talked with her sisters and ate and sang, happier than she ever was at home. She was so happy then, with everyone there for the holidays. *Of course.* It hits me. Why didn't I think of it sooner? Of course she was happiest then. Christmas was the only time she got to be with all her children at once.

Even if she had to play Tía Teresa.

One of my mother's last wishes was for us to throw a huge party on the one-year anniversary of her death. Marianela flew back to Peru, and she and I organized it, inviting 150 friends and family members just as my mother had instructed us on her deathbed.

After everyone went home, Meche and I were cleaning up and trading funny stories about my mom.

"Mechita," I said. "There's something I want to ask you."

"Dime, Silvita. What is it?"

"You were here when my Mom had J come over. When you tied him to the chair?"

"What?

"My mom said that after what happened to me, she called J. And while he was here, she boiled water, and you both tied him to a chair."

"We never tied him to any chair. We wouldn't do that."

"But she said she had the water boiling," I pushed, suddenly needing it to be true. "She had water boiling in that big aluminum pot, the one you used to wash all the cleaning rags with bleach? That one. And that once he was tied to the chair, she poured the hot water on him poco a poco and told him it was for what he had done to me."

Meche was wide-eyed.

"No, Silvita. I remember he did come over one time after you told her what he'd done. But your mother just told him never to come back."

"But she said the water was scalding. And that she told him why she was doing it. She said, 'This is to avenge the damage you did to my daughter.'"

Meche set her hand on my arm, her eyes soft.

"It's been a long day," she said kindly.

The slow, excruciating way my mother detailed pouring of the water; the fieriness and determination of her words; they had all swept me along on her story of revenge. The way she told the story, with so much color and pain and vengeance in her voice, she'd become the woman, the mother, I had always craved. One who would fight. Who would stand up. Who would take what she was owed. All she deserved. I'd been in awe of the strength she was able to summon. Finally. I'd never seen her like that in front of my father, but I always knew that's who she was deep down.

But the truth was more complicated. Perhaps she'd told herself that story because she needed to. Sometimes we have to tell ourselves stories to keep living.

I don't doubt that she wanted to take revenge. But her power, her voice, had been silenced by a lifetime of abuse, humiliation, racism, poverty. She wanted to stand up to men, to my father, and demand what was hers. *Ours.* To demand justice. Telling me she had overpowered J was her way of saying she was sorry. Of saying: *This is what I wish I could have done.*

There was so much my mother couldn't fix. So much she didn't have the strength to look at, but she wedged in all the beauty and joy and laughter possible to cushion the pain. To keep surviving in the ways that were available to her, even if that meant looking away, even if that meant staying silent. I don't know if learning the story was a lie hurt more because I wanted J to suffer so badly or because I wanted to believe my mother had fought for me.

And now here she is, doing what she always did best, distracting me—from the cold, from the darkness. She didn't support my climbing when she was alive, she was unable to stop the abuse or find justice, but she's here now, dancing me through the final hours. This is her love for me. I start to cry, but the tears come out as laughter.

"I love you, Mamita." I say it looking up into the ether, into the clear wide-open sky.

Chapter 19

෧෧෧෧

AT THE TOP OF THE WORLD

Viewed from the top, the shadows of the world's highest mountains are often perfectly triangular, even when the peak itself isn't. It's an optical illusion. Just the way a set of train tracks gets smaller and smaller until they form a peak on the horizon, the shadows of the mountains are so long that the human eye can't see where they end, so to us they appear as perfect pyramids.

I stop to catch my breath, and when I look up, my mother is gone and the strains of "Mi Burrito Sabanero" are lost in the howling wind. And in their place, just beyond Cho Oyu, Everest's neighbor to the west, sunrise is turning the horizon a dusky tangerine, and the shadow of Mount Everest appears, casting a perfect pyramid in the sky. Goose bumps sweep my arms. It's like some sort of mystical hologram.

Hallucinations must be setting in. First my mother, now this. I've heard about how lack of oxygen makes climbers see and do strange things. Pressing up the stepped ledges, I try to remember where I am, how dangerous it is; wiggling my fingers inside giant down mittens, I grip the jumar tighter in my hand, slide it up the rope, and step, listening for the sound of my crampons piercing ice. You are climbing a mountain, Silvia. This is real. Stay focused. But when I glance back, the pyramid is still there. It's growing, widening, rising higher in the sky, shadowing all the surrounding peaks. I try to dig for my camera, but it takes too much energy. Everything takes too much energy.

The early pyramids were shaped to mimic rays of the sun and act as spiritual staircases for pharaohs to climb to the sky. It was their ramp to God. I wonder if that's what this is for me too. Maybe I had to climb this high to see the true shape of a shadow. To see what it can become when you're above it. No longer a dark, menacing cloak, or even a friendly refuge, but something exalted. What if everything I've been looking for is not just in the shadows but is the shadow itself? And everything I did to get here, not just the climbing, but the last decade of pain and wonder and pushing my every limit, was all so that I could see a shadow from a different perspective.

I take a deep breath, sucking down as much air as I can, and let go, sighing, as my insides flood with tingly warmth. If I had to turn around right now, it would be okay. I don't even need to make it to the top. Maybe I never did. Even if I don't summit, I've still climbed Everest.

* * *

Thousands of feet down, the cloud cover has a crumbled quality, and in the early morning light it's hard to tell the clouds from the band of Himalayan peaks. After hours of climbing a wildly steep but broad face, we make it up the rocky steps and onto a semi-flat ledge, stopping to pant after each step. The path narrows until the earth we're standing on shrinks to a knife's edge no more than three feet wide. We keep walking, inching really. I feel like I'm running a slow-motion marathon through mud. One side of the path is protected by a huge snow wall, and the other is fully exposed—a seemingly endless abyss. Soon we reach a big rocky thumb and pull ourselves up and over. I press my body as close to the cold stone as I can, saying a prayer of thanks for its solidity. At the top, I see another exposed rocky hilltop, maybe a hundred yards above us.

My god. That's it. *The summit!*

I let out a muffled shriek and point wildly, yelling into Chewang Dorji's ear. "That's it, that's it! It's so close. The summit."

I made it. I start to cry. Cold little tears skid down my cheeks.

"No!" says Chewang Dorji. "No summit. We must still climb Hillary Step, and after, the summit is far."

"Oh shit."

"No tears," he says. "No yelling. Save all your oxygen!"

Suddenly exhausted, I want to collapse. To plug up my tears, I have to turn on the inner commander, that machine inside me that can tune out everything and keep going no matter what. The same engine that powered my survival and plenty of my destruction. The one that landed me in lots of trouble, but suddenly here, at 28,000 feet, it is exactly what I need. Against all bodily logic, we start inching down the backside of the rocky thumb. The trail gets even skinnier. We've slowed to a crawl. Every single step takes incredible effort. I need food or water but can't stomach either, and it's too dangerous to swing my pack around or turn to reach for anything.

When I look up again, we're just below the Hillary Step. A practically vertical rock outcropping made up of four huge boulders, or steps, it's the final technical challenge before the summit, and it's infamous. A traverse that would be tricky even if our bodies weren't actively shutting down. During last year's earthquake, the biggest boulder cracked away from the Step and fell down the mountain. Rumor says it is now easier to climb the Step. More a snowy vertical climb than a high-stakes scramble. It still looks tremendously difficult.

The Step itself is a big dome, and without the main boulder, it's a pretty straight shot up. But the path, a thin line flattened by the boots before us, is still no more than three feet wide—*maybe*—and totally exposed. It slopes down steeply on either side and drops away to nothing.

Holding back tears, I follow the fixed line up with my eyes. As I squint through the sun, now blaring high in the sky, what I see ahead looks more like a grocery store checkout line than the path up Mount Everest. The path is congested with people standing single file in colorful puffy suits, all waiting to take their next step.

There's only one rope. The way down must be on the other side of the mountain. Escalators, maybe. Yes, yes. A nice, paved path. Something like that. Just the thought relaxes me. This ridge seems too exposed, too dangerous, for people to be ascending and descending at the same time. There's no way that two people could stand on this path, let alone pass each other.

How far is the summit after this? I should know every inch of this climb in my mind. Have the landmarks and inclines committed to memory. But I never studied the route, and it's a little late for a geography lesson. Chewang Dorji had said a long way, but it feels like we've been walking forever and getting nowhere. I'm losing track of time and space.

Even though the Hillary Step has been "simplified," it still feels like the final test. To pass effectively, we have to switch between two safety carabiners with half-frozen hands in huge bulky mittens, with absolutely zero margin for error.

Everything feels both immediate and far away.

Pay attention. Stay alert, Silvia. My blood thumps through my body. I can feel it thickening. Slowing down. Every breath is the universe collapsing. My thoughts bubble into little clouds above my head. I try to jostle myself back into my body. Your body is the only thing that matters. Trust it. Trust your body. Don't think. Just move. Motion, concentration. Pay attention. You could fall at any minute. It's like balancing on the teeth of a shark.

And then they start coming.

A string of people passing us on the way down. Mostly men. Outliers who summited around six-thirty in the morning. Oh my God, we're sharing the same line? This is crazy. This is totally insane. And not only are they coming, but they have priority. Fighting against gravity, they're more likely to trip. Also, their oxygen must be running low. The time they have left to survive in the Death Zone is ticking away. Most climbers who don't make it back from Everest die on the way down from the summit. Now I see why. It looks physically impossible to let them pass without anyone tipping right off the mountain, but it's being done. We do all these impossible things. Outrageous things that are normalized. Death isn't something we're dancing with. She is the shark, waiting, mouth wide open, for someone to fall, to snap her jaws shut.

"Excuse me, excuse me," climbers say, sliding past.

"Congratulations," I exclaim breathlessly, half out of respect, half out of terror.

Two, four, *five* people pass.

When Sherpas go by, they lean so far out around the line that the stamps their boots leave behind are less than a foot from the edge. I can't help holding my breath as I watch them pass. I'm woozy and light-headed.

The sun is out, and the wind is minimal. It's a perfect day, but the longer I stare at the void, the sheer foreverness of the blue sky around us, the more nervous I am that my carabiners aren't placed properly. Or that my alpine harness will come undone—a terrible mistake that I won't notice until it's too late.

Halfway up, I see Brian making his way down. When he gets closer, I can see by the brightness in his eyes that he made it to the top.

"Congratulations, mate, I am so proud of you," he exclaims happily as he squeezes past. "You're almost there."

I've never heard sweeter words.

When Chewang Dorji and I pull ourselves to the top of the Step, I let out a sigh of relief. I can see the summit now—the actual summit. Twenty minutes, Chewang Dorji says. The terrain is moderate, and we walk slowly and easily, the stress beginning to fall away.

Climbers keep coming down, sharing congratulations both ways.

I feel like we're walking the Everest red carpet.

Danny passes on his way down. "Congratulations, Silvia!" he says.

"Danny Boy!" I say. "Congratulations."

He nods and keeps walking. We have enough oxygen for only twenty minutes at the top. Part of me is still wondering if there's another, more comfortable route I'll be able to take down the mountain when Chewang Dorji suddenly throws up his arms in victory.

The summit is a small, peaked slope, maybe ten feet by three feet, that drops away to nothing. Along its edges, two dozen people in summit suits—mostly red and orange and yellow—are clustered together facing away from the trail. The top of the world looks like a convention of astronauts. Their shadows fall back onto the snow in long strips. What are they looking at? It's not until we get closer that I realize we're here.

We're here. I made it.

Trudging toward the crowd, I see they're huddled next to a tiny mound of snow blanketed in layers of prayer flags. This is the border of China and Nepal, really where China, Nepal, and Tibet intersect. Climbers take turns raising their country flags over their heads for a photo, pumping their fists in the air or flashing a thumbs-up in giant mittens. I raise my mittened hands in celebration, then turn to Chewang Dorji and Kami Rita and pull them into an embrace before hugging all the Sherpas around me. Then anyone who looks open to a hug. Most people are snapping a quick photo, then turning right back and heading down the trail.

I can feel the emotion pouring out of me. I need a minute to myself, and I have an offering to make. I make my way to a less-crowded ledge higher up on the summit where someone has hammered a short makeshift post into the ground. From here, I have unobstructed views over Tibet and China. Snow-covered peaks run into massive swaths of brown earth. Some people have asked why I didn't start climbing in Peru. The peaks of the Cordillera Blanca are stunning, some as high as 22,000 feet. They would have been a logical choice, the mountains that my maternal grandmother called home. It was the native medicine of my country that led me to the mountains. But the answer isn't so simple. I think maybe it's easier to climb mountains far from home first.

The wind starts to pick up, churning powdery snow into a whorl around my head.

I kneel into the snow and start to cry. Tears of joy. Tears of loss. Bittersweet tears. Surreal tears. Each wave has its own feeling. Its own crest. Staring down at Tibet, I let them come. For once, I welcome them. Finally able to shed the armor. I don't have to fight anymore. I made it. I'm at the top of the world.

I set my backpack down next to the post and unzip the top pocket. I pull out the white khata and tie it around my neck, thinking of the nuns.

"I made it!" I want to yell into the ether, but it's better to keep them praying until I'm down the mountain safely.

Thank you, I whisper instead, bowing.

Then I pull out the yellow khata from the girls at Shakti Samuha and tie it around the post. All these miles, I carried the wishes of the girls in my pack, and now I hope the Mother will hear their dreams.

Anything is possible for them. I know it. I pull out my first prayer flags, the ones I bought with the girls in Kathmandu, and wrapped inside of them are the three small photos that have driven this entire journey, not just to Everest, but to all the mountains and through everything that came along with them.

The first is Lori in Shanghai. Wearing jeans and red lipstick with a sly smile, she's standing in front of the Oriental Pearl Tower. She loved that tower. On every peak I've summited since her death I leave the same picture. Making a copy became part of my packing ritual. My way to honor her. My vigil candle. At the top of every continent, I am closer to her star. Breathing in the cosmic dust that she's become.

The second photo is of my mother in 2011, on her sixty-seventh birthday, a year and a half before her death. We're at La Bistecca, and she's posing with an ice cream sundae—her all-time favorite dessert. A sparkling candle burns down low, and the ice cream melts as we shout for her to make a wish already. I see myself reflected in her smile. Her laugh. *Mi Madre. Mamita. Chomolungma. Sagarmatha. Everest.*

There are so many ways to say *mother*.

Everest has shown me that it is not just a role to play or a person to call your own, but an action. *Mother* is a verb.

The final picture is me in first grade. In a turquoise tracksuit, twin pigtails running down my back, wearing a strained smile. It's the picture I couldn't stand to look at for years. The photo that I found in my apartment in the Marina and tried to hide away. The same girl who visited me in the ayahuasca vision that led me here. I had never brought a photo of myself to leave at a summit. It felt weird leaving a picture of myself. But here it's different. Here I'm leaving little Silvita with the Mother.

I prop the picture up against the stake, trying to wedge it into the crunchy snow, but the wind flips it forward. Snatching it up, I brush off bits of snow and notice something I'd never seen before.

On the wall behind me in the photo is a snowman. A snowman I crafted from cotton balls that day in first grade, preparing for the Peruvian Christmas. He wore his hat crooked and smoked a corncob pipe. For a little girl from Lima who'd never seen snow or the mountains, I'd crafted a snowman out of stories and dreams.

The photo had become such an emblem of trauma that I'd missed its backdrop entirely.

But it was right there. Snow had been at my back all along. The mountains had always been behind me. I come from the blood of the mountains. Its terrain is my lineage, but the pain I inherited from the women of my family kept me away for so long. That little girl knew. She called me home. All I had to do was hold her hand and follow along. To walk freely through the mountains as she asked.

In return, she gave me back my life.

As my final moments at the summit tick away, I feel safe in a way I never have before. All raw nerves and a beating heart, I'm exhausted to the bone, but I've kept the most important promise I ever made—a promise to myself. Closing my eyes, I see the little girl pulling me toward peaks I didn't yet understand. She showed me that the journey to healing is not brightly lit. That more often it's a long climb through a maze of shadows, an icy forever you think will never melt. Other times, it's just pinpoints of light flickering in the dark. Tiny moments of illumination you have to follow. To hunt. Healing is not about reaching the top; she showed me. It's about the moments when you might not make it.

Even in the shadows, we are climbing.

Even in the dark, we are getting somewhere.

People talk about conquering fear the same way they talk about conquering mountains. *Conquer* is a word you hear a lot in mountain climbing. I never liked it. The word sounds like a violation. Something in my physiology, in my history, maybe, reacts to it. The world around me, the world of the men, of the bold, of those who strive and achieve and get things done, who like to conquer. On Everest there are many who come to conquer.

But conquering is not healing. Conquering is not merging; it's not collective. Conquering is an individual act. When we climb to conquer, we are climbing alone.

We do not conquer Everest, just like we do not conquer trauma. Instead, we must yield ourselves to the chasms and unexpected avalanches. Trust in the long, unknowable journey of the climb.

If we are lucky, Everest allows us to ascend. And not like the priests taught us in school. It's not a final, rapturous ascension. You fight for every step, and when you arrive, even at the top of the world, your feet are still on the ground.

In one of the last interviews Junko Tabei gave in her life, she reflected on standing at Everest's summit. She'd battled Japan's ideas of women in the 1970s, her own physical setbacks, logistical nightmares, and all the naysayers who said she'd never make it. But after everything she overcame, when she stepped onto the summit, she was calm.

"I didn't shout anything," she recalled. "But I thought: 'Oh, I don't have to climb anymore.'"

Now, I know exactly what she meant.

Here, I've slammed the rage and sadness from my body by scaling icy ridges and surviving nights alone listening to the rumble of avalanches. Everest taught me how to feel danger in a way that I could use. It taught me that I want to live this life, this messy, painful life.

Sometimes, it takes a long walk to see how far you've come.

Reaching the top isn't about the accomplishment. It's about walking in the shadows long enough to see the other side, about learning how to roll with other women and men, and how to lean on and support others instead of white-knuckling life alone. It's about letting people brush up against you, even if they are headed in a different direction. It's about sharing the journey, the stories, and the pain.

It's knowing that climbing with others is the safest way to climb and the surest way to heal.

With no more of this mountain left to climb, I'm back where I began.

"Lori, I love you," I say, touching my mitten to her photo one last time.

"Mamita, I love you. I did it. I made it. I couldn't have done it without you." I touch her photo as well.

"And you, Silvita, I love you too," I say.

And in that moment I know she is whole and where she belongs. At the top of the world, where there are no more shadows.

No whistles.

Where she is finally safe.

I pull on my backpack. "Okay," I say aloud. "Here we go."

And with that, I take my first slow step back down.

Knowing that for me, there are still more mountains to climb.

ACKNOWLEDGMENTS

Countless people have taken the journey to create this book with me, and I am grateful for all of you. Thank you!

And some of you directly pushed me up this mountain of a book and deserve all of my gratitude:

Lara Love Hardin, my agent, my mischievous soul sister, thank you for making time for that infamous "tea talk" and for listening, sharing the vision, and walking with me every step of the way.

To Ty Gideon Love, Boo Prince, Mariah Sanford, Janelle Julian, Rachel Neumann, Staci Bruce, Cody Love, Julia Dunn, and Stacie Sheftel, thank you for all your daily support.

To the generous Dr. Rachel Abrams, thank you for your kindness of heart introducing me to the Idea Architects family and Doug Abrams—for your boldness in creating a purposeful agency to share our stories.

To the amazing Nina St. Pierre—your heart, soul, and gift of words are forever etched in this book. Our collaboration is undoubtedly one of the highlights of my life. Thank you!

To my international family: Caspian Dennis, Sandy Violette, and the rest of the team at Abner Stein. Camilla Ferrier, Jemma McDonagh, Brittany Poulin, and the rest of the team at The Marsh Agency. Thank you for bringing this book around the globe.

To my original editor, Maddie Jones, your passion and care from the very beginning are the reason I can even type this.

To my editor, Shannon Criss, thank you for stepping up and diving in and bringing this book full circle. My immense gratitude to the most hard-working and dynamic team at Henry Holt: Amy Einhorn, Sarah Crichton, Ruby Rose Lee, Maggie Richards, Caitlin O'Shaughnessy, Allison Carney, Jason Liebman, Maia Sacca-Schaeffer, Christopher Sergio, Hannah Campbell, Jason Reigal, Meryl Levavi, and Clarissa Long. THANK YOU!

To the extraordinary women at WME: Sylvie Rabineau, Carolina Beltran, and Sarah Self. Thank you for your boldness in championing this journey and allowing me to live a dream come true.

To Jill Fritzo PR and her stellar team: Jill, Michael, Charlie, Stephen, Kelly. Thank you for all your guidance and your hard work in sharing the messages in this book.

To my chosen family: Sheryl and Quentin Dahm, thank you for allowing me to share my truth, and for your love and support along the way. To Nicole Heinrich, my therapist, thank you for holding my "orchestra" while embarking on the most painful and challenging times. To my Bay Area friends and family: Emily Lawson, Atul Patel, Lisa Kristine, Ryo Sakai, Sam Hardin, Marta Ayala, and Jen Watt. Thank you for listening, and giving me the emotional support and encouragement I needed, and for feeding me all during the pandemic. To my nieces and nephews: Andrea, Alvaro, Santiago, Ana, Rolando, Matthew, Teresa, Nico, Lucas, Olivia, and Charlotte—thank you for sweet innocence, unconditional love, and for inspiring me to lead by example. To my brothers and sister, Eduardo, Marianela, Ramiro, Rolando, and Miguel—thank you for embracing me as who I am.

And to my beautiful Lori, my mother Teresa "Telle Petelle," and papa Segundo: thank you for guiding me from afar and allowing my heart to find the light even during the darkest of times. Helene, thank you for believing in me and giving me the strength to heal my heart, and inspiring me to take such a bold leap of faith.

To all the friends and climbers that I met during many of my expeditions and on my training hikes and trips, some who are not in this story—from the beautiful local indigenous women in Papua who trekked along with me in silence so that I wouldn't get lost again in the jungle, to the botanist on a random corner store in Punta Arenas who gave me blessed rose water and told me to trust this journey. To all the random souls who shared food, conversations, and anecdotes as I lugged my heavy backpacks and tires, thank you for making me feel seen, for sharing your humanity, and for making me feel that I'm not alone. To the random smiles, acknowledgments, and the hundreds of "you're almost there"s—you all got me here. Thank you!

And finally, to all the courageous girls and boys worldwide—this is for you to step out of the shadows and climb.

ABOUT THE AUTHOR

Silvia Vasquez-Lavado is a humanitarian, mountaineer, explorer, social entrepreneur, and technologist living in San Francisco. In 2014 she launched Courageous Girls, a nonprofit that helps survivors of sexual abuse and trafficking find their inner strength and cultivate their voices by demonstrating their physical strength. Courageous Girls has had projects in Nepal, India, the United States, and Peru. Vasquez-Lavado was recognized by *Fortune* magazine as one of the Heroes of the 500 in 2015. CNET named her one of the twenty most influential Latinos in Silicon Valley. She has also been recognized by the Peruvian government as one of the "Marca Perú" ambassadors (country brand ambassadors). She is a member of the Explorers Club and one of the few women in the world to have completed the Seven Summits.